The Dialectica Therapy Prime

How DBT Can Inform Clinical Practice

The Dialectical Behavior Therapy Primer

How DBT Can Inform Clinical Practice

Beth S. Brodsky, PhD

Associate Clinical Professor of Medical Psychology
Department of Psychiatry
Columbia University College of Physicians and Surgeons
Research Scientist New York State Psychiatric Institute
New York, NY, USA

Barbara Stanley, PhD

Professor of Clinical Psychology
Department of Psychiatry
Columbia University College of Physicians and Surgeons
Research Scientist New York State Psychiatric Institute
New York, NY, USA

A John Wiley & Sons, Ltd., Publication

This edition first published 2013 © 2013 by John Wiley & Sons, Ltd

Wiley-Blackwell is an imprint of John Wiley & Sons, formed by the merger of Wiley's global Scientific, Technical and Medical business with Blackwell Publishing.

Registered Office
John Wiley & Sons, Ltd, The Atrium, Southern Gate, Chichester, West Sussex, PO19 8SQ, UK

Editorial Offices
9600 Garsington Road, Oxford, OX4 2DQ, UK
The Atrium, Southern Gate, Chichester, West Sussex, PO19 8SQ, UK
111 River Street, Hoboken, NJ 07030-5774, USA

For details of our global editorial offices, for customer services and for information about how to apply for permission to reuse the copyright material in this book please see our website at www.wiley.com/wiley-blackwell.

The right of the author to be identified as the author of this work has been asserted in accordance with the UK Copyright, Designs and Patents Act 1988.

All rights reserved. No part of this publication may be reproduced, stored in a retrieval system, or transmitted, in any form or by any means, electronic, mechanical, photocopying, recording or otherwise, except as permitted by the UK Copyright, Designs and Patents Act 1988, without the prior permission of the publisher.

Designations used by companies to distinguish their products are often claimed as trademarks. All brand names and product names used in this book are trade names, service marks, trademarks or registered trademarks of their respective owners. The publisher is not associated with any product or vendor mentioned in this book.

The contents of this work are intended to further general scientific research, understanding, and discussion only and are not intended and should not be relied upon as recommending or promoting a specific method, diagnosis, or treatment by health science practitioners for any particular patient. The publisher and the author make no representations or warranties with respect to the accuracy or completeness of the contents of this work and specifically disclaim all warranties, including without limitation any implied warranties of fitness for a particular purpose. In view of ongoing research, equipment modifications, changes in governmental regulations, and the constant flow of information relating to the use of medicines, equipment, and devices, the reader is urged to review and evaluate the information provided in the package insert or instructions for each medicine, equipment, or device for, among other things, any changes in the instructions or indication of usage and for added warnings and precautions. Readers should consult with a specialist where appropriate. The fact that an organization or Website is referred to in this work as a citation and/or a potential source of further information does not mean that the author or the publisher endorses the information the organization or Website may provide or recommendations it may make. Further, readers should be aware that Internet Websites listed in this work may have changed or disappeared between when this work was written and when it is read. No warranty may be created or extended by any promotional statements for this work. Neither the publisher nor the author shall be liable for any damages arising herefrom.

Library of Congress Cataloging-in-Publication Data
Brodsky, Beth S.
  The dialectical behavior therapy primer : how DBT can inform clinical practice / Beth S. Brodsky, Barbara Stanley.
    p. ; cm.
  Includes bibliographical references and index.
  ISBN 978-1-118-55624-5 (ePDF) – ISBN 978-1-118-55659-7 (emobi) – ISBN 978-1-118-55660-3 – ISBN 978-1-118-55661-0 (epub) – ISBN 978-1-119-96893-1 (softback : alk. paper)
  I. Stanley, Barbara, 1949– II. Title.
  [DNLM: 1. Borderline Personality Disorder–therapy.   2. Cognitive Therapy–methods.   WM 190.5.B5]
  RC569.5.B67
  616.85′852–dc23
                                                          2013002841

A catalogue record for this book is available from the British Library.

Wiley also publishes its books in a variety of electronic formats. Some content that appears in print may not be available in electronic books.

Cover image © GettyImage
Cover design by Cyan Design

Set in 10/12.5pt Times by SPi Publisher Services, Pondicherry, India
Printed and bound in Singapore by Markono Print Media Pte Ltd

1   2013

"Start where you are. Use what you have. Do what you can."
                                                    Arthur Ashe

This quote embodies the kind of encouragement that DBT provides for patients and, in true dialectic form, helps them move beyond where they are, develop more than what they have, and do more than what they can.

Contents

About the Authors	ix
Foreword	xi
Acknowledgments	xiii
1 Introduction	3
Part I Theoretical, research, and clinical foundations	**13**
2 When DBT is indicated: The patients, the clinicians, and the evidence	15
3 BPD: Treatable or untreatable?	27
4 BPD: Diagnosis, stigma, and phenomenology	33
5 Understanding and treating self-harm behaviors in BPD	45
6 The ABC's of DBT – the theoretical perspective	63
7 The ABC's of DBT – overview of the treatment	75
Part II Using DBT in clinical practice	**83**
8 Commitment and goal setting	85
9 The DBT tool kit: The essential DBT strategies and what happens in the individual session	101
10 Skills training: The rationale and structure	125
11 Skills training: The four skill modules	135
12 Between-session contact and observing limits	153
13 Management of suicidal behavior	177
14 The Safety Planning Intervention	185
15 The three C's of consultation	193
16 DBT case formulation	205
17 Beyond Target 1 – Therapy and "quality of life" interfering behaviors	221
18 The end of treatment	239
Index	245

About the Authors

The authors of this book are, in a sense, unlikely candidates to write a volume on Dialectical Behavior Therapy (DBT), a form of cognitive behavioral therapy (CBT). Both authors were originally trained in psychodynamic models of psychotherapy. However, also conduct clinical research on suicidal behavior and nonsuicidal self-injury. In an effort to provide effective treatment for the suicidal and self-injuring individuals that they were studying, they found psychodynamic treatment approaches wanting. This led them to a DBT-intensive training conducted by Marsha Linehan at the University of Washington and the development of a research program investigating the efficacy of DBT and other CBT approaches to chronically suicidal and self-injuring individuals. The DBT model not only seemed to be effective and helpful to patients, but it also suited the personal style of the authors, allowing room for them to be their "genuine and natural selves" while maintaining professionalism. They introduced DBT at their home institution, Columbia University, where the basic therapy training model for psychiatric residents and psychology trainees is psychodynamic in nature, and where graduates with psychotherapy practices primarily adopt a psychodynamic approach. As such, the authors have spent a lot of time bridging psychodynamic and cognitive behavioral concepts and techniques. In doing so, they have considered how many aspects of DBT – the model, the way of thinking about patients and their problems, as well as the techniques – can be used by clinicians who practice other models of therapy or who primarily do psychopharmacology. This volume is the result of their years of practicing and teaching DBT.

Clinical psychologists, Barbara Stanley, PhD, and Beth Brodsky, PhD, are internationally recognized experts in suicide, self-injury, and borderline personality disorder (BPD). They are both on the faculty of the Columbia University College of Physicians and Surgeons, in the Department of Psychiatry. They have received an NIMH grant to develop a curriculum on teaching DBT to psychiatry residents in training. The only other DBT grant given under this program was to the treatment developer, Dr. Linehan.

Dr. Stanley is Professor of Clinical Psychology and the Principal Investigator of an NIMH-funded grant comparing the efficacy and studying the mechanisms of action of DBT and antidepressants in the reduction of suicidal behavior and self-injury in BPD. She is the author of numerous professional articles and chapters, is a frequently invited speaker on BPD, suicidal behavior, and DBT and has participated in several NIMH work groups and review groups. She serves as editor-in-chief of the Archives of Suicide Research. With her colleague, Dr. Gregory Brown, she developed the Safety Planning Intervention that is used throughout the Veterans Health Administration, state mental health systems, and on crisis hotlines across the United States. She was awarded the American Foundation for Suicide Prevention Research Award and the New York State Suicide Prevention Center Research Award. She is a DBT trainer for Behavioral Tech, LLC.

Dr. Brodsky is Associate Clinical Professor and the lead DBT therapist in Dr. Stanley's treatment study. She serves as a supervisor of interns and psychiatry residents learning DBT. She, too, is the author of many articles and chapters on BPD, DBT, suicide, and self-injury and is a frequently invited speaker on BPD, suicidal behavior, and DBT. She serves on the editorial board of the *Archives of Suicide Research*. She is also a member of the Virginia Apgar Academy of Medical Educators at Columbia University.

Drs. Stanley and Brodsky have been active collaborators for several years. They also have DBT-based private practices in New York City and are frequently called upon to provide consultation on "difficult" patients with BPD for mental health professionals who are not trained in DBT. They have found that mental health professionals from a wide spectrum of clinical training can be helped to improve their work by applying DBT principles. In this book, they draw on their extensive experience and summarize their understanding of the phenomenology of BPD, and of the theoretical principles and treatment techniques of DBT.

Foreword

Borderline Personality Disorder (BPD) is a serious and underrecognized public health problem. It is relatively common – almost 2% of the general population and more than 20% of psychiatric outpatients have this diagnosis. These are people who suffer a great deal themselves and are often a cause of great suffering for their loved ones. BPD can be expensive to treat but even more expensive not to treat. And it can be deadly – the suicide rate in BPD is 10%.

The bad news is that currently available medications help just a little bit, or not at all. The good news is Dialectical Behavior Therapy (DBT). This is a very effective psychotherapy that helps therapists help their patients to find the way out from the maze of their previously self-destructive behavior. Marsha Linehan first developed DBT three decades ago, and it has since provided much needed guidance for clinicians and welcome hope for patients and their families. DBT is a wonderful, evidence-based treatment widely used around the world.

But DBT has one serious problem – it requires a lot of training for the therapist and a lot of commitment, time, and effort for the patient. The complete DBT package is simply not practical for many clinical situations. It always seemed to me that there was a place for a simpler, less demanding application of DBT techniques to everyday clinical practice. This book fills that niche. It will help clinicians incorporate aspects of DBT into their work with patients whenever the whole DBT treatment is impractical.

Marsha Linehan is a friend of mine. But I could never convince her of the value of this kind of "DBT light." Another friend, Barbara Stanley along with her long time colleague, Beth Brodsky, now fill the gap. Their book provides a comprehensive introduction to DBT and a very accessible approach toward integrating DBT with other psychotherapy techniques. This approach will be useful to everyone who works with borderline patients – those experienced in DBT will find many pearls; those with no prior DBT training will find a complete toolkit.

The authors received DBT-intensive training with Dr. Linehan and were inspired by her to conduct extensive research on its effects. The ideas in this book are a product of their years of experience in conducting the full DBT model in clinical and research settings, as well as in training and teaching DBT to psychologists, psychiatry residents, and other mental health providers. Their rich clinical experience comes through in the many vivid case examples. The authors present a practical DBT-informed interventions and hands-on, step-by-step guidance to help clinicians become more effective in the management of suicidal and self-harm behaviors and in making decisions about hospitalization of their patients.

Although the book is targeted mainly to clinicians, it will also be a very useful read for patients, family members, and loved ones. It provides hope for a happier and more stable future and concrete guidance on how to get there.

Allen Frances, MD

Acknowledgments

There are many individuals to thank for their help and support in the writing of this book – our families, our colleagues and editors, and especially our patients, from whom we have learned so much. But we particularly want to acknowledge Dr. Marsha Linehan, the developer of Dialectical Behavior Therapy. Her ideas about treatment and understanding borderline personality disorder are nothing short of genius. Her approach transformed the way we treat patients. Marsha is one of the very few individuals who has moved our field forward by a quantum leap. Her original text, *Cognitive Behavior Therapy for Borderline Personality Disorder*, is an amazingly dense work with gems of clinical insight packed into every page, and we base our work on this original text. The inside of Barbara's textbook jacket is filled with several columns of notations and associated pages of paragraphs that she found to be deeply insightful and helpful. Beth's copy of Linehan's text is filled with bookmarked pages and highlighted passages. In our team meetings, we have included readings of these paragraphs, and they always served as the basis for thought-provoking and interesting team discussions. We have often thought that many of these paragraphs could easily have been expanded into chapters because there is clearly so much behind each of these ideas. We express our deepest gratitude to Marsha and hope that this volume, meant to be a readily accessible guide to clinicians and patients, expresses our desire to remain true to the spirit of the DBT model.

Beth would also especially like to thank her husband, Amir Shaviv, and son, Natan, for their loving support, enthusiastic encouragement, and their patience and understanding during the writing process, and Barbara would like to express her appreciation to her children, Melissa and Thomas, who always provide balance, support, and great joy, and to her late husband, Michael, who continues to be a source of inspiration.

The Dialectical Behavior Therapy Primer

How DBT Can Inform Clinical Practice

Chapter 1

Introduction

For whom is this book intended?

In this volume, we hope to provide (a) an accessible, easy-to-understand primer for clinicians wanting to adopt Dialectical Behavior Therapy (DBT) as their treatment approach; (b) guidance, tools, and, more importantly, a way of thinking about treating borderline personality disorder (BPD) for clinicians who want to incorporate aspects of DBT principles and techniques into their practice but do not wish to adopt the entire model and (c) an introduction to DBT for the patients and their families and friends who want to learn the basics of this treatment approach. While becoming proficient in DBT requires intensive training, supervision, and feedback on therapeutic performance, there are many DBT principles, strategies, and techniques that can be understood and utilized by clinicians using other therapeutic modalities and models. For example, psychopharmacologists who have knowledge of DBT may better understand and manage their BPD patients' medication requests and suicidal behavior. Furthermore, their clinical approach to patients with BPD may be enhanced by a better understanding of the importance of validation (a central DBT concept) with this population. While we recommend utilizing DBT as developed since that is what has the empirical support behind it, we recognize that not all clinicians will choose to do so. And we believe that, whatever the treatment approach, clinicians can benefit from incorporating aspects of DBT into their practice. Thus, the primary purpose of this book is to provide a clinically oriented, user-friendly guide to understanding and utilizing the principles and techniques of DBT.

The challenge of treating Borderline Personality Disorder and disorders of emotion dysregulation

Individuals with BPD and disorders in which there is pervasive emotion dysregulation generally present many challenges in psychotherapeutic treatment for even the most trained and dedicated clinicians. The BPD diagnosis is one of the most stigmatized of the mental illnesses, notorious for treatment resistance [1], high treatment utilization [2],

---

The Dialectical Behavior Therapy Primer: How DBT Can Inform Clinical Practice, First Edition.
Beth S. Brodsky and Barbara Stanley.
© 2013 John Wiley & Sons, Ltd. Published 2013 by John Wiley & Sons, Ltd.

high dropout rates, high comorbidity with other diagnoses [3], and recurrent suicidal and non-suicidal self-injurious (NSSI) behaviors [1]. Therapist burnout with this population is common. The severity and chronicity of BPD symptoms cause individuals with the disorder and those involved with them a great deal of anguish and frustration. The clinicians treating those with the disorder are not immune to this sense of frustration and, consequently, act in ways that they find uncharacteristic and, ultimately, not helpful, despite initial and perhaps long-sustained intentions to help. Why?

More specifically, we ask, *"Why do mental health clinicians who are ordinarily empathic and who have chosen the helping profession as their career become exasperated, off balance, or unwilling to continue trying to help certain patients? Why may they resort to measures they would not take with their other patients?"*

Most psychotherapists have a story to tell regarding their most "difficult" patient. Chances are this patient was either clearly diagnosed with BPD or was given multiple Axis I diagnoses that shifted over time and, in retrospect, was best understood as BPD. What is it about BPD that individuals with this disorder are experienced as "difficult" and even as the *most* difficult patients to treat? Are their problems more severe than those diagnosed with schizophrenia or bipolar disorder? We do not think so.

Is it the fact that their problems are often manifest in the interpersonal domain that creates the difficulties?
Is it that their triggers to extreme emotional dysregulation may seem trivial and unpredictable to the therapist?
Is it that the emotional dysregulation itself is experienced as so extreme by the clinician that it is difficult to tolerate?

We think that all three factors contribute to the problems clinicians report in working with patients with BPD and severe emotion dysregulation problems. Clinicians become "burned out" and discouraged by the difficult symptomatology presented by borderline patients. These patients experience intense anger, sometimes directed at therapists and at any other person to whom they become emotionally attached. They engage in disturbing and frightening self-destructive behaviors including suicide attempts, nonsuicidal self-injury, and substance abuse. These behaviors are often triggered by interpersonal interactions, including even well-intentioned therapeutic interventions.

Individuals with BPD can be very dependent on those around them for self-definition and self-esteem [4]. They often develop an intense need for concrete contact with people important to them. This need for contact can be experienced as overwhelming and impossible to satisfy. Furthermore, the functioning of individuals with BPD is highly mood-dependent, can fluctuate dramatically, and can depend on the "emotional valence" of the situation. For example, individuals with BPD can do extremely well in work or school settings where they meet with success and positive feedback. Their underlying vulnerability may not be seen or provoked. To those who do not fully appreciate the nature of the disorder, this can create the impression that individuals with BPD are capable of high functioning in all circumstances and are deliberately behaving in a "helpless, manipulative" manner when their functioning is compromised by their emotional state or by the nature of their interpersonal relationships. So, the same individual who can produce a high-quality well-researched legal brief may fall apart when her boyfriend cancels a date at the last minute because of work commitments. On a very basic level, it does not seem possible that the dysfunctional behaviors are genuine. But they are.

These are some direct quotes from therapists with whom we have consulted or supervised.

> *My patient with BPD is so unbelievably manipulative. She gets great grades at that Ivy League college she attends and does independent research for one of her professors that draws great praise. Yet she gets distraught and can't function if her boyfriend doesn't call her or if I'm a few minutes late for our appointment. She's so melodramatic and self-centered. I find myself continually annoyed with her.*
>
> *I have a really "bad borderline" who keeps calling me and I can't stand to take her calls any more. She never has a good reason for the calls. Everything is an emergency to her.*
>
> *I'm sick and tired of my borderline patient's repeated suicide gestures and the inevitable calls from the ER in the middle of the night. Next time she does it, I'm going to tell the ER that she has been terminated from my care.*

This type of clinician response is not an infrequent occurrence when the patient is diagnosed with BPD. We have been suicide researchers and clinicians for many years and experienced a sense of our own limitations as we began to do psychotherapy with suicidal and self-injuring individuals who had BPD. We were both trained in a traditional psychodynamic model which we found did not provide the tools or a useful framework to help our patients manage their suicidal urges, their self-injury, their out-of-control emotions, and their relationships. Many clinicians who have sought our advice and consultation in working with their BPD patients have echoed this experience.

Why are we focusing on the clinician's reactions here instead of the enormous suffering of individuals with BPD? Because we recognize that BPD is a very common disorder and many individuals with BPD are desperately in need of treatment, and, therefore, most clinicians are likely to be asked to treat individuals with BPD. Some clinicians choose (when they have the option) not to treat this population or are not as helpful as they might be. By helping clinicians feel and, in fact, be more capable in working with individuals with BPD, we hope to decrease the suffering of the patients afflicted with this disorder who seek treatment. Are there approaches in which clinicians can better maintain a sense of balance and perspective while being understanding of and helpful to their patients with BPD? DBT offers one such approach.

What is DBT?

DBT is a treatment for individuals with pervasive emotion dysregulation and has quickly become a psychotherapeutic treatment of choice for individuals with BPD, particularly for those with suicidal and self-injurious behaviors, the population for whom the treatment was originally developed [5]. It was not until Marsha Linehan, the treatment developer, worked with patients with chronic self-injury and suicidal behavior that she concluded that her patients had the diagnosis of BPD in common. And, thus, DBT became a treatment for BPD, and more recently is being more broadly considered to be a treatment for severe emotional dysregulation, a core feature of the BPD diagnosis [6]. But its focus on self-harm behaviors lent it to adaptations for similar problems in which there is a pattern of self-destructive behaviors, such as substance abuse and eating disorders. Furthermore, in clinical practice, DBT has been extended for use with individuals who have a broad range of difficulties with regulation of emotions.

The beauty of DBT is that, through its structure, it provides a *road map* for clinicians (and their patients) to navigate the path toward improving the lives of multiproblemed patients with chaotic, crisis-driven, and often self-destructive patterns of living. The structure of DBT focuses therapists and patients on crucial problems that must be addressed (e.g., suicidal behavior and self-injury), helps them stay on track, and prevents detours that can easily be taken when the patient has a crisis-driven life. This road map keeps the therapeutic dyad moving toward mutually agreed upon goals.

The basic components of DBT include individual psychotherapy (conducted in a fairly structured manner); skills training, which typically takes place in a weekly seminar-type format and during which skills are taught to help individuals with severe emotion regulation problems; intersession patient coaching; and clinician team consultation to provide support to fellow therapists and to help each other stay on track in their work with this multiproblem population. These components are described to the patient in the initial sessions (pretreatment phase) so that the patient's agreement to be in DBT is with full knowledge of the treatment components and expectations for each of these components. There is misunderstanding by some in the field that DBT is only about teaching skills in a group format. And while the skills component is crucial, it is only one component. There are no studies yet that demonstrate that skills alone or added to other forms of treatment are effective. However, in our clinical work, we have certainly seen where it has been beneficial for patients who are struggling in other forms of therapy but do not wish to leave that treatment, to add a skills training group to their therapeutic experience. Interestingly, the recommendation for a DBT skills group often comes from the primary therapist who adheres to a model other than DBT. In order for this arrangement to be helpful to the patient, the primary therapist must be open to helping the patient apply the skills.

Why the name DBT? The B (behavior) in DBT is easy to understand. DBT is rooted in principles of behavior therapy with an emphasis on the application of learning principles, including operant and classical conditioning. And while it is a form of cognitive behavioral therapy (CBT), most adaptations of CBT place an emphasis, while not excluding the other, on either the cognitive or behavioral aspects of a CBT model and can be described as emphasizing the cognitions or behaviors, that is, big C (CbT) versus big B (cBT) approaches. The orientation of DBT is cBT, whereas Aaron Beck's approach is CbT [7]. These differences are more than an academic distinction because they determine the route these approaches take to change. The term "dialectical" in DBT requires more clarification. Dialectics is a philosophical concept that includes several assumptions: (a) all things are connected; (b) change is inevitable and continual; and (c) opposites can be integrated to develop a closer approximation of the truth. It is this last point that it is stressed in DBT and is at the core of the ongoing and continual explicit balance of acceptance and change that we will describe as present throughout the treatment [7].

As clinicians and researchers who have taken a particular interest in understanding and improving treatment efficacy for individuals with BPD, we have been inspired and informed by DBT. In particular, we have come to see that the philosophical assumptions underlying DBT serve to both orient and maintain morale in the clinician, a major aspect of improving treatment for individuals with BPD. As one patient put it, "Oh yes, I was in DBT therapy. It helped me but it also helped the therapist feel better about working with me."

Helping therapists feel better about treating individuals with BPD is no small feat. Of course, therapists would not "feel better" unless they were able to experience a sense of increased efficacy – their patients showed up for sessions, stayed in treatment, and improved. We believe that the theoretical stance inherent in DBT, as well as the specific interventions, effectively targets both the clinician and the patient.

The usual clinical training can leave clinicians ill-equipped to accurately interpret and intervene, and, therefore, be effective in the face of the severity and multitude of problems experienced by individuals with BPD. Notably, many standard approaches do not have protocols for treating and managing suicidal behaviors and nonsuicidal self-injury. In fact, some training programs refrain from exposing their trainees to suicidal patients with BPD because it is felt that they are too "difficult." We maintain that this is the ideal time because of the available support and structure. However, there has been little guidance for clinicians in tolerating and minimizing the emotional toll of frantic calls for help, the seemingly "bottomless pit" of dependency needs, the emotional intensity, lability, unpredictability, and genuine extreme sensitivity of these individuals. Conventional ideas regarding boundaries and limit setting do not prepare clinicians for finding the appropriate balance between autonomy and dependence in BPD patients. Nor are they particularly effective.

Many individuals with BPD experience therapeutic "neutrality" as uncaring and this, in turn, can breed resentment in a clinician who feels that their well-meaning efforts are being willfully misinterpreted. Furthermore, in BPD, what is neutral clinician behavior can be misread as "rejecting," "angry," "disinterested," or worse, as tacit approval of maladaptive and self-destructive behavior. While it is important for those with BPD to learn that they have a tendency to misread, they may experience this as too upsetting early on in treatment and withdraw before they have the opportunity to address this.

Toward this end, we present a clear, comprehensive summary of DBT principles and techniques illustrated with rich clinical vignettes. It should be noted that while we have tried to stay as true as possible here to the DBT model as developed by Linehan, our writing is inevitably affected by our training and our experience in applying the model. Thus, we also include DBT-informed conceptualizations and interventions that we have developed based on our experience over the years of conducting DBT in both research and clinical settings with individuals at risk for self-harm behaviors. We try to state explicitly where our thinking is informed by the DBT model but is an expansion of it.

"Top 10 questions" therapists ask about working with individuals who have BPD

We have identified the "top 10" most frequently asked questions about how to effectively intervene with borderline patients. While we set the questions in a neutral format, they are often asked with a great deal of anger, worry, and judgmental tone. We note the questions here and will demonstrate throughout the book how DBT effectively addresses each of these questions.

1. How can clinicians maintain empathy for their borderline patients?
2. What can clinicians do to help patients who are extremely sensitive to criticism tolerate change interventions and not leave prematurely in response to a change-oriented intervention?
3. How do clinicians help patients manage their chronic suicidal ideation, threats, and gestures in an outpatient setting without becoming dysregulated themselves? How can clinicians refrain from becoming either overly anxious and overreactive or disinterested and immune to suicide ideation and behaviors?
4. Are there effective therapeutic techniques for directly treating nonsuicidal self-injury and other destructive behaviors?
5. How do practitioners maintain limits when they fear it will trigger suicidal behavior and how do they refrain from inadvertently reinforcing suicidal behavior?
6. How do clinicians offer availability while placing manageable limits on between-session phone calls and requests for contact? In other words, how can clinicians expand their boundaries when appropriate without stretching them too far and how do clinicians keep from stretching them further and further and then abruptly ending the relationship?
7. How do clinicians handle emotionally dysregulated patients' angry and frantic requests for help in an effective manner?
8. When should an individual with BPD be hospitalized and how can clinicians avoid unhelpful, repeated hospitalizations?
9. What are the ways of effectively managing behaviors that are referred to as "splitting" in treatments where there are multiple clinicians?
10. How do practitioners assess capability in BPD patients and help patients set realistic goals and achieve a good quality of life?

How does DBT help the clinician?

By tackling these and other questions, we encourage clinicians to learn to view the BPD diagnosis and its treatment from within the framework of DBT. While DBT is a method of treatment based in CBT, it is also firmly embedded in a theoretical perspective about the nature of the disorder. In our experience, a DBT perspective particularly helps clinicians to see, from the patient's perspective, what it is like to suffer with the disorder. It removes pejorative expressions about the "badness" of a patient (e.g., manipulative or provocative) and discusses problems in a descriptive, nonjudgmental manner. In so doing, DBT immediately helps clinicians change their emotional reaction to patients.

DBT challenges and requires a relearning of certain basic conventions regarding the nature of doing therapy. For example, the term "treatment resistance" is absent from the DBT model. "Treatment resistance" is a concept from psychodynamic psychotherapy and a term that has become ubiquitous in therapeutic parlance to describe what the patient is doing to oppose the process of therapy. From a psychodynamic perspective, resistance is considered to be both conscious and unconscious, stemming from an individual's reluctance toward and defense against thinking about or facing certain feelings or experiences [8]. But the absence of this terminology in DBT does not mean that difficulties in the therapeutic relationship go unaddressed. Quite to the contrary, they are inquired about and addressed explicitly in each and every session. However, these difficulties are described as "therapy-interfering behaviors," a term that, in our opinion, carries a more neutral tone. In DBT, both the patient's and therapist's behaviors can be therapy-interfering, and both are the subject for discussion and resolution in sessions.

Through discussion of our experiences and those of the clinicians with whom we have consulted and supervised, we share how we have come to understand the emotional and behavioral world of individuals with BPD. We suggest that the nature of the disorder can transact with particular assumptions underlying the practice of some other forms of psychotherapy to exacerbate symptoms, and contribute to demoralization and clinician burnout. Our perspective is that, in order to retain these individuals in treatment, to reduce symptoms, and to increase capacity for positive life experience, clinicians need to carefully consider their assumptions and interpretations, and to assume greater responsibility for treatment failure. At the same time, they also need to engage the patient in taking shared responsibility for their treatment and for staying safe. The dialectic worldview, when applied to the treatment of BPD, provides clinicians with a viable theoretical approach. We take pains to illustrate how the dialectic philosophy underlies each DBT intervention, and how integral this way of thinking is to the effective practice of DBT.

Overview of the book

This book has two main parts. The first part, Chapters 2–7, lays the theoretical foundation and presents the empirical evidence for how DBT informs our understanding of the phenomenology of BPD and self-harm behaviors. The second part, Chapters 8–18, provides a clinical guide to incorporating DBT interventions into clinical thinking and practice.

In accord with these aims, in Chapter 2 we describe who (patients and clinicians) should consider doing DBT. We also discuss the qualities needed in therapists to work with individuals who grapple with chronic suicide ideation. We review the empirical basis for the efficacy of DBT with various diagnostic populations. We present the experiences of trainees from all mental health disciplines regarding the value of learning DBT. We also make recommendations to guide clinicians in performing an honest assessment regarding whether they are ready, willing, able, and open to "turn their minds" to the DBT way of thinking and intervening.

Chapter 3 explores the history and myth of BPD untreatability and the modifications that make DBT more effective in treating this population. Chapter 4 describes the stigma that has developed around the BPD diagnosis, by highlighting the historical aspects of the BPD diagnosis that relate to our current understanding of the disorder and treatment response. We describe and illustrate the subjective experience of the individual with BPD, informed by the theoretical perspective of DBT.

Chapter 5 provides a comprehensive review of what we currently know about the phenomenology of suicidal and nonsuicidal self-injury in BPD, including a DBT-informed conceptualization for understanding self-harm behaviors in BPD.

Chapters 6 and 7 provide an overview of DBT. In Chapter 6, we review the ABC's of DBT theory, describing what it means to take a dialectic therapeutic approach, and reviewing the assumptions underlying DBT theory and interventions. We elucidate the role of explicit validation in DBT, and describe the learning theories integral to DBT change interventions. In Chapter 7, we review the ABC's of DBT interventions, reviewing the four stages of DBT and the four modalities of DBT – individual psychotherapy sessions, group skills training, between-session coaching, and the DBT consultation team. We provide a clinical vignette to illustrate the multipronged DBT approach.

Chapters 8 through 18 provide step-by-step guidelines for using DBT techniques. Chapter 8 reviews the initial stages of DBT treatment strategies for making a commitment to and establishing goals for treatment. Chapter 9 describes the structure of an individual therapy session and the use of the diary card, agenda setting, and behavioral chain analysis to target treatment goals. Stylistic and dialectical strategies such as self-disclosure, irreverence, and use of metaphor are reviewed and illustrated. Chapters 10 and 11 describe the skills training component of DBT and how non-DBT individual therapists can enhance the learning of skills in their patients. Chapter 12 addresses between-session contact, in vivo skills coaching, and the DBT approach to observing boundaries. Chapter 13 provides guidelines for managing suicidal behavior from a DBT perspective and how to balance the emphasis on building a "life worth living" while guarding patient safety. Chapter 14 reviews the Safety Planning Intervention (SPI) developed by Barbara Stanley and Dr. Gregory K. Brown. Chapter 15 addresses the DBT approach to collaboration with colleagues, including consultation with third-party treaters, the DBT approach to "splitting," and how therapists who treat individuals with BPD can find support. In Chapter 16, we present the guidelines for conceptualizing a case from the DBT perspective and present case material to illustrate how case conceptualization informs treatment planning. In Chapter 17, we review a DBT-informed approach to the treatment of behaviors other than self-harm behaviors. For example, we illustrate DBT approaches to addressing therapy-interfering behaviors such as lateness and medication non adherence. We propose a DBT-informed way of thinking about how to assess and set realistic quality-of-life goals for individuals with BPD, in the face of their severe fluctuations in level of functioning. In our concluding Chapter 18, we discuss the various DBT ways of thinking about the end of treatment, including issues related to highly lethal suicide attempts and suicide.

We invite clinicians and individuals who care about someone with BPD to be open to viewing BPD from a perspective that can increase empathy for their plight, while at the same time feel more equipped to not become overwhelmed by it. Or, to use DBT language, we invite readers to take a dialectical stance, to be willing to validate the difficulty and pain of individuals with BPD, to view them and their behavior without judgment, while at the same time observing their personal natural (nonarbitrary) limits.

References

1. Mehlum, L. (2009) Clinical challenges in the assessment and management of suicidal behaviour in patients with borderline personality disorder. *Epidemiological Psychiatric Sociology*, 18 (3), 184–189.
2. Bender, D.S., Dolan, R.T., Skodol, A.E., et al. (2001) Treatment utilization by patients with personality disorders. *American Journal of Psychiatry*, 158 (2), 295–302.
3. Eaton, N.R., Krueger, R.F., Keyes, K.M., et al. (2011) Borderline personality disorder co-morbidity: Relationship to the internalizing–externalizing structure of common mental disorders. *Psychological Medicine*, 41 (5), 1041–1050.
4. Stanley, B., Siever, L.J. (2010) The interpersonal dimension of borderline personality disorder: Toward a neuropeptide model. *American Journal of Psychiatry*, 167, 24–39.
5. Koerner, K. (2012) *Doing Dialectical Behavior Therapy. A Practical Guide*, Guilford Press, New York.
6. Linehan, M.M. (1993) *Cognitive Behavior Therapy for Borderline Personality Disorder*, Guilford Press, New York.
7. Beck, J. (2011) *Cognitive Behavior Therapy: Basics and Beyond*, Guilford Press, New York.
8. Cabaniss, D.L., Cherry, S., Douglas, C.J., et al. (2011) *Psychodynamic Psychotherapy: A Clinical Manual*, Wiley-Blackwell, Oxford, pp. 150–151.

Part I
Theoretical, research, and clinical foundations

Chapter 2

When DBT is indicated: The patients, the clinicians, and the evidence

In this chapter, we describe the conditions for which DBT is indicated, the types of clinical populations that might best benefit from DBT from both an evidence-based and a clinical perspective, how familiarity with DBT contributes to a clinician's training and way of thinking and working, and the characteristics of clinicians who perhaps should not consider trying to work with the patient population we describe. It may seem rash to suggest that not all clinicians are suited for this work but, in our experience, there are some therapists who, despite training and supervision, are unable to develop sufficient tolerance of the suicidal feelings and emotional dysregulation that is required to work effectively with BPD.

> **Key points**
> - What does it mean to be an evidence-based treatment?
> - What can an understanding of DBT add to a clinician's ability?
> - When should you, as a clinician or patient, consider DBT treatment as the treatment of choice?
> - Patient characteristics – who is a good candidate for DBT and who is not?
> - Clinician characteristics – what abilities and characteristics are desirable in a DBT therapist and when should you consider not practicing DBT?

If you have treated individuals with BPD without specialized training in the treatment of this disorder, it is likely that you feel that you could improve your skills in managing and working with repeated high-risk, anxiety-producing behaviors such as suicide attempts or threats, chronic suicidal ideation, or nonsuicidal self-harm behaviors. Or perhaps you may feel challenged about how to maintain boundaries while stretching them at times to provide patients with BPD with what they need. And, once a boundary is stretched, do you feel that you cannot return to the prior limit? You may be uncertain about how to withdraw additional support from a rejection-sensitive patient when a time of crisis has passed.

The Dialectical Behavior Therapy Primer: How DBT Can Inform Clinical Practice, First Edition.
Beth S. Brodsky and Barbara Stanley.
© 2013 John Wiley & Sons, Ltd. Published 2013 by John Wiley & Sons, Ltd.

Perhaps you have had patients whose interpersonal hostility or intense dependency needs do not get adequately addressed with the delivery of treatment as usual (TAU). And, despite giving more time and effort than usual, the work does not progress smoothly and both your patients and you can become demoralized. You may even have had trouble maintaining hope for these patients and want to give up on them.

Or possibly, you are a consumer of mental health treatment who has had years of psychotherapy, which at best has provided some insight and support, or at worst has felt to be harmful or useless and has left you still struggling with dysregulated emotions, thoughts, and behaviors that greatly interfere with your quality of life. You may have experienced psychotherapy as not meeting your needs to learn basic skills for managing behaviors and emotions. You may have felt misunderstood or frustrated by standard "talk" therapy in which the therapist provides support and insight but little direction into how to translate this into day-to-day functioning. We have done consultations with many patients with BPD after their previous therapy came to a disastrous end with the patient and therapist clashing and either the therapist terminated the treatment precipitously or the patient fled in anger. These patients are wondering if DBT will offer a different outcome. A frequent refrain from these individuals is, "I know all about why I am doing what I'm doing. I just don't know what to do instead."

What do we know about the effectiveness of DBT to address these concerns? We will review the empirical basis for the efficacy of DBT in various clinical populations, as well as discuss the issues to consider in deciding whether and when to proceed with DBT.

DBT is an evidence-based treatment

What does it mean to be an evidence-based treatment? A number of randomized clinical trials (RCTs), the scientific gold standard for determining treatment efficacy, have been conducted that document DBT's efficacy in reducing suicidal and self-harm behaviors in this population. In RCTs, research participants are randomly assigned to either the study treatment group or to an alternative comparative study group – usually another treatment group. Thus, Linehan's first RCT compared DBT to TAU in the community [1]. Her second RCT compared DBT to "treatment by experts" (TBE) in the community [2]. The random assignment of participants to two or more treatment conditions is the best way to control for any bias that might occur when individuals select or are selected for a particular study treatment. In RCTs, all efforts are made to control for other possible confounding variables. In addition to random assignment, participants in each study group are compared on demographic and other clinical characteristics in order to identify any possible differences (other than the treatments themselves) between the two study groups that might impact on that group's response to the treatment. If differences in any of these other variables are found between the two groups, for example, age, then this variable is controlled for using statistical and study design methods.

DBT has also been adapted to treat destructive behaviors in other clinical populations. There is an evidence base for DBT efficacy in treating eating disorders (binge eating disorder and bulimia nervosa [3–5]), posttraumatic stress disorder (PTSD) [6], substance abuse [7–9], suicidal and self-harming adolescents [10–12], inpatient populations, partial hospitalization, and forensic settings [13–18].

When is DBT indicated?

Empirically based indications for DBT

If you are a clinician wondering if DBT is the indicated treatment for your patient, here are some guidelines. DBT is most clearly indicated, based on empirical findings, for individuals diagnosed with BPD and who regularly engage in self-harm behaviors. If you are treating someone with BPD who has chronic suicidal ideation, and who engages in either suicidal or nonsuicidal self-harm behaviors, DBT would not only be of help to the patient but, as we intend to illustrate, would give you effective clinical tools to manage risk and stay positively engaged with the patient. DBT has also been shown to reduce treatment dropout in this difficult-to-engage population. Thus, the increased efficacy in reducing suicidal behaviors, along with increased treatment engagement, should translate into increased hopefulness regarding treatment.

DBT for eating disorders

There is also empirical basis for the efficacy of DBT in binge eating and purging behaviors [3, 4]. DBT has been adapted to treat eating disorders in individuals with and without BPD. A DBT approach conceptualizes dysregulated eating behaviors from the perspective of the biosocial theory (see Chapter 4). In individuals who binge eat and/or purge, emotional vulnerability might stem from a biological disruption in the body's ability to signal hunger and satiety. The clinical researchers who adapted DBT for binge eating behaviors identify specific features of the invalidating environment that contribute to the development of binge eating and bulimia, such as body-shape and weight-related teasing, as well as family history of distorted cognitions and behaviors around weight and eating. DBT for eating disorders targets emotional dysregulation as a way to reduce binge/purge behaviors [5].

A randomized controlled trial comparing DBT adapted for binge/purge behaviors with a waiting list condition found that DBT was more effective in reducing binge/purge behaviors, although there were no differences between the groups in terms of changes in their ability to regulate emotions [3]. In trial comparing DBT for binge eating disorder (DBT-BED) to an active comparison group therapy intervention, the DBT group had fewer treatment dropouts, and showed greater efficacy in the reduction of binge eating at the end of the 20-week treatment period. However, these reductions did not extend into the 3-, 6-, and 12-month follow-up periods [4].

DBT for suicidal adolescents (DBT-A)

DBT has been adapted by Alec Miller, Jill Rathus, and Marsha Linehan for the treatment of suicidal adolescents (DBT-A) [10]. DBT-A includes a multifamily skills training group that has parents and teens learning the skills together. They have defined specific dialectical dilemmas and secondary targets (see Chapter 16) for adolescents, which are targeted in the skills training sessions. Family therapy sessions are another addition to the standard DBT model. Finally, some adolescent-friendly skills, called "walking the middle path" (see Chapter 10 on skills), have been added to the DBT skills manual for DBT-A.

As of this writing, the first RCT to test the efficacy of DBT versus TAU is under way in Norway [11]. However, studies using a pre-post design have shown promise for DBT as effective in the reduction of psychiatric hospitalizations, suicidal ideation, general psychiatric symptoms, and symptoms of BPD in highly symptomatic adolescents [12].

Posttraumatic stress disorder

Until recently, childhood abuse and trauma were not addressed in Stage 1 DBT treatment until suicidal and self-harm behaviors were under control. Standard exposure therapies for trauma [19] have excluded individuals who are at risk for suicidal behavior for fear that exposure therapy might exacerbate suicide risk. However, a new protocol based on prolonged exposure has recently been developed to add to standard DBT for the treatment of PTSD behavior in individuals with BPD and PTSD who engage in suicidal and self-injuring behaviors [6]. In a pre-post feasibility study, 13 women meeting criteria for PTSD and BPD who engaged in recent self-harm behaviors received DBT plus the prolonged exposure (PE) protocol. One year of DBT resulted in a decrease in PTSD symptoms so that a majority of the women no longer met criteria for PTSD. In addition, there were decreases in suicidal ideation, dissociative symptoms, guilt, shame, anxiety, and depression. There was no evidence that the PE protocol increased urges to self-injure.

When is DBT indicated: Clinical basis

As researchers, we are deeply involved in and devoted to the rigorous scientific testing of psychotherapy treatments. At the time of this writing, we are in the process of conducting a randomized controlled trial funded by the National Institute for Mental Health (Barbara Stanley Principal Investigator) comparing six months of standard DBT to six months of treatment with antidepressants (selective serotonin uptake reinhibitors) to determine which treatment is more efficacious in the reduction of suicidal and self-harm behaviors in individuals diagnosed with BPD.

While we understand that we cannot make scientific claims for the efficacy of DBT for the treatment of various psychiatric symptoms, and in clinical populations that have not yet been subjected to randomized controlled trials, we can anecdotally report that we have experienced effectiveness in the application of our DBT expertise to the treatment of various other behaviors and with individuals other than those who meet full criteria for BPD. Individuals who do not meet full criteria for BPD may nevertheless have significant traits of BPD that are amenable to DBT treatment. In particular, we have found that DBT can be quite effective in targeting impulsive/destructive behaviors such as assaultiveness or anger management problems, promiscuous sexual behaviors and sex addictions, stealing, reckless driving, and gambling.

Often, interpersonal difficulties and avoidance behaviors severely impair the social and vocational functioning of individuals who have significant avoidant, borderline, or paranoid personality traits. DBT can be effective in treating interpersonal difficulties such as tendencies to misinterpret the intentions of others, interpersonal avoidance behaviors, difficulties in skillful self-assertion, limitations in the ability to empathize with and validate the experiences of others, and lying. Avoidance behaviors, in general, can also be targeted using DBT interventions and skills training.

A history of not doing well in either insight-oriented or supportive psychotherapy may be another indication for DBT. Patients who have experienced difficulty in tolerating psychotherapy because they felt invalidated either by too much emphasis on change or lack of a directive stance on the part of the therapist may be good candidates for DBT. These patients might tend to interpret therapists as being overly critical or uncaring, which would lead to negative therapeutic alliance or early dropout. The dialectic approach that balances validation and change, as well as the active stance of the therapist in DBT, might lead to better treatment engagement.

Why should a clinician learn DBT?

DBT training is intensive, and takes a lot of time and effort to learn. Becoming well versed in DBT can require a radical shift in how clinicians conceptualize patients, as well as what it means to do psychotherapy and the role of the therapist. Doing DBT also demands greater availability and involvement with patients than some other treatment approaches. To be a DBT therapist you need a willingness to take on difficult patients with high-risk behaviors, hostile/dependent interpersonal styles, and limited and ineffective ways of coping that makes progress slow and can make engagement and therapeutic alliance more challenging.

Over the years, we have provided DBT training to trainees from all disciplines of the mental health profession: psychiatry residents, psychology interns and externs, social work students, as well as more seasoned clinicians – clinic directors, attending psychiatrists, emergency department staff – who were interested in gaining skill in DBT. In all cases, the training was elective and not a required part of their training program.

The training typically consist of intensive didactic training along with individual DBT case assignment and DBT team supervision. Trainees also lead DBT skills training groups. In all of these cases, the trainees are challenged in at least one, but usually all, of the following ways: by having to field between-session calls from their patients, handle suicidal crises, or worry about patients who did not show up and did not call. They also struggle with maintaining a positive stance toward patients who engaged in "therapy-interfering behaviors" including not showing up, showing up and being extremely hostile, expressing a level of neediness that felt unquenchable and unmanageable, or making extremely slow progress.

Despite the challenges, these trainees invariably considered learning and conducting DBT to be an extremely gratifying clinical training experience, one that positively impacted on their personal development as a clinician. In particular, these clinicians identified the following aspects of the training that were the most valuable for them:

1. They developed a greater ability to feel empathy for and to manage negative reactions toward their BPD patients.

    My training in DBT taught me the power of validation and empathy when working with patients with borderline personality disorder. I came to understand more fully that most of these patients have been told that the way they think and act is "wrong," "bad," "lazy," and that they come to expect this is how they will be treated by everyone they come in contact with. By trying to understand how their thoughts and actions work for them has opened doors for change for my patients and made working with them much more enjoyable.

My training in DBT over the last few years has greatly altered my conceptualization of clients and transformed my practice. In the past I have felt helpless and at a loss treating clients with BPD. Yet, now that I have some training in DBT I am better able to connect and help clients change and grow. The DBT training helped me to understand clients' suffering and maladaptive behaviors from a very different perspective. Thus, I believe the patients feel better understood; using validation is so powerful.

The exposure to the DBT model, in particular the dialectic between acceptance and change, has greatly impacted my view of my patients. In particular, I notice that I constantly try to find the "golden kernel" to validate in my patient's experience, especially when they are not immediately able to see it. I often see patients' current functioning as their best attempt to feel safe in the world and therefore I'm constantly looking for ways that it makes sense and ways that it can be improved. The DBT training has made me see my role as a nonjudgmental collaborator. Therefore, I often try to hold the nonjudgmental stance and merely observe what the patient is telling me and the result of any actions they may have taken. I now often ask the question, "How did that work for you? Was it effective?" whereas before I may have asked "why did you do that?" or "how did that make you feel?" In this way, I feel that I see my role less as a mirror, sounding board, or holding space and more as an active participant in acceptance and change with the patient.

Most importantly, really learning the difference between your own anxiety vs. a situation calling for emergent action was key. I learned to tolerate my own anxiety as my fairly sick patients often presented me with some very stressful situations, and I developed a better idea of when situations called for appropriate actions vs. choosing to sit with and contain my patients' anxieties. Patients benefitted from my acquired wisdom, because in learning this I was modeling anxiety tolerance and mindful action for them.

2   They developed greater confidence and effectiveness in managing suicide risk.

I think the most important way that DBT impacted me was to help me to feel more confident treating a suicidal patient. I felt I had a well-structured framework for how to ask about suicidality and discuss interventions. Suicidal patients are much less scary for me than before my DBT training.

A huge advantage of learning DBT as a resident was how it changed my comfort level in working with suicidal and other high risk patients. I learned how to speak frankly with patients about the meanings of suicidal or self-injurious thoughts, and how to collaborate with them in measuring acuity and risk rather than feeling that I as the psychiatrist had to be 100% responsible for considering and managing that.

What I really found helpful and still find helpful is how DBT, as a whole, can be very effective with Target 1 [suicidal] behaviors. The prioritization of behaviors is incredibly helpful as it orients both the patient and me towards what needs to be addressed first.

Using the skills to manage these symptoms not only helped contain the patients but also helped me to form a solid alliance.

The ability to tolerate a high level of risk in recurrently suicidal patients and still feel hopeful about their prospects makes working with this population much less anxiety provoking. I think these concepts should be an integral part of psychiatric training.

3   DBT gave them tools to understand self-destructive behavior and to intervene.

I feel that the behavioral analyses we conducted in DBT transformed the way I viewed maladaptive behaviors – that while patients would say they wanted to stop them, there were ways that the behaviors served some function for them, and it was important to discuss the pros and cons of behaviors when trying to modify them.

I now help clients focus on the here and now rather than the past (as I was trained to do earlier). I try to refrain from judgment and instead validate while also helping clients identify their maladaptive behaviors. Using a diary card and chain analysis (tools I never used before in my psychodynamic work) has also been really useful with particular clients. Furthermore, helping clients become more aware of their judgments and "all or nothing thinking" has been extremely useful and often a catalyst for change. In line with this, I am often reminded to move towards the long-term treatment goals by tackling much smaller goals that are more manageable (having realistic expectations for everyone).

4   Personal growth as a therapist.

I have also noticed a change within my boundaries. I am constantly thinking about what my personal boundaries or limits are that I need to communicate and observe. This thought process as well as other aspects of the training has made me much more genuine with my patients and I believe this makes the work more transparent.

One of the biggest pieces that learning DBT gave me was that it helped me to bring more of myself into the room. I didn't have to just quietly nod my head – I was encouraged to be active and to share concrete advice. Partly this is because DBT encourages thoughtful clinician self-disclosure and this can be used to normalize that everyone gets dysregulated at times and behaving skillfully can be difficult for all of us. This helps to bring clinician and client onto more equal footing and encourages collaboration. DBT also helped me to be more transparent and explicit with my clients about my thinking in general and about treatment planning.

Learning DBT… really provided a deeper understanding of certain therapeutic principles. I think this happened by adding a new vantage point on what we had already learned about affect, how patients develop within a treatment, the importance of alliance and the containing function of the therapist. The role of the therapist as a model became much clearer as I disclosed more with my DBT patient than I had in my previous psychodynamic experience. It increased my flexibility for conceptualizing my patients and creating a formulation for their experience. I was no longer thinking primarily about conflict and uncovering unconscious affects, but I was thinking even more about development, what skills had my patient not yet acquired, and what did she need to practice with me from a behavioral standpoint in order to act more adaptively in her other relationships? My ability to absorb and tolerate strong affects was certainly strengthened by learning DBT, which obviously lent itself to my work with non-DBT patients as well. I was even more attuned to the important of alliance, because if there was a rupture in alliance I was sure to hear about it from my patient, and we could talk about it and have a dialogue about it. This was one of the ways in which my DBT patient taught me, and modeled for me, about how to think about alliance and keep it in mind even with patients who might NOT be bringing it up.

5   Patients and therapist have a more positive therapy experience.

I never imagined how much I would enjoy working with borderline patients, but the changes promoted by DBT within my patients became a source of inspiration for my work. It is remarkable how much of the treatment is internalized by the patients and how meaningful it has been for me to learn and practice the skills as well. The support from the supervising team is fantastic. The non-judgmental stance from this orientation has allowed me to continue bringing my own style into the room and observing unbelievable changes in my patients.

It can be very liberating for patients to be able to conceive of and then make measurable gains, and of course, it is gratifying for us (as clinicians) as well – particularly when working with "difficult" patients that others have given up on. Finally, I think DBT very elegantly and simply (two qualities which can be undervalued in our field all too often) explains basic but necessary skills that many people use intuitively but would ordinarily be unaware of.

6   Collaboration with colleagues and peers.

The trainees found the DBT team to be a positively unique supervisory experience. In particular, they expressed that the team collaboration and support added a new dimension to their work as therapists.

Which clinicians are not suited to doing DBT

Through our training experiences we have also come to understand that not every clinician is suited to become a DBT therapist. Although the main thrust of this book is to encourage openness to DBT and the treatment of BPD, we respect that many clinicians have other talents and interests, and little desire to take on the challenge of working with BPD and other severe disorders, or to make themselves available in the way that DBT requires. We promote the exposure of trainee-level clinicians to DBT to both increase openness to the model and contribute to professional development in general. We have observed a number of factors that characterize those clinicians who do not naturally embrace the DBT model.

1   As DBT is becoming a treatment of choice for suicidal individuals with BPD and is gaining popularity and support from insurance companies, some clinicians might take on DBT training from a feeling of obligation or from calculations of increasing their marketability, even if they would prefer not to work with this population.

2   Many clinicians, even at the level of trainee, may already be extremely identified with or entrenched in the psychodynamic conceptualization of the treatment frame and the therapeutic stance. This results in a reluctance to or discomfort with taking a directive therapeutic stance, being more transparent and collaborative, and using self-involving self-disclosure, as is integral in DBT. Relatedly, these clinicians may be unwilling or feel a sense of burden regarding being available between sessions for skills coaching. They may not be comfortable addressing their own therapy-interfering behavior directly with a patient, or may not be able to internalize the assumption that the treatment or the therapist is the problem rather than the patient. Some clinicians are constantly translating DBT concepts into psychodynamic terms, and are not willing or able to accept the radical differences or become able to clinically conceptualize from a DBT perspective.
3   Some clinicians experience intense anxiety about suicidality and self-harm and cope with it by taking on too much responsibility for the patient's safety. The anxiety interferes with the clinician's ability to work collaboratively with the patient to share the responsibility. Ultimately, resentment builds up leading to clinician burnout.
4   Not all clinicians are interested in working with lower-functioning patients with multiple and severe difficulties in living. They do not have the patience for or have difficulty recognizing the areas of slow progress, and become easily demoralized by the frequent setbacks. And, while many individuals with BPD are not low-functioning, there is a significant number who are.
5   It is extremely difficult for some to maintain a validating stance toward BPD patients in the face of their interpersonal hostility, persistent self-harm behaviors, and intense dependency needs. These clinicians, with good therapeutic intentions, tend to understand and interpret neediness and aggression in a way that might seem invalidating to the patient.
6   Many clinicians would rather work more independently and are not willing to be committed to working with a peer supervision team, an integral aspect of DBT, for support and assistance in maintaining a validating stance.

Summary

Clinicians should consider incorporating DBT into their clinical practice for the treatment of self-harm behaviors and other impulsive/destructive behaviors related to BPD and for patients who generally have difficulty regulating their emotions. DBT has been adapted for and has been shown through research to be effective in treating suicidal adolescents, individuals with symptoms of bulimia nervosa, and PTSD. In clinical practice, DBT can be used for the treatment of impulsive/destructive behaviors such as unsafe sexual practices and sexual addictions, anger outbursts, and assaultiveness. DBT can also target the interpersonal difficulties and avoidance behaviors of individuals with borderline, avoidant, and paranoid personality traits.

Although learning DBT may require a radical shift in therapeutic conceptualization and the learning of new interventions, particularly for clinicians trained in a traditional psychodynamic or supportive model, it can contribute to an increased sense of professional growth as a clinician. Despite the challenges, DBT provides tools that increase capability for clinical progress in working with a high-risk, treatment-resistant population. DBT training increases confidence and ability to treat individuals at risk for suicidal behavior.

Anyone considering training in DBT should honestly assess whether they are open to the radical shift in treatment frame, the active therapeutic stance, and the increased clinician availability that is required to be effective with DBT interventions. Mostly, in order to be a good candidate for becoming a DBT therapist, a clinician must be willing to take and maintain a validating stance toward individuals with severe impairments in behavioral, emotional, and interpersonal functioning.

References

1. Linehan, M.M., Armstrong, H.E., Suarez, A., et al. (1991) Cognitive-behavioral treatment of chronically parasuicidal borderline patients. *Archives of General Psychiatry*, 48, 1060–1064.
2. Linehan, M.M., Comtois, K.A., Murray, A.M., et al. (2006) Two-year randomized controlled trial and follow-up of dialectical behavior therapy vs. therapy by experts for suicidal behaviors and borderline personality disorder. *Archives of General Psychiatry*, 63 (7), 757–766.
3. Safer, D.L., Telch, C.F., Agras, W.S. (2001) Dialectical behavior therapy for bulimia nervosa. *American Journal of Psychiatry*, 158, 632–634.
4. Safer, D.L., Robinson, A.H., Jo, B. (2010) Outcome from a randomized controlled trial of group therapy for binge eating disorder: Comparing dialectical behavior therapy adapted for binge eating to an active comparison group therapy. *Behavioral Therapy*, 41 (1), 106–120.
5. Wisniewski, L., Safer, D., Chen, E. (2007) Dialectical behavior therapy and eating disorders, in *DBT for Clinical Practice* (eds L. Dimeff and R. Koerner), Guilford Press, New York, pp. 174–221.
6. Harned, M.S., Korslund, K.E., Foa, E.B., et al. (2012) Treating PTSD in suicidal and self-injuring women with borderline personality disorder: Development and preliminary evaluation of a dialectical behavior therapy prolonged exposure protocol. *Behaviour Research and Therapy*, 50 (6), 381–386.
7. van den Bosch, L.M.C., Verheul, R., Schippers, G.M., et al. (2002) Dialectical behavior therapy of borderline patients with and without substance abuse problems: implementation and long-term effects. *Addictive Behaviors*, 27, 911–923.
8. Linehan, M.M., Dimeff, L.A., Reynolds, S.K., et al: (2002) Dialectical behavior therapy versus comprehensive validation therapy plus 12-step for the treatment of opioid dependent women meeting criteria for borderline personality disorder. *Drug and Alcohol Dependence*, 67, 3–26.
9. Linehan, M.M., Schmidt, H.I., Dimeff, L.A., et al. (1999) Dialectical behavior therapy for patients with borderline personality disorder and drug-dependence. *American Journal of Addictions*, 8, 279–292.
10. Miller, A., Rathus, J., Linehan, M.M. (2007) *Dialectical Behavior Therapy with Suicidal Adolescents*, Guilford Press, New York.
11. Rathus, J.H., Miller, A.L. (2002) Dialectical behavior therapy adapted for suicidal adolescents. *Suicide and Life Threatening Behavior*, 32, 146–157.
12. Mehlum, L., Tørmoen, AJ., Ramberg, M., et al. (2012) Dialectical behavior therapy for adolescents with recent and repeated suicidal and self-harming behavior and borderline traits – first randomized controlled trial. At the 46th Annual Convention of the Association for Behavioral and Cognitive Therapies, National Harbor, MD, November, 15–18.

13. Bohus, M., Haaf, B., Stiglmayr, C., et al. (2000) Evaluation of inpatient dialectical behavior therapy for borderline personality disorder: A prospective study. *Behavioral Research in Therapy*, 38, 875–888.
14. Swenson, C.R., Sanderson, C., Dulit, R.A., et al. (2001) The application of dialectical behavior therapy for patients with borderline personality disorder on inpatient units. *Psychiatric Quarterly*, 72, 307–324.
15. Barley, W.D., Buie, S.E., Peterson, E.W., et al. (1993) Development of an inpatient cognitive-behavioral treatment program for borderline personality disorder. *Journal of Personality Disorders*, 7, 232–240.
16. Simpson, E.B., Pistorello, J., Begin, A., et al. (1998) Use of dialectical behavior therapy in a partial hospital program for women with borderline personality disorder. *Psychiatric Services*, 49, 669–673.
17. McCann, R.A., Ball, E.M., Ivanoff, A. (2000) DBT with an inpatient forensic population: The CMHIP forensic model. *Cognitive Behavioral Practice*, 7, 447–456.
18. Trupin, E.W., Stewart, D.G., Beach, B., et al (2002) Effectiveness of dialectical behaviour therapy program for incarcerated female juvenile offenders. *Child and Adolescent Mental Health*, 7, 121–127.
19. Foa, E. (2011) Prolonged exposure therapy: Past, present, and future. *Depression and Anxiety*, 28 (12), 1043–1047.

Chapter 3

BPD: Treatable or untreatable?

DBT was originally developed to treat suicidal and self-harm behaviors in individuals with BPD. In this chapter, we review the modifications that DBT makes to the usual treatment approaches, modifications that increase efficacy of psychotherapy in the treatment of BPD, and the myth that BPD is an untreatable condition.

Key points

- The myth of untreatability of BPD
- Modifications of "psychotherapy as usual"
- Evidence-base for the treatability of BPD

The myth of BPD untreatability

Alice, a patient in DBT, attended her individual psychotherapy session the prior week in a state of intense distress, triggered earlier in the day by a comment made by her psychology professor. The professor gave a lecture on BPD during which she told the class that she refused to treat patients with the diagnosis because they were "extremely sick"; they did not stay in treatment and therapy just didn't "work" for them.

Alice was understandably upset by this. She had a desire to challenge the professor and reveal that she was in DBT and that it was an evidence-based treatment shown to be effective in treating BPD. However, she decided that it was not in her best interest to do so. But not verbalizing her opinion resulted in a sense of confusion in which she started to doubt her judgment about DBT, and she questioned whether the treatment was, in fact, helping her. While she felt that the treatment was useful, her fragile sense of self made her vulnerable to such stark invalidation by someone in a position of authority and with solid professional credentials. Alice came to her next session doubting both her decision to engage in DBT and her sense that she had made any progress. Her therapist spent a good part of her individual psychotherapy session validating and grounding her in her knowledge that she was indeed getting better in treatment.

The Dialectical Behavior Therapy Primer: How DBT Can Inform Clinical Practice, First Edition.
Beth S. Brodsky and Barbara Stanley.
© 2013 John Wiley & Sons, Ltd. Published 2013 by John Wiley & Sons, Ltd.

Case example

Alice is a 24-year-old white female who is in graduate school and works part time as an office administration assistant. She lives alone but has a boyfriend she has been seeing for one year off and on. She has a significant history of anxiety and mood symptoms from childhood, beginning around the time she was sexually molested by a 15-year-old male cousin multiple times between the ages of 5 and 6. Alice has symptoms of PTSD related to this childhood abuse, including nightmares and flashbacks that have persisted up to the present time. A sexual assault at age 21 exacerbated her symptomatology and contributed to its chronic nature. Alice also had concerns about her weight and appearance dating back to childhood, and she developed symptoms of anorexia during her freshman year of college. She restricted her food intake and exercised excessively. She binged periodically during periods of restriction. At this time, her menstruation ceased for approximately six months and she was about 15% under her ideal body weight. Currently, she is maintaining a normal weight and binge eats when she is under stress.

Alice also reports a period of heavy and regular alcohol consumption that began near the end of her sophomore year in college. During that period, which lasted for approximately six months, she reported having several drinks daily, frequent intoxication, and continued use despite her awareness of the problems drinking was causing: lateness turning in assignments, missing classes, poor grades. Although she has significantly reduced her use of alcohol, she still engages in periodic binge drinking.

Alice meets all nine of the criteria for the *DSM-IV* diagnosis of BPD. She has a history of six suicide attempts, with the first at age 13, the most serious occurring within the context of being intoxicated at a party and experiencing rejection from a male friend in whom she had a romantic interest. She impulsively broke a glass and used it to cut herself deeply on the wrists. She received 15 stitches and required blood transfusion and was hospitalized for a week. All of her suicide attempts have been impulsive and are triggered by interpersonal interactions with family members or boyfriends. Only one suicide attempt (her first at age 13) appears to have happened within the context of a major depressive episode.

Alice is an only child – her parents divorced when she was four years old. Her father moved out of state but remained in close contact and would either visit or have Alice visit him a few times each year. Alice had her first contact with the mental health system at approximately age 13. She saw a psychologist in private practice for approximately one year for the treatment of "adjustment difficulties" when her mother remarried. She sought treatment again when during her sophomore year in college because she developed anorexia. She did not attend treatment regularly and discontinued after six months. Shortly thereafter, she was hospitalized for a suicide attempt; she started her first trial of antidepressant medication and worked briefly with several different psychiatrists. She reports that she had difficulty finding a psychiatrist who could really understand her. She felt criticized and unsupported by most of the treatment providers with whom she came in contact. Later in college, she went into treatment again with a psychologist. During this treatment, she was hospitalized for a second time following a high-lethality suicide attempt and was asked to take medical leave from college. Her therapist also terminated treatment with her at that time stating that she was "too high risk." She moved back to live with her parents and attended weekly psychotherapy sessions for almost a year until she went back to college. She started treatment with another psychologist but only attended two sessions because she thought the therapist was cold and distant. She has never been in treatment with the same mental health provider for more than a year.

We present the case of Alice to illustrate the type of borderline patient that her professor had in mind but who can indeed benefit from treatment. Alice typifies the patient that the professor refused to treat – someone with a long history of treatment-resistant borderline symptomatology, co-morbid mood, eating and substance use disorders, treatment dropout, and therapy-interfering behavior that resulted in therapist burnout.

DBT is ideally suited to specifically address the types of challenges presented by patients such as Alice. Through the details of Alice's DBT treatment (as well as through a number of other composite case examples), we will illustrate in the later chapters how the DBT approach and interventions can engage such patients while lessening therapist burnout and the inclination for the therapist to terminate the treatment as one of Alice's therapists did. But DBT is not the only treatment that approaches these problems. In fact, adaptations of therapeutic approaches for BPD symptoms began nearly 75 years ago even before the diagnosis was fully described.

Modifying "psychotherapy as usual"

As early as the year 1938, American psychoanalyst Adolf Stern observed that certain individuals (those who presented psychopathology which would later serve as a basis for the *DSM* criteria for a diagnosis of BPD) did not improve within psychoanalytic treatment. He developed modifications [1] to make the conventional therapeutic approach of the day more effective for his identified "borderline" group of patients [2]. Stern implemented these adaptations to prepare these patients to eventually be able to tolerate a traditional psychoanalytic approach, or to "make them analyzable in the strict sense of the term" [2].

Some of the modifications that he proposed seem to be the precursors of the types of BPD-specific interventions incorporated into DBT and other psychotherapies geared to the treatment of BPD [3–5]. Stern determined that these patients required a more "reality-determined" relationship with the therapist, one that would provide more support and reassurance to them in experiencing and facing their painful emotions. Toward this end, he recommended having them sit in a chair facing the therapist rather than lying on the couch. He also cautioned against extended periods of silence on the therapist's part, since this would interfere with the "reality relationship" and would leave patients in "painful doubt" of what the therapist thinks about them.

Stern seemed to understand two very important characteristics of individuals with BPD: that uncertainty about what a person is feeling toward them is extremely difficult even if what the person is feeling is not negative, and that silence on the therapist's part is filled in with negative attributions. He suggested that the therapist be ready to provide sustenance and assurance, which includes paying attention to what the patient feels toward the therapist and not ascribing it primarily to transference and resistance. As mentioned earlier, resistance refers to what the patient is doing to oppose the process of therapy. Transference is a psychoanalytic concept that refers to the feelings that a patient has toward a therapist [6, 7]. Although these feelings can be related to actual characteristics of the therapist, more often the term "transference" is used to refer to feelings the patient has toward others, or wishes or fantasies that the patient has about the therapist (that are not related to actual characteristics of the therapist), that the patient "transfers" onto the therapist. The patient's feelings toward the therapist are interpreted (transference interpretations) to uncover and bring into awareness these wishes, fantasies, and/or feelings toward others that the patient may not be aware of. Stern felt that with this identified group of patients it was helpful to give more credence to the patient's understanding and intuition regarding the therapist's motives and behaviors.

A "reality-determined relationship," more support and reassurance, a more active stance on the part of the therapist including less silence, less emphasis on transference interpretations, and most of all, an honest belief in the patient's perspective – these are the "deviations" from psychotherapy as usual that can enhance the effectiveness of psychotherapy to engage and make progress with the borderline patient.

As we will see in detail through this book, DBT is defined by these types of interventions. The assumptions underlying the DBT therapeutic stance and DBT-informed interventions (see Chapters 6 and 7) represent a direct challenge to the assumptions of psychotherapy as usual. For example, the treatment frame in DBT is expanded to include between-session availability for additional in vivo support outside of the therapy office. Also, DBT's central emphasis on validation requires the clinician to be a real person in the room and puts the patient's perspective first. Distortions in the patient's perspective are only addressed after all of the valid aspects of the patient's experience have been identified and highlighted. The DBT therapist is mandated to take a very active stance in both validating as well as encouraging the patient to change.

Evidence-base for the treatability of BPD

It has been nearly two decades since Marsha Linehan first published the results of her randomized controlled trial comparing standard manualized DBT to TAU in treating self-harm behaviors in BPD. In this study, BPD individuals randomized to the DBT treatment group demonstrated a significantly higher reduction in suicidal and self-harm behavior than did those in the TAU group [8]. Also in this study, those in the DBT treatment condition had fewer hospitalizations and stayed in treatment longer (had fewer treatment dropouts) than those in the TAU condition. The reduction of self-harm behaviors in the DBT group was maintained over a six-month follow-up period, and the DBT group also showed fewer inpatient hospitalization days than the TAU group over the course of a one-year follow-up period [9].

Interestingly, in this study, depression declined in both groups while the self-harm effects were confined to the DBT group. From this, we can see that DBT appears to be as effective as other treatments for depressive symptoms but has specific behavioral effects.

In another study, a two-year randomized controlled trial of DBT versus "therapy by experts" in the community [10], research participants receiving DBT were significantly less likely to make a suicide attempt, required less hospitalization for suicidal ideation, and had lower medical risk associated with suicide attempts and nonsuicidal self-injury.

In addition to Linehan's findings, a number of well-controlled RCTs of DBT have been conducted across independent research teams, in the United States, Canada, and Europe. In a meta-analysis [11] of eight randomized trials comparing DBT to either TAU or TBE, DBT was found effective in reducing suicidal behavior in individuals with BPD. However, across studies, DBT was not shown to have a lower dropout rate than the comparison treatments. Only one of these RCTs compared DBT to another BPD specific treatment [12].

Summary

Unfortunately, we are not shocked by the view of Alice's psychology professor. However, we see it as a harsh reminder of the need to debunk the myth of BPD untreatability. The misconceptions and stigma regarding the BPD diagnosis and the inability to make progress in treatment seems to stem from attempts to shoe horn the treatment of BPD into models of treatment for other disorders. It just does not fit. More recent treatment models take into account the severe behavioral and mood dysregulation as well as the extreme interpersonal sensitivity of BPD and do better at maintaining patients in treatment and making progress toward change. Since the first clinical use of the term "borderline" was to describe a group of patients that could not tolerate the frame of psychoanalytic psychotherapy, "borderlines" originally, by definition, were those who did not respond to treatment.

However, we present empirical evidence in support of the treatability of BPD. We describe how "treatment as usual" has been modified, to more effectively target and address BPD pathology, its symptoms, and behaviors.

For reasons that are unclear (but about which we have some idea that we share in Chapter 4), the BPD diagnosis has been stigmatized to the extent that the lack of effectiveness of "treatment as usual" treating BPD has been viewed as a function of the illness, rather than as a failure of the treatment. With the latest empirical findings regarding the efficacy of DBT, it is clear that insistence on "one therapy fits all" has contributed to the persistent misconception that BPD is not treatable. We are writing this book so that clinicians can become more aware of and be able to incorporate new ways of thinking about and intervening, and ultimately become more willing to, and better at, treating individuals with BPD.

References

1. Stern, A. (1938) Psychoanalytic therapy in the borderline neuroses. *Psychoanalytic Quarterly*, 14, 190–198.
2. Stern, A. (1938) Psychoanalytic investigation and therapy in borderline group of neuroses. *Psychoanalytic Quarterly*, 7, 467–489.
3. Clarkin, J.F., Yeomans, F.E., Kernberg, O.F. (1999) *Psychotherapy for Borderline Personality Disorder. Focusing on Object Relations*, American Psychiatric Publishing, Inc., Washington, DC, pp. 33–70.
4. Kellogg, S.H., Young, J.E. (2006) Schema therapy for borderline personality disorder. *Journal of Clinical Psychology*, 62 (4), 445–458.
5. Bateman, A., Fonagy, P. (2010) Mentalization-based treatment for borderline personality disorder: A practical guide. *World Psychiatry*, 9 (1), 11–15.
6. Cabaniss, D.L., Cherry, S., Douglas, C.J., et al. (2011) *Psychodynamic Psychotherapy: A Clinical Manual*, Wiley-Blackwell, Oxford, p. 217.
7. Gabbard, G.O., Horowitz, M. (2009) Insight, transference, interpretation and therapeutic change in the dynamic psychotherapy of borderline personality disorder. *American Journal of Psychiatry*, 166 (5), 517–521.
8. Linehan, M.M., Armstrong, H.E., Suarez, A., et al. (1991) Cognitive-behavioral treatment of chronically parasuicidal borderline patients. *Archives of General Psychiatry*, 48, 1060–1064.

9. Linehan, M.M., Heard, H.L., Armstrong, H.E. (1993) Naturalistic follow-up of a behavioral treatment for chronically parasuicidal borderline patients. *Archives of General Psychiatry*, 50, 971–975.
10. Linehan, M.M., Comtois, K.A., Murray, A.M., et al. (2006) Two-year randomized controlled trial and follow-up of dialectical behavior therapy vs. therapy by experts for suicidal behaviors and borderline personality disorder. *Archives of General Psychiatry*, 63 (7), 757–766.
11. Kliem, S., Kroger, C., Crosfelder, J. (2010) Dialectical behavior therapy for borderline personality disorder: A meta-analysis using mixed-effects modeling. *Journal of Consulting and Clinical Psychology*, 78 (6), 936–951.
12. Clarkin, J.F., Levy, K.N., Lenzenweger, M.F., et al. (2007) Evaluating three treatments for borderline personality disorder: A multiwave study. *American Journal of Psychiatry*, 164 (6), 922–928.

Chapter 4

BPD: Diagnosis, stigma, and phenomenology

Top 10 question to be addressed in this chapter:

How can clinicians maintain empathy for their borderline patients?

In this chapter, we will review the history as well as the current conceptualizations of the BPD diagnosis, theoretical perspectives on the etiology of the disorder, and the phenomenological experience of having the disorder. We will propose that stigma regarding BPD, and misconceptions regarding its treatment resistance, stem from certain reality-based challenges as well as from iatrogenic factors.

> **Key points**
> - The origins of the term "borderline personality disorder" and current diagnostic issues
> - The stigma of BPD
> - The experience of "being borderline"

As clinicians who have an admitted bias toward the destigmatization of the BPD diagnosis, we nevertheless readily admit that the negative reputation of BPD is based on certain realities regarding the difficulties that these patients present. It is clear that the nature of the behavior exhibited by individuals with BPD can be extremely anxiety-provoking, more so than in most other psychiatric disorders. These individuals present with chronic suicidal ideation, self-harm, and impulsive, self-destructive behaviors. They can experience extreme, seemingly unpredictable fluctuations in mood, level of functioning, and interpersonal relatedness. They also have severe interpersonal sensitivity and limitations in interpersonal functioning, which manifests in the form of hostile, paranoid behaviors that challenge the patience and compassion of the most caring, well-intentioned clinician.

The Dialectical Behavior Therapy Primer: How DBT Can Inform Clinical Practice, First Edition.
Beth S. Brodsky and Barbara Stanley.
© 2013 John Wiley & Sons, Ltd. Published 2013 by John Wiley & Sons, Ltd.

These persistent personality traits often do not respond to traditional forms of psychotherapeutic and psychopharmacological interventions.

To gain some perspective, however, let us step back and consider how we have come to understand the BPD diagnosis.

The BPD diagnosis

History

The conceptualizations of borderline pathology and borderline personality originate in psychoanalytic theory. In fact, the term "borderline" was historically identified and was applied to a subset of individuals who did not respond to psychoanalysis, providing the original basis for the ongoing misconception of BPD untreatability.

As we reviewed in Chapter 2, the term "borderline" was first introduced by American psychoanalyst Adolph Stern in 1938 [1, 2] to describe individuals who seemed to lose reality testing at times but did not exhibit full-blown delusional thinking. He identified a certain subset of patients who did not seem to respond well to psychoanalytic treatment, called them the "borderline group," and described them as "bordering" between neurosis and psychosis. In the 1940s, psychoanalyst Robert Knight [3] described "borderline states" from the perspective of ego psychology, and described "borderline disorder" as a failure to consistently perform the ego functions of integrating thoughts and feelings into functional responses and behaviors. Thus, an example of an ego function is the ability to "reality test." Individuals who suffer from psychotic disorders suffer from a pervasive compromise in their ability to perceive reality, and therefore have impaired ego functioning. Individuals with "borderline disorder," as conceptualized by Knight, can have distorted perceptions of reality under certain emotionally distressing circumstances. According to Knight, these lapses in reality testing distinguish the "borderline states" from the higher "neurotic" level of ego functioning, in which reality testing remains intact across most situations.

The term "borderline personality" was later introduced in the 1960s and 1970s by psychoanalyst Otto Kernberg, within the context of personality disorders and object relations theory. Object relations theory of psychic development postulates that at early stages of development, the human infant perceives primary caregivers as either all bad or all good. Through the normal course of development, the individual becomes increasingly able to synthesize the split of bad and good perceptions, leading to a more holistic and realistic view of other individuals [4, 5].

Kernberg provided a more distinct diagnostic description of individuals with what he termed as a "borderline personality organization" [5]. According to his formulation, disruptions in the early caregiving environment prevent these individuals from overcoming earlier developmental splits in their internal representations of self and other. The failure to overcome these splits, according to Kernberg, results in a reliance on "primitive defense mechanisms" such as splitting, projective identification, and dissociation. The defense mechanism of "splitting" refers to an extreme polarization of good and bad feelings toward important attachment figures, such as love and hate, or attachment and rejection. "Projective identification" involves the projection of an unwanted or unacceptable thought or feeling into another person and then acting in such a way as to make that other person experience the projected thought or feeling as if it were his or her own. The defense of dissociation operates by causing a disconnection from unacceptable thoughts or feelings. This disconnection can be experienced as a loss of memory, or the loss of the ability to accurately perceive body sensations, or a loss of a current sense of reality. These defenses are considered to be "primitive" because they can, at times, result in a disruption of the individual's ability to perceive reality. According to psychodynamic theory, these unconscious mechanisms, as well as what Kernberg termed pathological aggression, underlie the poor impulse control, variability in reality testing, affective dysregulation, and interpersonal difficulties presented by these patients.

This conceptualization of borderline personality is broader than the current *Diagnostic and Statistical Manual of Mental Disorder* (*DSM*) [6] definition of BPD, which was introduced by Gunderson and Singer in 1975 [7] and supported by empirical work.

While personality disorders were included in the first two versions of the *DSM*, it was not until the third version in 1980 [8] that BPD was included as a diagnostic category in the *DSM*. At this point in time, there was a marked shift from psychoanalytic conceptualizations of diagnoses to psychiatric nosology. The *DSM* applied an atheoretical medical model based on symptoms to create classifications and diagnostic entities that can have more consistency for clinical and research purposes. This shift was heralded by the advent of new psychopharmacological agents that targeted symptoms of psychosis, depression, and anxiety. A multiaxial diagnostic system was created in which "clinical" disorders were placed on Axis I, distinguishing them from personality disorders, which were placed on Axis II of this system.

What does it mean to have a personality disorder?

All of the research and treatment development regarding BPD until now has been based on the definition of BPD according to the third and fourth editions of the *DSM*. *DSM-V* retains the criteria for BPD as laid out in *DSM-IV*. In the *DSM-IV*-TR [6], a personality disorder is defined as "an enduring pattern of inner experience and behavior that deviates markedly from the expectations of the individual's culture…, is pervasive and inflexible, is stable over time that causes distress and impairment." The pattern of inflexibility is manifest in various aspects of the individual's experience and functioning. It affects the individual's perception and interpretation of themselves and others, and the way in which the individual experiences emotions, including the range, intensity, and appropriateness of the individual's ability to control their impulses. Thus, in general, to have a personality disorder means to have a set of firmly entrenched personality traits that are problematic and not very amenable to change.

Thus, according to the definition of BPD (Box 4.1) within the *DSM* diagnostic system, there are 256 ways of meeting criteria for BPD, making BPD theoretically a heterogeneous diagnostic group. However, in reality, there are many fewer symptom clusters that are typically found.

> **Box 4.1 *DSM* criteria for the diagnosis of BPD**
>
> Specifically, in the *DSM*, borderline personality disorder is described as "a pervasive pattern of instability of interpersonal relationships, self-image, and affects, and marked impulsivity beginning by early adulthood and present in a variety of contexts, as indicated by 5 or more of these 9 criteria":
>
> 1. Frantic efforts to avoid real or imagined abandonment
> 2. A pattern of unstable and intense interpersonal relationships characterized by alternating between extremes of idealization and devaluation
> 3. Identity disturbance: markedly and persistently unstable self-image or sense of self
> 4. Impulsivity in at least two areas that are potentially self-damaging
> 5. Recurrent suicidal behavior, gestures, or threats, or self-mutilating behavior
> 6. Affective instability due to a marked reactivity of mood
> 7. Chronic feelings of emptiness
> 8. Inappropriate, intense anger, or difficulty controlling anger
> 9. Transient, stress-related paranoid ideation or severe dissociative symptoms

The stigma of BPD

Why is BPD viewed differently than other psychiatric disorders?

This "pervasive pattern of instability of interpersonal relationships, self-image, and affects, and marked impulsivity," along with poor treatment response, has contributed to BPD being stigmatized among mental health professionals, who often use terms such as "difficult," "manipulative," "demanding," "bad," and "attention-seeking" to describe their BPD patients [9–12]. As we have suggested [13], this stigma may predispose mental health clinicians to view certain behaviors as interpersonal demands rather than symptoms.

We propose that there are several aspects unique to the BPD disorder that, in transaction with typical therapeutic assumptions, make it more difficult for clinicians and involved others to attribute the manifestations of this disorder to a mental illness. Rather, borderline symptoms tend to be attributed to willfulness and a deliberate effort on the part of the BPD individual to be difficult. This is not the case regarding other psychiatric illnesses, particularly Axis I disorders, which are understood to be more biologically based than are personality disorders. Individuals who suffer from bipolar disorder or schizophrenia are rarely, if ever, regarded by clinicians to have deliberate control over their symptoms. For example, a study by Gallop et al. [14] found that nurses expressed less empathy for hypothetical patients with BPD than patients with schizophrenia.

This phenomenon was also evident in an informal yet systematic review of approximately 50 charts of patients (by coauthor Beth S. Brodsky) who had lengthy hospital stays during the 1980s. During the course of a long hospitalization, there were clear differences in the tone of treatment notes by nurses and other mental health providers in referring to patients who were diagnosed either with schizophrenia or BPD. In some cases, patients who were initially diagnosed with schizophrenia were re-diagnosed with BPD at some point during their hospital stay. For those who were diagnosed with BPD, the notes referred to manipulative behaviors on the part of the patients and indicated that the patients were purposefully choosing to engage in these behaviors in order to get something they wanted (or because they were not getting what they wanted). For those with schizophrenia, difficult behaviors were attributed to their illness.

Of course, the stigma of mental illness is not confined to BPD [15]. In major depression, family members and friends might have an invalidating stance, attributing symptoms to laziness and a poor work ethic, a tendency to whine and complain, and they may believe that depressed people can just "snap out of it" if they choose to do so. Studies provide empirical evidence that stigma regarding depression and seeking psychological treatment is greater among men, those with less education, and those living in rural areas [16].

We maintain that both patients and clinicians contribute to the cycle of stigma. Patients certainly can and do behave in ways that are extremely off-putting. They may say or do things that will make clinicians feel either angry and/or demoralized, and clinicians may react by getting angry, or losing interest, or caring less about the patient. By allowing themselves to be pushed away, however, clinicians contribute to patients' feelings of abandonment, which leads to further anger, disappointment, and ability to trust on the patients' part. For example, patients might accuse clinicians of not caring, and tell clinicians that nothing they are doing is helpful, or even worse, that it is harmful. Patients may say that they are not sure they want to continue working with their clinicians. In the face of hostile accusations, seeming lack of gratitude, and being told that they are not only helping but also actually hurting the patient, clinicians might believe and suggest that the best thing would be for a patient to find another clinician. This is experienced by the patient as further rejection.

In addition, it can be quite demoralizing for clinicians to have patients who clearly have many strengths, yet do not seem to make much progress due to severe fluctuations in mood and functioning. It is difficult to fully appreciate patients' limitations, which may lead clinicians to highlight patients' competencies and interpret their lower functioning as a deliberate or at least semiconscious attempt to communicate desire for attention or increased caregiving. However, it is important for clinicians to keep in mind that a core feature of BPD is mood lability and dependency, which severely impairs the ability to maintain an even level of functioning across situations.

By understanding BPD as a disorder like any other, clinicians can more easily avoid burnout and remain involved with even the patients they consider to be the most challenging. This in turn can create a therapeutic environment in which patients can become less anxiety-provoking and/or hostile/dependent. As we will illustrate in later chapters, DBT provides guidelines for the clinician to maintain a more therapeutic stance vis-à-vis BPD patients. In general, the assumptions of DBT and the emphasis on validation that inform the basic stance toward the patient (see Chapter 6) help reframe clinician expectations regarding what BPD patients "should" need or be able to do in therapy. The DBT team (see Chapter 15) provides validation and support for the clinician, who has the demanding task of maintaining an accepting and validating therapeutic regard toward their difficult BPD patients.

Our main point is that BPD is one of the few diagnoses in which the stigma exists not just in laymen but also among the *mental health providers* toward their patients. We propose that there is a transaction between specific aspects of BPD pathology with the myth of untreatability that contributes to this stigma. We speculate that the following characteristics of individuals with BPD contribute to a tendency on the part of clinicians to assign them more responsibility for their symptoms:

1. *Individuals with BPD utilize mental health services more extensively than patients with Axis I disorders* [17]. However, patients also have a high dropout rate, more revolving door hospitalizations, higher recidivism, and do not seem to respond to standard forms of care. Thus, although they present for treatment, they do not seem to be able to utilize treatment to make positive gains in functioning. Rather than view this as a possible limitation of what the mental health system has to offer, these patients are usually blamed for not being able to get better. The assumption is that the treatment should work, and if it does not, the patient is not utilizing the treatment properly, is uncooperative, or is not motivated.
2. *Variability in functioning due to mood dependency.* Individuals with BPD experience extreme shifts in mood state, and their thoughts and behaviors are strongly influenced by their current mood state. Thus, even when they are not in a major depressive episode, a transient depressed mood state can result in extreme lack of motivation and inability to maintain normal functioning. Similarly, when in a euthymic or hypomanic mood state, individuals with BPD are often highly engaged in functional social and vocational activities. The fluctuating and unpredictable nature of mood states, along with the strong dependency on a positive mood state in order to maintain functioning, leads to the attribution of blame on patients and the assumption that they are willfully refusing to maintain functioning.
3. *Variability in functioning due to environmental/interpersonal stress.* Similarly, in highly structured, less stressful situations in which emotional arousal is relatively low, individuals with BPD can exhibit a high level of vocational and social competence. However, in circumstances of increased stress (usually interpersonal or perceived failure), they decompensate severely, and the emotional dysregulation that results compromises their level of functioning. The fact that they demonstrate the capability for higher levels of functioning leads to the assumption that they have more control over their behaviors, and that they are "choosing" to not function at these times.
4. *BPD patients feel extremely needy, yet can also be help rejecting.* They require more clinician time and effort, yet can feel unsatisfied with the clinician's efforts to help. The interpersonal nature of BPD can be manifest at times in a hostile/dependent interaction. This, in turn, can be taken personally by caregivers and experienced as a lack of gratitude.
5. *Despite mounting evidence to the contrary, a biological and genetic basis of BPD is dismissed or minimized.* Substantial research has been done to document the biological and genetic factors contributing to Axis I disorders such as major depressive disorder, bipolar disorder, and schizophrenia, and for psychopharmacological treatment for these disorders. Similar research on BPD is not as extensive, in part, because until recently the existence of the disorder was questioned. However, preliminary findings support the role of biological and genetic factors related to BPD traits of aggression and impulsivity [18], and disruptions in interpersonal affiliative behaviors [19]. Environmental factors such as childhood abuse and trauma have also been found to both contribute to [20–22] and interact with biological factors in the etiology of BPD. This research is in its infancy and proposed models of the interaction between possibly genetic and biological factors with environmental life events in the etiology of BPD are just beginning to be investigated [23–25].

Understanding the etiology of BPD, as well as the day-to-day experience of someone who has BPD, can also contribute to a more empathic and less stigmatizing view of the disorder.

The biosocial theory of the etiology of BPD

Linehan postulates that emotional dysregulation is at the core of BPD and the self-destructive behaviors associated with it. According to the biosocial theory of the etiology of BPD, this emotional dysregulation results from a transaction between an inborn emotional vulnerability and an emotionally invalidating environment.

The biologically based emotional vulnerability is characterized by three components:

1 *High sensitivity.* Minor perturbations result in intense reactions.
2 *High reactivity.* An intense, quick reaction to stimuli in the environment.
3 *Prolonged activation.* Long recovery time following emotional arousal. The emotional arousal often includes a physiological component.

This combination of factors, particularly the slow return to baseline equilibrium, can result in individuals becoming emotionally aroused and dysregulated in response to an upsetting event prior to returning to a regulated emotional state from an earlier distressing event.

The "invalidating environment" refers to an ongoing pattern of unsatisfactory responses on the part of the primary caregiver to the emotional expressions of the emotionally dysregulated individual, responses that communicate to the individual that his or her emotional experience is wrong or inappropriate in some way. One type of invalidating environment consists of caretakers who may be unable to perceive, understand, and validate the individual's emotional intensity, and therefore do not provide conditions in which the individual can learn how to regulate their emotional experience. Thus, for example, a well-intentioned caregiver might try to comfort a child by telling him that he has no reason to feel angry or frightened. While such a seemingly innocuous invalidating response might not present a problem for an emotionally regulated individual, a predisposition to emotional dysregulation increases an individual's vulnerability to this type of communication over time to the development of pervasive dysregulation in emotion, sense of self, and behavior.

The most egregious example of an invalidating environment would be one in which sexual or physical abuse or neglect was present. Besides being a clear example of invalidation of the child's needs, the experience of childhood abuse and neglect is often characterized by much inconsistency and conflict as the child experiences both nurturing and abuse/neglect from the same caretaker. Given the high prevalence of reported childhood abuse among individuals with BPD [20–22], abuse cannot be ignored as contributory to the etiology of BPD. However, less explicit forms of invalidation such as repeated dismissal or denial of a child's emotional experience and reinforcement of maladaptive coping mechanisms can also lead to severe impairment in self-regulation [26].

A transaction between these two elements, in which the emotional sensitivity leads to increased reactivity, especially in interpersonal situations, and in which a caregiver's invalidating responses exacerbates the emotional vulnerability, leads to behavioral dysregulation. When emotionally vulnerable individuals feel that their emotions have been invalidated, they tend to ratchet up the expression of their emotional experience, which often includes engaging in destructive or self-destructive behaviors, in order to get a nurturing response from the invalidating environment. As their behaviors escalate, they are intermittently reinforced, making them very difficult to unlearn. For example, if a young child expresses fear of monsters in his room, his mother might try to reassure him by telling him not to be silly. Instead of feeling reassured, the child now not only feels frightened, but he may feel that there is something wrong with his feeling of fear, that it is silly, and this might make him feel even more in need of reassurance. He may end up having a temper tantrum in his room because he is left alone with his feeling of fear and doesn't know how to manage it. At this point, his mother might come in and try to help him calm down. This nurturing response reinforces the temper tantrum behavior and the child learns that this is the way to get his mother to help him when he is frightened.

"Being borderline"

Can this conceptualization of the etiology of BPD help us understand the daily experience of "being borderline"? Why do individuals with BPD behave in such an erratic manner, alienate the people that care about them, and engage in self-destructive behaviors?

What seems clear is that individuals with BPD experience a pervasive sense of badness, which requires a constant effort to resist. Their deep sense of unworthiness and worthlessness makes them more vulnerable to feeling disappointed and rejected. They have extreme difficulty trusting and accepting their inner emotional experience; they are very judgmental and rejecting of their own reactions. They believe that their natural emotional reaction is incorrect, bad, stupid, or an overreaction. This leads to self-invalidation and self-condemnation. They experience their emotions with a high intensity that is accompanied by physiological arousal and strong urges to act. This contributes to the feeling that they are controlled by, not in control of, their emotions.

There is empirical evidence that individuals with BPD, when compared with those with other personality disorders, such as histrionic, narcissistic, obsessive–compulsive, or dependent, experience a much higher level of dysphoria. Those with BPD spend a much higher percentage of time feeling overwhelmed, worthless, empty, abandoned, betrayed, or very angry. Cognitively, individuals with BPD spend a higher percentage of time feeling misunderstood, thinking that no one cares, that they are bad, believing that they are evil and that they are damaged, and they spend almost half of their time thinking about killing themselves [27].

Several factors predispose BPD individuals to react to interpersonal stressors with self-injury. Leibenluft et al. [28] suggest that the dysphoria experienced by these individuals has a primitive quality that belongs to an earlier developmental stage. Cognitive capabilities to recognize and verbally express dysphoric affect are absent or not well developed, possibly resulting from early trauma, which might arrest cognitive development.

Individuals with BPD maintain a very tenuous hold on self-worth, which makes them particularly reliant on external indicators and others for proof of worthiness. Because their emotions are so dysregulated, they find upsets and disappointments very difficult to tolerate. Because of their reliance on others for worth, interpersonal difficulties are particularly upsetting. Thus, pervasive feelings of badness and extreme self-criticism, along with tenuous self-worth bolstered by external forces, lead them to be extremely vulnerable to interpersonal disappointments, which are experienced as an assault on their tenuous self-esteem. They respond frantically, experiencing dysregulated anger at both the cause of upset and toward themselves. These feelings of badness, anger at self, and self-criticism for being so vulnerable lead to suicidality and self-injury.

> ### Case example
>
> **The case of George illustrates the daily experience of having BPD**
>
> George is a 28-year-old white man who has been in a relationship with a girl for about four months. He lives with roommates. He has a master's degree and works sporadically as a Web designer. He has a long history of depression, mood swings, anger outbursts, and substance abuse. He presents for treatment because he struggles with feelings of self-hate that sometimes lead to the self-harming behavior of head banging. Although he has never made a suicide attempt, he has frequent thoughts of killing himself and at times he becomes actively suicidal, with a plan to jump into the path of an oncoming train. He also has difficulties accepting direction from authority figures, which interferes with being able to hold down a job for any length of time. He has anger outbursts, which have resulted in losing friends and girlfriends in the past, and the loss of his jobs and relationships exacerbates his feelings of self-hate. George has periodic binge drinking behavior and also sometimes abuses methamphetamine.
>
> George meets seven out of nine criteria for the *DSM* diagnosis of BPD. He tends to idealize people and jobs, and then quickly becomes disillusioned and feels that everyone and everything about the job is horrible. He has impulsive substance use binge behaviors and also drives recklessly at times. He experiences intense rages and has frequent anger outbursts. He experiences emptiness, and he has trouble knowing exactly what he wants to do professionally. He also meets the criterion for nonsuicidal self-injury and suicidality. His mood is unpredictable and shifts quickly, and when he is in one type of mood, it is almost impossible for him to remember feeling any other way.
>
> George has many strengths – he is extremely intelligent, creative, and talented; is physically attractive; and can be very sweet and affectionate in his relationships. However, despite considerable academic and vocational achievements, he cannot sustain a sense of being comfortable in his own skin. He feels that he needs constant reassurance and positive affirmation from his jobs and his relationships, and, as soon as there is an absence of positive feedback, he feels empty and down on himself, and sinks into feelings that he is a terrible person, angry, low-achieving, and unlovable. These feelings are constantly lurking under the surface even when he is euthymic. He feels constantly weighed down by his feelings of emptiness and low self-esteem. These feelings affect his ability to maintain any gain and this, in turn, results in feelings of hopelessness and demoralization.
>
> George attends his psychotherapy sessions regularly but he is often in a very foul mood, dwelling on feeling very angry or victimized by a boss or his parents, and he rejects his therapist's efforts to offer other ways of examining himself and his life. He becomes suspicious of the therapist's attempts to help and feels that the therapist isn't being honest and doesn't really care about him. At times, he is in a better mood, reporting positive developments at work or in his relationships. At these times, he experiences himself and appears to others as quite competent and likeable. However, he gets easily triggered by interpersonal interactions and quickly deflates to a depressed and angry state. He makes little progress on his treatment goals and continues to challenge his bosses, lose jobs, use substances, and spiral into feelings of hopelessness and self-hate.

George is the type of patient that clinicians might find difficult to remain engaged with due to his difficulty in staying engaged with himself and any project or relationship with which he gets involved. George's strengths lead people, including his therapist, to expect a certain level of engagement and ability to move forward. However, these strengths are undermined by deep feelings of rage, emptiness, and self-hate, which feel very intractable. George's mistrust of and inability to engage with his therapist might also lead the therapist to become frustrated and less able to understand George's pain. Unless the therapist is trained to and supported in remembering that George's off-putting behaviors are manifestations of his self-hatred and ongoing distress, the therapist is at risk of joining in the feelings of hopelessness and demoralization.

Summary

We acknowledge the very real clinical challenges posed by individuals with BPD and how the erratic, self-destructive behaviors along with interpersonal hostility and extreme neediness contribute to the reputation of BPD as a difficult clinical population to treat. However, we also speculate that specific characteristics of BPD pathology transact with and challenge the usual treatment approaches, resulting in a loss of clinical perspective that places the responsibility of treatment failure on the patient rather than on the treatment, the therapeutic dyad, or the clinician.

We make the case that clinicians can maintain a less stigmatized and more accepting stance if they keep the concept of BPD as a disorder in the same way that schizophrenia, bipolar illness, and depression are disorders in the forefront. Toward this end, we present the DBT biosocial theory of the etiology of BPD as well as clinical and research findings that document the suffering experienced by BPD individuals on a daily basis. We intend to illustrate in future chapters how the assumptions of DBT, the biosocial theory of the etiology of BPD, the emphasis on validation, and the role of the DBT team in supporting the therapist are all ways in which DBT facilitates the destigmatization of BPD.

References

1. Stern, A. (1938) Psychoanalytic investigation and therapy in borderline group of neuroses. *Psychoanalytic Quarterly*, 7, 467–489.
2. Stern, A. (1938) Psychoanalytic therapy in the borderline neuroses. *Psychoanalytic Quarterly*, 14, 190–198.
3. Knight, R.P. (1953) Borderline states. *Bulletin of the Menninger Clinic*, 17 (1), 1–12.
4. Kernberg, O.F. (1967) Borderline personality organization. *Journal of the American Psychoanalytic Association*, 15 (3), 641–685.
5. Kernberg, O.F. (1984) *Severe Personality Disorders: Psychotherapeutic Strategies*, Yale University Press, New Haven.
6. American Psychiatric Association. (2000) *Diagnostic and Statistical Manual of Mental Disorders* (4th ed., text rev.), American Psychiatric Association, Washington, DC.
7. Gunderson, J.G., Singer, M.T. (1975) Defining borderline patients: An overview. *American Journal of Psychiatry*, 132 (1), 1–10.

8. American Psychiatric Association. (1980) *Diagnostic and Statistical Manual of Mental Disorders* (3rd ed.), American Psychiatric Association, Washington, DC.
9. Gallop, R., Wynn, F. (1987) The difficult inpatient: Identification and response by staff. *Canadian Journal of Psychiatry*, 32, 211–215.
10. Nehls, N. (1998) Borderline personality disorder: Gender stereotypes, stigma, and limited system of care. *Issues in Mental Health Nursing*, 19, 97–112.
11. Fraser, K., Gallo`p, R. (1993) Nurses' confirming/disconfirming responses to patients diagnosed with borderline personality disorder. *Archives of Psychiatric Nursing*, 7, 336–341.
12. Stone, M., Stone, D., Hurt, S. (1987) Natural history of borderline patients treated by intensive hospitalization. *Psychiatric Clinics of North America*, 10, 185–206.
13. Aviram, R.B., Brodsky, B.S., Stanley, B. (2006) Borderline personality disorder, stigma, and treatment implications. *Harvard Review of Psychiatry*, 14 (5), 249–256.
14. Gallop, R., Lancee, W.J., Garfinkel, P. (1989) How nursing staff respond to the label "borderline personality disorder." *Hospital and Community Psychiatry*, 40 (8), 815–819.
15. Link, B.G., Phelan, J.C., Bresnahan, M., et al. (1999) Public conceptions of mental illness: Labels, causes, dangerousness, and social distance. *American Journal of Public Health*, 89, 1328–1333.
16. Jones, A.R., Cook, T.M., Wang, J. (2011) Rural–urban differences in stigma against depression and agreement with health professionals about treatment. *Journal of Affective Disorders*, 134 (1–3), 145–150.
17. Bender, D.S., Dolan, R.T., Skodol, A.E., et al. (2001) Treatment utilization by patients with personality disorders. *American Journal of Psychiatry*, 158 (2), 295–302.
18. Foti, M.E., Geller, J., Guy, L.S., et al. (2011) Borderline personality disorder: Considerations for inclusion in the Massachusetts parity list of "biologically-based" disorders. *Psychiatric Quarterly*, 82 (2), 95–112.
19. Stanley, B., Siever, L.J. (2010) The interpersonal dimension of borderline personality disorder: Toward a neuropeptide model. *American Journal of Psychiatry*, 167, 24–39.
20. Herman, J.L., Perry, J.C., van der Kolk, B.A. (1989) Childhood trauma in borderline personality disorder. *American Journal Psychiatry*, 146, 490–495.
21. Ogata, S.N., Silk, K.R., Goodrich, S., et al. (1990) Childhood sexual and physical abuse in adult patients with borderline personality disorder. *American Journal of Psychiatry*, 147, 1008–1013.
22. Brodsky, B.S., Cloitre, M., Dulit, R.A. (1995) Relationship of dissociation and childhood abuse in borderline personality disorder. *American Journal of Psychiatry*, 152 (12), 1788–1792.
23. Goodman, M., New, A., Siever, L. (2004) Trauma, genes, and the neurobiology of personality disorders. *Annals of the New York Academy of Science*, 1032, 104–116.
24. Livesley, J. (2008) Toward a genetically-informed model of borderline personality disorder. *Journal of Personality Disorders*, 22 (1), 42–71.
25. Distel, M.A., Middeldorp, C.M., Trull, T.J., et al. (2011) Life events and borderline personality features: The influence of gene-environment interaction and gene-environment correlation. *Psychological Medicine*, 41 (4), 849–860.
26. Linehan, M.M. (1993) *Cognitive Behavior Therapy for Borderline Personality Disorder*, Guilford Press, New York, pp. 10–12.
27. Zanarini, M.C., Frankenburg, F.R., DeLuca, C.J., et al. (1998) The pain of being borderline: Dysphoric states specific to borderline personality disorder. *Harvard Review of Psychiatry*, 44, 224–225.
28. Leibenluft, E., Gardner, D.L., Cowdry, R.W. (1987) The inner experience of the borderline self-mutilator. *Journal of Personality Disorders*, 1 (4), 217–324.

Chapter 5

Understanding and treating self-harm behaviors in BPD

Suicidal and nonsuicidal self-injurious behaviors (SIB) constitute tremendous challenges for the clinician in treating BPD. The difficulty in predicting risk and reducing these behaviors, and in distinguishing between suicidal and nonsuicidal self-harm, creates confusion and anxiety for clinician and patient alike. DBT was specifically developed to be effective in reducing these behaviors in individuals with BPD, as well as to give the clinician effective tools and support in doing so. Conducting DBT with suicidal individuals with BPD in both research and private practice settings over the years has informed our understanding of these behaviors in this population. In this chapter, we present a comprehensive review of what is currently known regarding the emotional and physical experience of individuals with BPD who intentionally harm themselves, either by attempting suicide or engaging in nonsuicidal self-injury. We then describe a DBT-informed formulation regarding how to more effectively intervene toward the prediction, prevention, reduction, and eventual elimination of these behaviors.

> **Key points**
>
> - Defining the problem – the confusion surrounding self-harm behaviors and its prevalence in BPD
> - The distinction between suicidal behavior and nonsuicidal self-harm and also the ways in which they sometimes overlap
> - The experience of self-injury – its function, the triggers, and vulnerabilities that increase its likelihood, and its aftereffects
> - How the experience of being suicidal in individuals with BPD may differ from suicidal individuals with other disorders
> - Clinical approaches to investigating the nature of self-injury toward reduction and prevention

The Dialectical Behavior Therapy Primer: How DBT Can Inform Clinical Practice, First Edition. Beth S. Brodsky and Barbara Stanley.
© 2013 John Wiley & Sons, Ltd. Published 2013 by John Wiley & Sons, Ltd.

Individuals with BPD engage in a wide continuum of self-harm behaviors ranging from nonsuicidal self-injury, such as superficial cutting and burning, to nonlethal and sometimes lethal suicidal behavior. Chronic self-harm behavior, performed with serious, ambiguous, and/or no intent to die, presents one of the main clinical challenges in working with this population. Many clinicians refuse to treat people with BPD because of the sense of burden, confusion, stress, and liability of working with these behaviors.

Treating individuals at risk for suicidal and self-harm behaviors can be stressful, as is true for any clinician working with patients who have a life-threatening illness. At the same time, it can be an extremely rewarding and productive experience to help someone refrain from cutting themselves after years of doing so or to assist someone in grappling with suicidal urges and seeing these urges diminish over time. Through conducting DBT with many suicidal and self-injuring patients with BPD over the years, both in clinical and research settings, we have developed a way of thinking about and understanding this behavior, one that has given us a greater sense of efficacy and hope in treating these behaviors.

The problem

Confusion surrounding self-harm behaviors

Individuals who engage in deliberately inflicted self-harm behaviors often feel disturbed, frightened, and ashamed. However, at the same time, there can also be a profound sense of relief associated with engaging in these behaviors. The intensity and the conflicting nature of the emotional experience create a confusing picture for both the patients and those who care for them. Self-harm behaviors cause extraordinary physical and emotional suffering, while at the same time serve as a way of coping and relieving psychic pain.

While there are many motives that self-injurers report for engaging in this behavior that are described later in this chapter, individuals with BPD sometimes report that they engage in self-harm behaviors in order to substitute physical suffering for emotional pain. For them, physical pain is easier to tolerate and plainly visible. Emotional pain feels intolerable, partly because it is mostly invisible to others, and, therefore, these individuals have difficulty knowing whether their emotional suffering is real. Physical damage, however, provides concrete proof of emotional suffering. Furthermore, individuals with BPD have difficulty decoding their emotional experience and tend to self-invalidate and minimize their inner experience. By hurting themselves physically, they provide a physical demonstration of how upset they are. They think, "I must be upset, look what I have done to myself." Also, the physical pain gives a more "valid" reason to feel bad. Another cause for confusion is that, although the nonlethal self-harm behavior causes physical damage, it can also serve as a compromise between not hurting oneself and committing suicide. In the individual's mind, it "satisfies" the need to self-harm but gives permission to go on living. This compromise can make it frightening for both the patient and the clinician to work toward the patient relinquishing the behavior. The cycle of self-injury is difficult to interrupt because it can become reinforcing and perpetuates itself because it does, indeed, "work" by making the self-injurer feel better, for example, less anxious, less dysregulated, and less angry.

Overreacting to suicidal behavior

Professionals and family members can, at times, ascribe suicidal intent to NSSI. Clinicians understandably become anxious about the risk for suicide and often react to self-harm behavior by deciding to hospitalize the patient. However, such a course of action may be unnecessary and even counterproductive if the individual has already decided that it is permissible to go on living. Unnecessary hospitalization can cause a disruption of the individual's functioning, which for many is already tenuous, leading to loss of work or school dismissal and fear, anger, or withdrawal by family and friends [1, 2]. These consequences can ultimately lead to an increase in hopelessness and suicidality [3] and do not further longer-term treatment goals.

Part of the problem is that typical clinical training for suicidal crisis management mainly consists of negotiating "contracts for safety." When patients cannot contract for safety, a visit to the emergency room (ER) or psychiatric hospitalization is often considered as the only option to prevent suicidal behaviors. While hospitalization is the most guaranteed method to prevent a suicidal behavior in an immediate time period, it can be overutilized and, therefore, not a long-term strategy for the treatment and prevention of suicidal and nonsuicidal self-harm behaviors. Furthermore, resorting to hospitalization does not help the patient learn to develop strategies for long-term coping with suicidal urges. Hospitalization and contracting for safety, which constitute the core of standard clinical training for suicide risk management, are not directly applicable to NSSI where the self-harm is deliberate yet has no clear suicidal intent. Also, there is little empirical evidence for the effectiveness of "safety contracts" in preventing suicidal behavior [4].

Underestimating suicide risk

In an opposite scenario, the low medical lethality and seemingly minor precipitants associated with many self-injury episodes may contribute to the misperception that suicidal threats do not need to be taken seriously [5]. Clinicians and family members interpret repeated episodes of self-injury, suicidal ideation, and threats as interpersonal manipulations and attempts to seek attention. A "boy who cried wolf" reaction may develop as professionals and families become habituated to chronic nonsuicidal self-injury and low-lethality suicide attempts. They may become complacent and, therefore, underestimate or neglect genuine suicide risk. The case of Sarah illustrates this dilemma.

Case example

Sarah is a 25-year-old single woman who lives alone and works as a babysitter during the day. She is able to function well at work, but often has difficulty when she returns home in the evening. She has chronic suicidal thoughts and feelings of hopelessness about ever being able to have the life she wants, including getting married and having a family. Sarah has several good friends in the community on whom she relies for emotional support. She has very conflicted relationships with her parents and siblings, who reside in the same town. When Sarah is not spending time with friends, she watches television continually and binge eats. Whenever she interacts with her family, her suicidal

(Continued)

> (*Continued*)
>
> ideation increases. She has never made a suicide attempt, but at these times she will wrap an electrical cord around her neck when she is distressed. She spends some time fiddling with the cord but does not tighten it around her neck. She then calls her friends and tells them that she is sitting in her apartment with a cord around her neck thinking about killing herself. These friends usually rush to be with her at these times. Twice in the past, a friend has taken her to the Emergency Department, which made Sarah extremely angry. There have been a few times when a friend called the mobile crisis team to check on her. When the team came to make an assessment, Sarah maintained that she had no intention of actually killing herself, and the crisis team left. This has happened so many times that one day when Sarah called her friend after having lost her job and feeling very hopeless about finding another one, and threatened to kill herself, the friend, who was not able to come over, decided that it was not necessary to call mobile crisis since Sarah has never actually made a suicide attempt. Sarah could not reach any of her other friends, she became frantic thinking about her financial predicament, and she called one of the mobile crisis team members who knew her well and told him that she was suicidal. She was not asked nor did she reveal the recent precipitants. The team had been to her apartment twice in the past month, and they did not take Sarah seriously and did not send the team. Sarah became increasingly distressed and this time she pulled the cord tightly around her neck in an attempt to kill herself. She bruised her neck and caused some damage to her throat. She became scared and went to a neighbor, who called 911 and helped her get to the Emergency Department, where she was evaluated and hospitalized.

In the face of suicidal threats and gestures, and low-lethality suicide attempts in which the intent to actually die is ambiguous, ongoing therapeutic interventions that inform clinical ability to determine and manage suicide risk are required. DBT helps to fill the gap by providing comprehensive clinical strategies to aid the clinician in effective outpatient suicide risk assessment and management. Another effective intervention that was partly informed by DBT is the SPI, developed by Stanley and Brown [6], which will be fully described in Chapter 14.

Definitions

In order to discuss the phenomenology and treatment approach to nonsuicidal self-injury (NSSI) and suicidal behavior, how we define them must be clear. The terms used to describe these behaviors and their definitions are unclear, and conflicting definitions are used. We use the terminology originally developed by suicide researchers at Columbia University and other universities and modified by the Centers for Disease Control (CDC) and widely used in the United States [7].

Suicide attempt

A *suicide attempt* is defined as a nonfatal self-directed potentially injurious behavior with any intent to die as a result of the behavior. A suicide attempt may or may not result in injury. While this definition may seem to be straightforward enough, the assessment of an individual's subjective intent is not. Intent may be difficult to determine through direct inquiry. Retrospective reports are at times not accurate descriptions of the individual's state of mind at the time of the self-injury, since they may be influenced by reinterpretation and by outcome. Thus, a patient may deny suicidal intent at the time of an overdose but the clinical and/or medical consequences (hospitalization for example) may be such that suicidal intent can be inferred by mental health providers and may become the way the patient comes to understand his own motivation and intent at the time. Furthermore, a behavior that began devoid of suicide intent can shift into becoming a frank suicide attempt. For example, a patient who took her usual dose of medication for sleep found that she was unable to fall asleep. She then took another dose thinking it would help and then impulsively decided that it would be best to "end it all" by taking all the remaining pills. Thus, she went from taking her prescribed medication to taking an overdose with intent to die. Similarly, individuals can engage in cutting behavior that begins as nonsuicidal in intent, but as they perform the behavior, mood and motives change and the behavior becomes suicidal in nature.

Clinically, suicidal intent is often deduced by more objective, external behaviors or factors, such as how medically lethal the self-injury is, or the circumstances, such as the unlikelihood of discovery during and immediately following the act surrounding the self-injury. This can lead to erroneous assumptions, particularly among individuals with BPD, who self-injure for many reasons and in whom the intent to die is often ambiguous.

Self-harm behaviors that are not actual suicide attempts

During the course of conducting suicide research, both clinical trials and investigations of suicide risk, it has become clear to us that individuals engage in behaviors that are clearly associated with increased risk for suicide, yet do not fit into the aforementioned definition of suicide attempt. The CDC has developed the following definitions of behaviors that should be included in a clinical assessment as well as in research studies in which suicidal behavior is an outcome measure.

Interrupted and aborted suicide attempts

Sometimes individuals make preparatory acts toward making a suicide attempt, but they do not go through with it. In the case of an *interrupted attempt*, an individual prepares to engage in a deliberate self-harm behavior with intent to die, but is prevented from doing so by the intervention of another person or persons. For classification purposes, the cutoff between calling such an act an interrupted attempt (as opposed to an actual suicide attempt) is that the interruption must occur before any self-harm behavior is conducted. For example, a husband finds his wife ready to ingest a handful of pills, and grabs them away from her. Once she ingests even one pill, this act is considered to be an actual suicide attempt.

In the case of an *aborted* attempt (or as termed by the CDC – attempt interrupted by self), the individual makes preparatory acts toward making a suicide attempt and is very close to acting on them, and stops himself before taking the first step. For example, a man may go to a roof of a tall building and stand at the edge preparing to jump. At the last minute, he backs away from the edge and decides not to go through with it.

Micro overdoses

In our research, we have identified another form of self-harm behavior that we have termed "micro-overdosing," which has either defied categorization, has been miscategorized, or has fallen through the cracks of our classification system in the United States. In the *International Classification of Diseases (ICD)*, this behavior would be classified as self-poisoning, although there is no *ICD* coding to specify undetermined intent [8]. An individual takes a higher dose of medication than is prescribed (or indicated on an over-the-counter bottle), but clearly not enough to cause any adverse physical consequences. The reported intent of this type of behavior varies. It can be to "feel better," to "fall asleep for a while," or to "calm down." Sometimes a micro-overdose is taken at one time while at other times the individual starts by taking the prescribed amount but then continues to take more if the effects are not felt quickly enough. This type of behavior is often either miscategorized as a suicide attempt (an "overdose") or is not classified at all as a self-harm behavior due to the absence of medical consequences, explicit suicide intent, and the lack of tissue damage required in NSSI.

Nonsuicidal self-injury

NSSI is defined as intentional self-destructive behavior performed with no intent to die. So what is the intent if not to die? Such self-injury with no suicidal intent can be understood within the context of BPD pathology (this behavior also occurs in several other disorders) as an effort to regulate emotions. Although suicidal intent is often ascribed to these behaviors by clinicians and family members, individuals with BPD are often quite clear that their intent is quite to the contrary, and that these behaviors are often used in order to feel better.

The term *self-mutilation* was commonly used in the past to describe nonsuicidal self-harm, but was found not be inclusive enough. Some forms of self-injury involve mutilation, such as cutting and burning. Others, such as head banging and hitting oneself, do not.

Yet, the term "self-mutilation" appears as a symptom of BPD in *DSM IV* [9] and continues to be used by clinicians and researchers [10, 11]. However, the terms "self-injury," "self-injurious behavior," and "deliberate self-harm" [12] have also been used interchangeably to describe behaviors such as skin-cutting, burning, self-hitting, self-biting, head banging, scratching, skin carving, and needle sticking or as the "deliberate, direct destruction of body tissue without conscious suicidal intent" [13]. Most confusing is the fact that in Europe and in the *ICD* [8], the term "intentional self-inflicted injury" is used to describe self-injurious behavior both with and without suicidal intent. Similarly, the term "parasuicide" refers to any deliberate self-harm performed with or without suicidal intent that does not result in death [14]. Thus, all nonlethal suicide attempts fall into the category of parasuicide, as do acts of NSSI. This term, although used in the first trial reports of DBT, is no longer used. Adding to the confusion, the term "suicide gesture" is sometimes used to describe very low lethality self-harm behaviors or threats that indicate a level of intent to die but that do not result in death.

NSSI has also been defined as "the intentional destruction of body tissue without suicidal intent and for purposes not socially sanctioned" [15, 16]. NSSI behaviors have been described as "repetitive, low-lethality actions that alter or damage body tissue without suicidal intent" [17]. However, this definition fails to clearly include some serious forms of self-injury in which individuals with BPD engage including head banging and self-hitting.

From these definitions, we can extrapolate that in order to distinguish NSSI from suicidal behavior, the bodily harm is deliberately self-inflicted with no intent to die. Thus, substance abuse and eating disorders do not meet these criteria because the bodily harm that results is not a directly intended consequence of the behavior. Favazza [18] suggests that in order to be called NSSI, these behaviors must be outside the realm of socially sanctioned forms of self-injury that are regarded as expressions of individuality and creativity. This would rule out behaviors such as tattooing and body piercing.

Determining suicidal intent

The intent to die is the main criterion that distinguishes an act of NSSI from a suicide attempt. Yet, intent is a subjective, phenomenological construct that is mainly determined through an individual's self-report, and thus vulnerable to intentional and unintentional distortion owing to current emotional state, poor recall, and reformulation of intent retrospectively. Relatively objective measures of suicide intent consist of inferences made from behaviors surrounding an act of deliberate self-harm, such as writing a suicide note, taking precautions against being seen or discovered, or communicating plans to someone prior to acting. These actions are important to consider when evaluating intent and suicide risk.

The medical consequences of an act, or the lethality of the chosen method, are also more objective measures of an individual's intent to die. Thus, if an individual reports no intent to die associated with a deliberate self-harm behavior, yet they used a highly lethal method (e.g., an overdose of many toxic pills), which resulted in serious health consequences or the need for medical hospitalization, it is difficult to confidently classify such a behavior as nonsuicidal.

Prevalence of suicide and NSSI in BPD

Within the context of the high frequency of nonlethal self-harm, it is easy to lose sight of the fact that the lifetime rate of completed suicide in BPD is 9–10% [19–21]. This high rate is comparable to the completed suicide rate in other high-risk diagnostic populations such as schizophrenia, major depressive disorder, and bipolar disorder [22]. Up to 75% of individuals with BPD in clinical populations have made nonlethal suicide attempts [23], with nearly 50% making at least one severe attempt [23]. Approximately 80% of hospitalized patients with BPD have engaged in NSSI [24]. These figures are derived from psychiatric inpatients and, therefore, may somewhat overestimate the incidence of these behaviors in the overall BPD population. However, in the general population, a striking number of individuals with BPD (25%) will attempt suicide at some point in their lives [25]. Furthermore, BPD appears to carry as much risk for suicide as schizophrenia and recurrent depression. All three confer high suicide risk [26].

NSSI, itself, is a risk factor for suicidal behavior, as 55–85% of self-injurers have made at least one suicide attempt [27–29]. As previously mentioned, this combination of suicidal behavior and NSSI is especially common in BPD [30–32].

Suicide attempt or NSSI?

Clinically, suicide attempts and NSSI can be quite distinct in an individual's mind [13], and are different in method and function, in addition to intent. For example, Brown et al. [33] found that self-reported reasons for NSSI in a sample of chronically suicidal women with BPD were to express anger, self-punish, and distract. Suicide attempts, on the other hand, were reported as intended to relieve the pain of others.

The usual method of suicide attempt in BPD is overdosing [34]. Although overdosing can be more amenable to low-lethality attempts, this does not necessarily imply less intent to die. A study of method choice, intent, and gender in completed suicide found that although women who commit suicide use less violent methods (overdoses and carbon monoxide poisoning vs. guns and hanging in men), there was no difference in their intent, based on objective measures of intent surrounding the suicide, such as whether they took steps against being discovered or wrote a suicide note [35]. Other methods used for NSSI are typically skin cutting and skin burning, often on the inside of the arms, and on the legs and stomach. Also common are self-hitting, head banging, self-biting, hair pulling, and skin picking [36].

The medical consequences of a suicide attempt and an act of NSSI might be similar due to miscalculations and distortions in the perception of lethality of a given act. Individuals with BPD who both self-injure and make suicide attempts tend to perceive their suicide attempts as less lethal than they actually are, with a greater likelihood of rescue and with less certainty of death [34]. They seem to lose their sense of judgment regarding how dangerous a behavior may be, possibly because of having had multiple experiences of nonlethal nonsuicidal self-harm. Thus, lower intent to die may not result in a lower level of medical lethality.

Nonsuicidal self-injurious behavior: Reasons and functions

Is the purpose of NSSI attention-seeking?

A common belief has been that NSSI is mainly designed to seek attention and to provoke and manipulate others. However, there is mounting clinical and empirical evidence arguing against this. NSSI is usually an extremely private behavior when performed and is often denied and hidden, since individuals who self-injure are frequently deeply ashamed of their self-injury. Approximately 50% of BPD patients hide the fact that they self-injure and do not let anyone know about it [37, 38]. Isolation from others almost always precedes the actual act of NSSI [39].

Individuals who self-injure do so in a state of feeling overwhelmed by their emotions, and are often unaware of or unconcerned about the effect they have on others [38]. Nevertheless, people do feel manipulated and provoked by NSSI, and the attention that results from NSSI can become reinforcing. Thus, even when the behavior is originally intended for purposes of affect regulation, the attention that results often becomes a learned and desired consequence.

The current theory and research regarding the reasons for engaging in NSSI is that NSSI serves both intrapersonal and interpersonal functions [10]. Within the person, NSSI helps an individual regulate affect [16] by resulting in negative reinforcement (the immediate reduction of distressing emotional states) and positive reinforcement (increase in feelings of calm, well-being, and even euphoria). In relation to other people, the consequences of NSSI can be positively reinforcing (increased caregiving response) or negatively reinforcing (through avoidance of stressful situations).

The phenomenological report of our patients corroborates the research findings that *affect regulation* is the number one reason for engaging in NSSI. NSSI reduces the emotional tension that stems from states of extreme distress, anxiety, anger, guilt, or shame [28]. NSSI also serves to *distract* from emotional pain [33]. In a manner similar to bulimia with all its rituals and preoccupation, NSSI episodes become an engaging activity and, therefore, serve as a distraction from distressing emotions and events. NSSI also serves as a form of *self-punishment* [1, 10, 33] "providing relief from a poorly articulated but intolerable state involving intense shame, remorse, and convictions of badness and alienation."

As stated earlier, individuals with BPD often need *concrete proof of their emotional distress*. Linehan [39] describes the process of self-invalidation that occurs in BPD, in which individuals believe that they are overreacting, or that they have no reason to be feeling the way they do, and, therefore, they are not and should not be feeling this way. A scar or bruise can provide the concrete evidence of their emotional state.

Also, because individuals with BPD easily become emotionally dysregulated, they often experience themselves as being out of control. Engaging in NSSI helps them to gain a *sense of control*. By harming themselves, they believe they are taking control of the out-of-control behaviors of others, or over the external events that cause their distress [40].

Some individuals with BPD, particularly those with a significant abuse or trauma history, respond to emotional overload by entering into a state of numbness or depersonalization. Although initially providing a sense of relief, this state often becomes distressing and extremely uncomfortable, and is hard to snap out of. NSSI seems to alleviate the numbness. Favazza [40] calls this function of NSSI "return to reality."

Patients also report that they engage in NSSI to vent their anger. Acting on angry feelings through self-harm seems safer and less guilt producing than expressing anger toward others [33, 40].

The experience of nonsuicidal self-injury

NSSI is a behavior that represents the end point of a series of events, thoughts, and feelings. The typical trigger is an environmental event that is either a real or perceived interpersonal loss [1, 38, 40]. An interpretation (cognition) of the event follows, which usually involves the individual blaming herself ("I must have done something wrong/am too needy, and now they are abandoning me."). Emotions escalate and become dysregulated so that they feel all-consuming and cloud judgment and cognition. Usually the feelings change to some form of self-hatred. The overwhelming emotions sometimes lead to a dissociative response in which the individual goes from feeling intense pain to feeling nothing other than the experience of numbness [41]. Either the painful feelings or the numbness begin to be experienced as a rising internal, physiological pressure. By self-injuring, the individual experiences an immediate sense of relief from the pressure [42] and a reinstatement of emotional equilibrium. How does NSSI result in a feeling of relief?

Some individuals report that they stop the self-injury when they begin to feel physical pain. Others stop when they see the blood, as if this is experienced as the release of the tension or the "letting out" of the bad feelings [43]. For reasons that are not clear, self-injury is remarkably effective in relieving the dysphoric state [5].

Physiological factors

While the relief may be associated with psychological factors such as relief of guilt through self-punishment, there is evidence of a physiological mechanism, such as the relief of one type of pain by inducing a counter-stimulus. Or, perhaps self-injury stimulates the release of a pain-reducing neurotransmitter such as an endorphin. A study by Stanley et al. [44] found reduced levels of endogenous opioids in the cerebrospinal fluid of self-injurers, suggesting that the opioid system is implicated in NSSI. They hypothesize that an opioid deficiency may result from ongoing childhood stress and trauma, and that self-injury might be a mechanism through which individuals try to correct the deficiency.

Dissociation, SIB, and the experience of pain

A few reports have documented that individuals with BPD who self-injure fall into two distinct groups related to whether or not they experience pain when they self-injure. According to Russ et al. [45], those individuals who do not experience pain during NSSI represent a more impaired population characterized by higher levels of depression, anxiety, impulsivity, dissociation, trauma symptoms, number of past suicide attempts, and prevalence of sexual abuse. Kemperman et al. [46] report that female patients with BPD who do not experience pain during self-injury discriminate more poorly between noxious thermal stimuli of similar intensity. They conclude that analgesia during self-injury is related to both neurosensory and psychological factors.

Neurobiology and neurocognitive factors

Neurobiological findings regarding the role of endogenous opioids and serotonergic functioning point to their possible role in suicidal injury and NSSI [47]. Serotonin has been implicated in suicide, suicide attempts, impulsivity, and aggression.

Neuropsychological studies are now under way investigating the relationship between lower serotonin, impulsivity, and cognitive thought processes that might impact on self-injury. For example, Keilp et al. [48] have identified an impairment of executive functioning among depressed patients who have made a previous high-lethality suicide attempt that is beyond that typically found in major depression. In BPD, neuropsychological correlates of decreased executive function and disinhibiting processes related to the dorsolateral prefrontal cortical regions are associated with suicidal behavior [49].

Similarly, the role of cortisol and the functioning of the neurological stress regulatory system (hypothalamic–pituitary–adrenal (HPA) axis) have also been studied in regard to risk for suicide and suicide attempt but not as much as a risk factor for NSSI. There is evidence that both childhood trauma and genetic factors (variations in HPA axis-regulating genes) interact to impact the stress regulatory system, and that stress dysregulation is a risk factor for suicide attempt [50]. Blunted cortisol response (a measure of dysregulation of the HPA axis) has been found in relatives of suicide completers [51], indicating a biological vulnerability for suicide.

Cognitive factors

Individuals who self-injure often have rigid and/or dysfunctional ways of thinking that lead to the increased likelihood of engaging in NSSI. For example, individuals with BPD often strongly believe that they cannot handle emotional pain, and that physical pain is easier for them to tolerate. They are certain that self-injury is the only way to obtain immediate relief from emotional distress. They are convinced that, by injuring themselves, they feel in greater control than if they allow themselves to experience their "out of control" emotions. Individuals believe that it is better to hurt themselves rather than express anger directly, that it is "wrong" to express angry feelings toward others, particularly people they care about. Self-punishers believe that they deserve to suffer [52].

Suicide attempts: Reasons and functions

The way many of us have been trained to think about suicide, the way the media portrays suicide, and the expected pattern of thinking and acting leading to a suicide attempt are based on the concept that being depressed is the most important factor contributing to a suicide attempt. The assumption is that someone who is seriously suicidal is a depressed individual who endures a protracted period of depressed mood, hopelessness, withdrawal, and isolation. Often, but not always, this depression is preceded by some form of psychosocial stressor, such as a significant loss in health, employment status, or the loss of someone close. Chronic depression can culminate in a feeling that life is not worth living and a profound sense of hopelessness that may lead to a suicide attempt. Following the attempt, the individual typically feels regret that the attempt was not "successful" and did not result in death.

Changing the way we think about suicidal behavior

This typical picture of the suicidal individual often does not apply to suicide attempts in BPD. There is preliminary empirical evidence identifying suicide risk factors unique to individuals with BPD, such as hospitalization, poor social adjustment [3], affective instability [53], impulsivity [54], and interpersonal triggers [55]. And suicide attempts serve an emotion regulation function similar to NSSI in individuals with BPD. Therefore, they tend to feel better, not worse, after making a nonlethal attempt.

Case examples

We present two case examples (Reprinted with permission from *Understanding and Treating Borderline Personality Disorder: A Guide for Professionals and Families*. (2005), American Psychiatric Publishing) that demonstrate how the conventional way of understanding suicidality is inadequate in explaining the suicidal states of many individuals with BPD.

> ### Case example: Candace
>
> Candace is a 22-year-old Hispanic, single young woman who engages in NSSI in order to manage feelings of anger, anxiety, and guilt. When she is angry at her boyfriend or another significant person in her life, she feels guilty for feeling angry; this leads to feelings of deep self-hatred, which she believes she cannot tolerate, and she begins to pinch her skin in order to feel physical pain that will distract her from these feelings. Sometimes the pinching leads to intense scratching until she draws blood. This provides a sense of relief from her emotions. The relief is experienced as feeling "back in control." Candace describes two low-lethality suicide attempts that she distinguishes from the NSSI. On two separate occasions, on the anniversary of the death of her father, she became extremely angry at her boyfriend for not acknowledging the difficulty of this day for her. She became hopeless, feeling that her boyfriend would never be able to understand her, and that she would always feel unbearably sad about losing her father and would be unable to get the help she needs to deal with it. She also felt that there is something wrong with her for feeling this way. These thoughts led to a decision to take an overdose of her medication in order to kill herself. On both occasions, as soon as she took about 10 pills, which were not enough to cause lethal harm, she felt a sense of relief that at least she had "done something" to take control of her situation and she no longer wished to die. She then fell asleep and had no other medical consequences from the overdose, and woke up feeling much better.

> ### Case example: Rachel
>
> Rachel is a 35-year-old Caucasian, single woman who has made approximately 20 suicide attempts since she was 13 years old. At least 15 of these attempts have required medical attention and hospitalizations. Rachel describes these attempts, as well as her chronic suicidal ideation, as her method of managing overwhelming feelings and avoiding confrontations and responsibility that she finds aversive. Many of the attempts occur without accompanying symptoms of depression. Rachel's last attempt occurred during a period of self-reported euthymic mood and stability. Rachel reports that she was in a good mood but became angry with her boyfriend over a few separate matters. Because Rachel has difficulty being direct interpersonally and has problems experiencing or expressing her feelings, she avoided a confrontation with her boyfriend. However, she began to ruminate about his behavior and thereby continued to feed the very emotions that she was trying to avoid. Rachel stated that the feelings of anger became overwhelming and soon turned to fear and anxiety. Rachel reported that, without much thought, she began taking prescription psychiatric medications one after the other, in the frantic effort to escape her state of misery. After taking a substantial number of pills, Rachel reported that she realized she "blew it" and called her boss, a friend, and her therapist, hinting that she was in trouble. She then passed out. Soon emergency help arrived and took her to the hospital where she needed medical care. After this attempt, as well as others, Rachel appeared bright, focused, and less anxious. She reported feeling motivated for change, willing to set goals, and functioned at an improved level. In addition, Rachel reported that she felt regret for her actions as she recognized that they disturb those that she loves. These feelings, she reported, replaced the anger she had felt previously. Likewise, Rachel's loved ones seem interested, careful, and cognizant of her feelings. Rachel reported that she felt more intimate with others and less fearful and alone. For a brief period, lasting up to a month, Rachel's emotional life felt manageable and enjoyable.

Discussion of case examples

It is clear that the usual way of understanding suicidal behavior does not apply to the behaviors of the two individuals presented in these cases. Clinicians may overlook the more immediate emotion regulation function of suicidal behavior in these individuals. As illustrated by these cases, individuals with BPD usually feel better following a suicide attempt. This may lead to the erroneous conclusion that the attempt was not genuine or was intended purely to manipulate a caregiving response from others. This conclusion is especially likely to be drawn if the suicide attempt results in a markedly improved mood. Although the mood improvement may be attributed in part to a caregiving response, the suicide attempt itself often provides psychological and physiological relief from extreme states of emotional dysregulation.

In addition, in these cases, both the NSSI and the suicide attempts occurred outside the context of a major depressive episode or depressed mood, and were triggered by seemingly minor interpersonal disappointments and upsets. Thus, in individuals with BPD, suicide risk may not be recognized when an individual is not reporting a classically depressed mood. And, the interpersonal nature of the triggers may seem insignificant (e.g., not "worthy" of a severe reaction), and the improvement in mood following a suicide attempt could lead others to underestimate the suicide intent associated with a low-lethality suicide attempt.

Treatment implications

Often in BPD, a suicide attempt is a reaction to a very transitory state of mind or situation. Based on our understanding of the phenomenology and function of self harm behaviors in BPD as efforts to self-regulate in the moment, we propose the following recommendations to increase the effectiveness of treatment and management of self-injury in this population. Treatment should directly and in an ongoing manner address the following goals: (a) the reduction of self harm behaviors; (b) explicit risk assessment even in the absence of spontaneously reported suicide ideation; and (c) collaborative problem solving between the patient and therapist to manage suicide ideation and urges including spikes in ideation of the chronically suicidal. This may include hospitalization.

Reducing self-injurious behavior

A comprehensive history taking should include a complete assessment of an individual's subjective experience of self-injury, its function, and intent. This would provide a customized profile of that individual's experience of self-harm and could inform the identification of specific aspects of the experience that could be targeted in treatment:

1 *Function of the self-injury*. An assessment of the individual's subjective experience regarding an episode of NSSI or a suicide attempt would allow for a nuanced understanding of the various previously mentioned functions of (both suicidal and non-suicidal) self-injury, such as emotion regulation, self-punishment, and self-validation.

With the enhanced awareness of the multiple functions of parasuicidal behavior, treatment could focus on the development of more skillful ways to achieve these goals.

2 *Intent of past suicidal and NSSI behaviors.* A detailed assessment of the intent associated with past self-injury behaviors would include distinguishing between self-injurious acts performed with and without intent to die. Intent would not be inferred solely by the circumstances, the extent of medical lethality, or the interpersonal consequences of the self-injurious event. Both the patient and clinician would be encouraged to validate the individual's subjective report of his or her intent, despite objective circumstances that might seemingly contradict it.

3 *Cognitions that contribute to self-injury.* As reviewed earlier, patients often have fixed or distorted beliefs that can lead to self-injury. For example, they may harbor the belief that they cannot tolerate emotional pain, or that the only way to handle their painful emotional state is through self-injury. Such beliefs, once recognized, can be modified through cognitive restructuring. Secondly, therapeutic interventions can increase awareness of how intense emotional arousal, and past trauma, can lead to distorted cognitions or interpretations of external events.

4 *Consequences of the self-injury.* Identifying the reinforcing consequences of the behavior can help us to understand the perpetuation of self-injury, as well as provide information about the ways to modify these reinforcement patterns, so as to promote more skillful behaviors. Secondly, distinguishing between intended and unintended consequences can aid both patient and clinician to clarify original intent versus learned intent with those in the past.

Distinguishing between suicidal injury and NSSI, which patients are often clearly able to do, can make both clinicians and patients better able to recognize actual suicide risk. In addition, recognizing the various functions of self-injury, not assuming the intent is solely to die, patients can gain more insight into how their behaviors affect the people close to them, which can provide an opportunity for improved interpersonal effectiveness.

Risk assessment and the decision to hospitalize

In deciding whether or not to hospitalize, clinicians must perform a balancing act between taking the risk of suicide seriously and increasing patients' capacity to safely tolerate chronic suicidal ideation on their own. Here again, a more comprehensive assessment of the subjective experience of a self-injurious patient can aid in the difficult task of recognizing when the risk for suicide requires hospitalization. The detailed history of the circumstances, triggers, cognitions, intent, behaviors, and contingencies of the specific patient can inform risk assessment in a particular moment in time by comparing the current circumstances, triggers, and interpersonal contingencies, and maintaining awareness of the day-to-day emotional pain experienced by individuals with BPD can reduce the burnout that might lead to underrecognition of suicide risk.

On the other hand, as we have noted, chronic suicide ideation and NSSI can also lead to multiple hospitalizations that severely disrupt the individual's ability to function, and that might be avoidable. Multiple disruptive hospitalizations can create a cycle that inadvertently further increases hopelessness and suicide ideation. We have stated that often, suicidal ideation and NSSI in BPD stem not necessarily from a strong intent to die, but rather from a desperate desire to manage and obtain relief from what feels like an intolerable emotional state. In other words, it can be an effort to stay alive. An outpatient treatment that can address the need for such relief and provide support for the individual to manage these states safely can reduce the need for revolving door hospital admissions. Indeed, in a prospective study of suicidal behavior in BPD, Soloff and Fabio [3] found that the number of hospitalizations increased the risk of suicide, while long-term risk for suicide was decreased by any outpatient treatment.

Gunderson and Ridolfi [1] describe the scenario in which multiple unnecessary hospitalizations create a patient who comes to view hospitalization as the only way her pain can be validated, and who presents herself as needing hospitalization even when the clinician does not believe it is necessary. They present a principle of "false submission": the clinician agrees to hospitalize, but works toward changing the meaning the patient ascribes to hospitalization.

However, in the case where all attempts to maintain outpatient functioning have not adequately reduced the imminent suicide risk, a very brief hospitalization can block the behavior and help the individual to tolerate the emotions until they subside.

Summary

Suicide risk assessment remains one of the main challenges in the treatment of BPD. The unpredictability and chronicity of suicidal ideation, suicide attempts, and NSSI in these patients can lead to unnecessary hospitalizations. On the other hand, the chronicity of suicidal ideation, the seemingly ambiguous intent to die associated with low-lethality suicide attempts, and the seemingly minor interpersonal precipitants for these behaviors, along with visible mood improvement following acts of suicide and NSSI, may lead to the erroneous assumption that intent to die among these patients is not to be taken seriously. We suggest that the application of conventional thinking about suicide risk prediction, such as the way in which we understand suicide in depressed patients, may be partly responsible for the under- or overestimation of suicide risk in BPD.

We have proposed a comprehensive approach to understanding the phenomenology of suicide attempts and NSSI, based on clinical and empirical findings that suggest that these behaviors serve an emotion regulation function in individuals with BPD. This approach includes understanding and distinguishing between intent to die and intent to find relief from emotional distress, and how these two sometimes overlap. From this perspective, we can expect that individuals with BPD are often not depressed when they try to kill or harm themselves and that personality traits such as impulsivity, affectively lability, as well as rejection sensitivity and other environmental factors, are just as likely to contribute to suicide risk.

The DBT interventions described in the following chapters (particularly Chapters 13 and 14, in which we review suicide intervention strategies and safety planning) provide clear guidelines for applying this understanding toward increased ability to assess and predict risk, as well as to make more well-informed decisions regarding hospitalization.

References

1. Gunderson, J.G., Ridolfi, M. (2001) Borderline personality disorder suicidality and self-mutilation. *Annals of the New York Academy of Sciences*, 932, 61–77.
2. Fine, M.A., Sansone, R.A. (1990) Dilemmas in the management of suicidal behavior in individual with borderline personality disorder. *American Journal of Psychotherapy*, 44 (2), 160–171.
3. Soloff, P.H., Fabio, A. (2008) Prospective predictors of suicide attempts in borderline personality disorder at one, two, and two-to-five year follow-up. *Journal of Personality Disorders*, 22 (2), 123–134.
4. McMyler, C., Pryjmachuk, S. (2008) Do 'no-suicide' contracts work? *Journal of Psychiatric and Mental Health Nursing*, 15 (6), 512–522.
5. Leibenluft, E., Gardner, D.L., Cowdry, R.W. (1987) The inner experience of the borderline self-mutilator. *Journal of Personality Disorders*, 1 (4), 217–324.
6. Stanley, B., Brown, G.K. (2011) Safety planning intervention: A brief intervention to mitigate suicide risk. *Cognitive and Behavioral Practice*, 19, 256–264.
7. Crosby, A. Ortega, L., Melanson, C. (2011) Self-directed Violence Surveillance: Uniform Definitions and Recommended Data Elements, Version 1.0. Centers for Disease Control, p. 21.
8. World Health Organization. (2008) *ICD-10: International Statistical Classification of Diseases and Related Health Problems* (10th Rev. ed.), World Health Organization, New York.
9. American Psychiatric Association. (2000) *Diagnostic and Statistical Manual of Mental Disorders* (4th ed., text rev.), American Psychiatric Association, Washington, DC.
10. Nock, M.K., Prinstein, M.J. (2004) A functional approach to the assessment of self-mutilative behavior. *Journal of Consulting and Clinical Psychology*, 72 (5), 885–890.
11. Nock, M.K., Prinstein, M.J. (2005) Contextual features and behavioral functions of self-mutilation among adolescents. *Journal of Abnormal Psychology*, 114 (1), 140–146.
12. Nock, M.K., Teper, R., Hollander, M. (2007) Psychological treatment of self-injury among adolescents. *Journal of Clinical Psychology*, 63 (11), 1081–1089.
13. Muehlenkamp, J.J. (2005) Self-injurious behavior as a separate clinical syndrome. *American Journal of Orthopsychiatry*, 75 (2), 324–333.
14. Linehan, M.M., Armstrong, H.E., Suarez, A., et al. (1991) Cognitive-behavioral treatment of chronically parasuicidal borderline patients. *Archives of General Psychiatry*, 48, 1060–1064.
15. Gratz, K.L., Hepworth, C., Tull, M.T., et al. (2011) An experimental investigation of emotional willingness and physical pain tolerance in deliberate self-harm: The moderating role of interpersonal distress. *Comprehensive Psychiatry*, 52 (1), 63–74.
16. Chapman, A.L., Gratz, K.L., Brown, M.Z. (2006) Solving the puzzle of deliberate self-harm: The experiential avoidance model. *Behavioral Research in Therapy*, 44 (3), 371–394.
17. Klonsky, E.D., Muehlenkamp, J.J. (2007) Self-injury: A research review for the practitioner. *Journal of Clinical Psychology*, 63 (11), 1045–1056.
18. Favazza, A.R. (1998) The coming of age of self-mutilation. *Journal of Nervous and Mental Disorders*, 186 (5), 259–268.
19. Stone, M., Stone, D., Hurt, S. (1987) Natural history of borderline patients treated by intensive hospitalization. *Psychiatric Clinics of North America*, 10, 185–206.
20. Gunderson, D. (1984) *Borderline Personality Disorders*, American Psychiatric Press, Washington, DC.
21. Fyer, M. (1988) Suicide attempts in patients with borderline personality disorder. *American Journal of Psychiatry*, 145, 737–739.

22. American Foundation for Suicide Prevention. www.afsp.org. Accessed on 8 January 2013.
23. Shearer, S.L., Peter, C.P., Quaytman, M.S., et al. (1988) Intent and lethality of suicide attempts among female borderline inpatients. *American Journal of Psychiatry*, 145, 1424–1427.
24. Roy, A. (1978) Self-mutilation. *British Journal of Medical Psychology*, 51, 201–203.
25. Bolton, J.M., Robinson J. (2010) Population-attributable fractions of Axis I and Axis II mental disorders for suicide attempts: Findings from a representative sample of the adult, noninstitutionalized US population. *American Journal of Public Health*, 100 (12), 2473–2480.
26. Qin, P. (2011) The impact of psychiatric illness on suicide: Differences by diagnosis of disorders and by sex and age of subjects. *Journal of Psychiatric Research*, 45 (11), 1445–1452.
27. Rosenthal, R.J., Rinzler, C., Wallsh, R., et al. (1972) Wrist-cutting syndrome: The meaning of a gesture. *American Journal of Psychiatry*, 128, 1363–1368.
28. Gardner, A.R., Gardner, A.J. (1975) Self-mutilation, obsessionality and narcissism. *British Journal of Psychiatry*, 127, 127–132.
29. Favazza, A.R., Conterio, K. (1989) Female habitual self-mutilators. *Acta Psychiatrica Scandinavia*, 79, 283–289.
30. Shearer, S.L. (1994) Phenomenology of self-injury among inpatient women with borderline personality disorder. *Journal of Mental Disorder*, 182 (9), 524–526.
31. Soloff, P.H., Lis, J.A., Kelly, T., et al. (1994) Self-mutilation and suicidal behavior in borderline personality disorder. *Journal of Personality Disorders*, 8 (4), 257–267.
32. Muehlenkamp, J.J., Ertelt, T.W., Miller, A.L., et al. (2011) Borderline personality symptoms differentiate non-suicidal and suicidal self-injury in ethnically diverse adolescent outpatients. *Journal of Child Psychology and Psychiatry*, 52 (2), 148–155.
33. Brown, M.Z., Comtois, K.A., Linehan, M.M. (2002) Reasons for suicide attempts and non-suicidal self-injury in women with borderline personality disorder. *Journal of Abnormal Psychology*, 111 (1), 198–202.
34. Stanley, B., Gameroff, M.J., Michalsen, V., et al. (2001) Are suicide attempters who self-mutilate a unique population? *American Journal of Psychiatry*, 158, 427–432.
35. Denning, D.G., Conwell, Y., King, D., et al. (2000) Method choice, intent, and gender in completed suicide. *Suicide and Life Threatening Behavior*, 30 (30), 282–288.
36. Nock, M.K. (2009) Why do people hurt themselves? New insights into the nature and functions of self-injury. *Current Directions in Psychological Science*, 18 (2), 78–83.
37. Brodsky, B.S., Cloitre, M., Dulit, R.A. (1995) Relationship of dissociation and childhood abuse in borderline personality disorder. *American Journal of Psychiatry*, 152 (12), 1788–1792.
38. Suyemoto, K.L. (1998) The functions of self-mutilation. *Clinical Psychology Review*, 18 (5), 531–554.
39. Linehan, M.M. (1993) *Cognitive Behavior Therapy for Borderline Personality Disorder*, Guilford Press, New York.
40. Favazza, A.R. (1989) Why patients mutilate themselves. *Hospital and Community Psychiatry*, 40 (2), 137–140.
41. Russ, M.J. (1992) Self-injurious behavior in patients with borderline personality disorder: Biological perspectives. *Journal of Personality Disorders*, 6 (1), 64–81.
42. Gardner, D.L., Cowdry, R.W. (1985) Suicidal and parasuicidal behavior in borderline personality disorder. *Psychiatric Clinics of North America*, 8, 359–403.
43. Klonsky, E.D. (2009) The functions of self-injury in young adults who cut themselves: Clarifying the evidence for affect-regulation. *Psychiatry Research*, 166 (2–3), 260–268.
44. Stanley, B., Sher, L., Wilson, S., et al. (2010) Non-suicidal self-injurious behavior, endogenous opioids and monoamine neurotransmitters. *Journal of Affective Disorders*, 124 (1–2), 134–140.

45. Russ, M.J., Shearin, E.N., Clarkin, J.F., et al. (1993) Subtypes of self-injurious patients with borderline personality disorder. *American Journal of Psychiatry*, 150, 1869–1871.
46. Kemperman, I., Russ, M.J., Clark, W.C., et al. (1997) Pain assessment in self-injurious patients with borderline personality disorder using signal detection theory. *Psychiatry Research*, 70 (3), 175–183.
47. Winchel, R., Stanley, M. (1991) Self-injurious behavior: A review of the behavior and biology of self-mutilation. *American Journal of Psychiatry*, 148 (3), 306–317.
48. Keilp, J.G., Sackeim, H.A., Brodsky, B.S., et al. (2001) Neuropsychological dysfunction in depressed suicide attempters. *American Journal of Psychiatry*, 158 (5), 735–741.
49. LeGris, J., van Reekum, R. (2006) The neuropsychological correlates of borderline personality disorder and suicidal behaviour. *Canadian Journal of Psychiatry*, 51 (3), 131–142.
50. Roy, A., Hodgkinson, C.A., Deluca, V., et al. (2012) Two HPA axis genes, CRHBP and FKBP5, interact with childhood trauma to increase the risk for suicidal behavior. *Psychiatry Research*, 46 (1), 72–79.
51. McGirr, A., Diaconu, G., Berlim, M.T., et al. (2010) Dysregulation of the sympathetic nervous system, hypothalamic–pituitary–adrenal axis and executive function in individuals at risk for suicide. *Journal of Psychiatry and Neuroscience*, 35 (6), 399–408.
52. Wenzel, A., Brown, G.K., Beck, A.T. (2008) *Cognitive Therapy for Suicidal Patients: Scientific and Clinical Applications*, American Psychiatric Publishing, Inc., Washington, DC.
53. Yen, S., Shea, M.T., Sanislow, C.A., et al. (2004) Borderline personality disorder criteria associated with prospectively observed suicidal behavior. *American Journal of Psychiatry*, 161 (7), 1296–1298.
54. Brodsky, B.S., Malone, K.M., Ellis, S.P., et al. (1997) Characteristics of borderline personality disorder associated with suicidal behavior. *American Journal of Psychiatry*, 154, 1715–1719.
55. Brodsky, B.S., Groves, S.A., Oquendo, M.A., et al. (2006) Interpersonal precipitants and suicide attempts in borderline personality disorder. *Suicide and Life Threatening Behavior*, 36 (3), 313–322.

Chapter 6

The ABC's of DBT – the theoretical perspective

Top 10 question to be addressed in this chapter:

What can clinicians do to help patients who are extremely sensitive to criticism tolerate change interventions in order to remain in treatment and not leave prematurely?

In this chapter, we will describe the theoretical underpinnings of DBT and how they inform treatment. Important DBT constructs such as the, dialectical approach, mindfulness, and balancing acceptance and change are described.

> **Key points**
> - The concept of the dialectic in DBT – balancing validation with change
> - DBT assumptions for treating BPD and how they are informed by the dialectic philosophy
> - Mindfulness orientation
> - Validation strategies and the emphasis on acceptance
> - Focus on change and the importance of learning theory
> - The case conceptualization in DBT and the importance of learning theory in the conceptualization

Overview of DBT theory

DBT was developed specifically for individuals that had difficulty remaining and engaging in treatments informed by other therapeutic approaches. As such, DBT uses strategies that are designed to help with treatment engagement. Validation and acceptance techniques are major vehicles for aiding in this process. At the same time, the treatment maintains a steady eye on the need for change and it is made clear from the outset that "acceptance only" is not sufficient. Thus, there is an ongoing and continual focus on balancing change and acceptance. This stance is reflected in one of the tenets of DBT that is often shared

---

The Dialectical Behavior Therapy Primer: How DBT Can Inform Clinical Practice, First Edition.
Beth S. Brodsky and Barbara Stanley.
© 2013 John Wiley & Sons, Ltd. Published 2013 by John Wiley & Sons, Ltd.

with patients, which is, "You are doing the best that you can but you have to do better." For individuals who are experiencing tremendous suffering, as most people with BPD are, this is unarguable. For the most part, they are doing what they know how to do to help themselves but if they do not improve, try harder, try new ways of coping, they will not alleviate their suffering. DBT therapists have this tenet at the forefront of their minds as they work with patients. In fact, DBT therapists can apply that same principle to their own work as clinicians.

The theoretical and philosophical underpinnings and the treatment strategies and case conceptualizations in DBT are directly linked. At the core of DBT is a dialectical philosophy, which encourages a synthesis of Zen contemplative practice (total acceptance) with the learning (change) principles of behavioral science [1]. In this chapter, we will describe how DBT provides the foundation for the DBT therapeutic stance and interventions.

The dialectical perspective in DBT

A dialectical worldview is the overarching perspective in DBT and is manifest in every aspect of the treatment. The "dialectic" refers to the way in which extreme opposites of experience are reconciled. The primary dialectic in DBT is the synthesis of total acceptance of individuals while at the same time insisting that they need to change (improve). The therapy strives to create a balance in acceptance of the patients' dysfunctions while helping patients modify their thinking and behavior. This synthesis is achieved through integration of Eastern Zen Buddhist principles with Western cognitive behavioral practice.

DBT *explicitly* emphasizes the need to balance change strategies with acceptance and validation techniques. This balance is important for two primary reasons. First, acceptance and change are important ingredients in any successful psychotherapy. Many problems and issues confronted in psychotherapy cannot be changed, for example, having a disabled child or attending a college that was not the first choice because the first-choice school rejected the patient. An obvious example is past childhood experiences. Patients are sometimes stuck in a place of nonacceptance about their past and, consequently, are unable to move beyond a stance that it "…should not have happened." While at first glance this stance may not seem so destructive, it can be. If an individual cannot accept and indeed embrace what has happened, it is impossible to change. Thus, acceptance and change have a dynamic interplay. Acceptance enables one to change, while change allows for increased tolerance and acceptance of what cannot be changed.

In conducting DBT, a balance between change and acceptance strategies is maintained within each intervention and over the course of the treatment. Complete validation and acceptance, without an emphasis on need for change, would represent an imbalance, which might result in the patient feeling demoralized and hopeless about the possibility of improvement. Conversely, focusing too intently on change can backfire. The patient can feel poorly understood and much criticized. Individuals with BPD are extremely sensitive to criticism and a therapist saying something as benign as "It would be good to do *x* instead of *y*" without validation of why they are doing *x* can be experienced as overly judgmental and critical. Such an imbalance might also increase a patient's self-blame and result in treatment dropout.

DBT interventions based on total acceptance of the individual include an emphasis on validation (which we describe later), reciprocal communication (warmth, genuineness, and responsiveness), and sometimes environmental intervention by the clinician on the patient's behalf. Change interventions (which will be more fully elucidated in later chapters) focus on problem solving, behavioral analysis (Chapter 9), commitment strategies (Chapter 8), psychoeducation, skills training (Chapters 10 and 11), exposure, cognitive modification, and coaching the client to deal with individuals in the environment on their own behalf (Chapter 15). The key point here is that the balance between acceptance and change is kept at the forefront of the clinician's mind in the approach to the patient.

DBT assumptions are informed by the dialectic

One of the unique aspects of DBT is that the underlying assumptions of the treatment approach are explicit and are shared at the outset with the patient, usually in the initial sessions. The dialectical stance results in several assumptions that underlie the DBT approach (Box 6.1).

The first explicit assumption is that patients are doing the best they can. At the same time, patients want to improve but they need to do better, try harder, and be more motivated to change. Furthermore, another assumption of the approach is that patients may not have caused all of their own problems, but they have to solve them anyway. DBT also assumes that the lives of BPD patients as they are currently being lived are unbearable. An additional assumption is that patients cannot fail in therapy; rather, if failure occurs, it is the treatment that fails [2]. Finally, clinicians who treat individuals with BPD need support. This last assumption arises from the fact that many treatments with complicated patients can get offtrack and are demanding, and clinicians doing this work need support to stay on track and remain effective.

These philosophical assumptions serve to enhance clinician and patient motivation, and inform the therapeutic stance at all times [3, 4]. For example, the first assumption encourages a nonjudgmental approach and discourages negative thinking on the clinician's part in the face of ongoing difficult patient behavior.

The second assumption validates the need for change, without blame or judgment, and promotes effective problem solving. Furthermore, it also underscores the belief that the clinician cannot save the patient – the patient needs to do most of the work with the help of the clinician. The clinician's role is to encourage self-care rather than to take care of the patient. Many "out of control" treatments where we have consulted with the therapist and/ or the patient are the product of the therapist assuming more and more responsibility for

---

Box 6.1   DBT assumptions

Patients are doing the best they can.
Patients want to improve.
Patients need to do better, try harder, and be more motivated to change.
Patients may have not caused all of their problems, but they have to solve them anyway.
The lives of BPD patients as they are currently being lived are unbearable.
Patients cannot fail in therapy.
Clinicians who treat individuals with BPD need support.

the patient. Ultimately, this results in the therapist feeling overburdened or overwhelmed or both, leading to withdrawal from the patient either through a precipitous termination (e.g., hospitalizing the patient for a rise in suicide ideation and telling the inpatient unit that the therapist is no longer willing to treat the patient) or becoming suddenly very limit-setting and emotionally disconnected, or visibly angry. For example, in response to a patient becoming increasingly depressed, the clinician may increase the number of sessions, then add periodic phone check-ins to see how the patient is doing, and then additional check-ins to the point where the therapist and patient are speaking for an hour or so on a daily basis. The patient's mood may not improve and may even worsen, and the clinician begins to feel resentful and overburdened but also unable to make changes for fear of making the patient worse. At some point, either the patient realizes that this is not helpful or the clinician gets "fed up" with how he feels taken advantage of despite the fact that he has created the situation.

The final assumption is that if the patient does not make progress, gets worse, or drops out of treatment, the burden of the failure is assumed by the therapy. That is to say, the therapy was not successful in enhancing patient motivation, and this assumption removes blame from the patient regarding lack of motivation. Patients with BPD are often blamed directly for their treatment failures. So this assumption is particularly helpful to patients who experience tremendous self-blame, which can be crippling and can inhibit them from extending themselves both in therapy and life generally. Whenever this assumption is explained to a new DBT patient who has been in treatment before, it is met with both surprise and pleasure, and sometimes a joking question, "You mean if this doesn't work out, it's the fault of DBT and not me?" Clinicians reading this may be thinking that their patients with BPD already externalize blame toward the clinician and the therapy. While that can certainly be the case, it usually stems from BPD patients' underlying sense that lack of progress in treatment is their fault.

What is mindfulness and where does it fit into the DBT model?

The Eastern philosophical tenets of acceptance and mindfulness are integral to DBT [5]. As we described earlier, an exclusive focus on change can be readily experienced as invalidating by traumatized or rejection-sensitive individuals, and it can result in early dropout or resistance to change within the treatment. It is almost as if patients feel that if they change, they admit that they were "wrong" and feel worse about themselves.

The concept of mindfulness is basic to increasing acceptance of oneself and other. The mindfulness orientation encourages total acceptance of the individual, viewing their destructive behaviors as the patient's best efforts to cope with unbearable pain.

Mindfulness, as defined by Jon Kabat-Zinn, means "paying attention in a particular way: on purpose, in the present moment, and nonjudgmentally" [6]. It is a state of being that includes enhanced awareness and ability to sustain attention in the here and now, to notice what "is" without the filter of what we want or think things should be.

At first glance, the concept of mindfulness seems very abstract and difficult to grasp, particularly for individuals with BPD. When we first started learning about and teaching mindfulness, we did not fully understand its relevance to psychotherapy and we feared that patients would have difficulty understanding or being able to relate to the idea. For example, it was hard to see how watching one's breath could be helpful in reducing suicidal urges. However, it did not take long to realize that not only were patients able to grasp the concept, they quickly incorporated the principles into their understanding of their difficulties, and the idea of mindfulness and mindfulness practice remains one of the most helpful of the skills interventions.

Mindfulness practice teaches acceptance through controlling and training the mind to observe and describe the present moment, without judgment. This promotes increased awareness of the current reality. In addition to cultivating an accepting stance toward the present moment, this training is also extremely useful in helping patients remain in the present rather than focusing on past worries or future fears. As patients fight urges to hurt themselves, mindfulness practice is very effective in helping them accept themselves and their situation. In this way, they can distance themselves from their negative self-judgments, which ultimately helps them to reduce the intensity of their urges. In Chapter 11, we will fully describe how mindfulness is taught in DBT, and how it underlies all of the DBT skills.

Validation

Validation is at the core of the acceptance/change dialectic and is a crucial aspect of the therapeutic approach in DBT. Validation is a strategy that is used in many forms of psychotherapy including supportive, psychodynamic, and client-centered therapy. However, in DBT, there is a unique explicit emphasis on validation, and DBT clinicians are trained to listen actively for any opportunity to validate. Linehan [7] presents the "essence" of validation in the context of DBT psychotherapy: "The clinician communicates to the client that her responses make sense and are understandable within her current life context or situation." Discussion of the patient's emotional experiences, suffering, and difficulty changing are some of the occasions for using validation.

Validation is much more than empathy. Empathy is the ability to correctly understand the patient's internal experience. Empathy is necessary but not sufficient. Furthermore, validation must be genuine and not patronizing, otherwise it can end up feeling hollow and can engender anger. Validation is highlighting the person and the behavior in terms of an external source of consensual or empirical "truth" or reality. Validation is also not synonymous with praise. The clinician cannot and should not avoid confrontation when necessary. Nor should the invalid be validated. For example, it would be counter therapeutic to validate the following statement by a patient: "He made me so mad, I just had to throw the phone at him." However, the patient's experience of anger can be validated. Similarly, the self-injuring patient who says "I had no other way to make myself feel better but to cut myself" can have the unbearable feelings that need to be relieved validated without validating the behavior of self-injury.

Validation strategies require the clinician to search for, recognize, and reflect to patients the validity inherent in their response to events. A validating clinician notices, amplifies, and reinforces valid responses. This can present quite a challenge – to find something to validate – when a patient presents with many destructive or ineffective behaviors, distorted cognitions, and misinterpretations of events and interpersonal motivations of others.

Validation is an explicit DBT intervention, and Linehan delineates six levels of validation [7]. The first three levels are universal to all modalities of psychotherapy, while levels 4, 5, and 6 are not. In general, the clinician should try to validate at the highest possible level. The levels are:

- *Level 1.* Active listening and observing. At this level, the clinician becomes a participant and an observer, maintaining awareness of where the patient is at the moment. An example of Level 1 validation might be when a therapist states, upon hearing a patient's description of an emotional episode, "I can see that this was very upsetting for you. You look as if you are still upset about it."
- *Level 2.* Accurate reflection and taking a nonjudgmental stance. The clinician accurately reflects back what the patient has verbalized regarding their thoughts, feelings, and experiences. Thus, when the patient describes feeling hurt and rejected by her boyfriend, the therapist might state: "When your boyfriend cancelled your dinner plans, you felt rejected and uncared for."
- *Level 3.* Articulating the unverbalized. The clinician presents insight interpretations regarding thoughts or feelings that the patient has not explicitly articulated. Only accurate interpretations are validating, and in DBT the clinician presents them as hypotheses or questions, not statements, and does not assume that an insight interpretation is accurate unless the patient acknowledges the possibility. This makes the approach much more collaborative and partners the therapist and patient to correct the therapist's "hunches" and develop an understanding to which both the patient and therapist agree. The clinician as "all-knowing" is avoided. This simple strategy of posing hypotheses rather than making statements or decrees is extremely helpful in avoiding therapeutic "tugs of war" in which the therapist defends an interpretation that the patient has rejected. A clinician might present a Level 3 validation in the following manner: "I know you feel hurt by your boyfriend. I am wondering if it is possible that you are also angry at him?"
- *Level 4.* Current unskillful behaviors, cognitive interpretations, or emotional experiences are considered to be valid within a historical and/or biological context. Thus, current behaviors may be valid in terms of having been learned in the past but they are not valid in the present situation. Or, behaviors may be valid in terms of antecedents (what came before) but not consequences, in terms of short-term but not long-term consequences. Unskillful emotional experiences or responses may be valid in the context of a biologically based mood disorder. A Level 4 validation strategy requires the clinician to conduct additional analysis of an unskillful behavior, thought, or feeling in terms of past context. For example, a patient with a history of emotional abuse may interpret a clinician's encouragement as insincere or even uncaring. The clinician might respond: "I know that your mother was very critical of you and that you believe that this was her way of caring about you. So, when I praise or cheerlead you, I wonder if you think that I am just saying these things but that I don't mean them and I don't care about you because I'm not being honest with you?"
- *Level 5.* Normalization – Thoughts and feelings are normalized and viewed as making sense within the present context. The clinician suggests that many or most people would feel this way in such a situation. For this level of validation, the clinician highlights feelings of pain and the difficulty of experiencing pain. Level 5 validation strategies also address the difficulty of changing, and the pain of having to use skills to tolerate

distress rather than escaping through unskillful behaviors. An example of a Level 5 validation is when a patient with an anger management problem was upset with himself for what he thought was "road rage" when he cut in front of another car in a traffic jam at a bridge toll. The therapist responded: "You won't get anywhere driving in New York City without cutting someone off in traffic. Most NYC drivers need to do that at one time or another. Although you do have trouble controlling your anger at times, this doesn't seem like one of those times."

- *Level 6.* The clinician is "radically genuine" with the patient. This can include confrontation of the invalid, refraining from treating the patient with kid gloves, cheerleading, acknowledging the patient's capacity for valid behavior in the future, and appropriately discussing the patient's impact on the therapist. When a patient accused her therapist of not caring whether her patients live or die, the therapist responded in a radically genuine manner, stating, "You may be very angry with me, but it is not okay to make such a hurtful accusation."

These six levels comprise three steps of validation:

1 active observing of what the patient is reporting;
2 reflection of the patient's feelings, thoughts, and behaviors in a nonjudgmental and nonauthoritarian manner, whereby the clinician phrases the reflection not as a pronouncement but more as a question;
3 direct validation of the "understandability" of the patient's response and experience.

We present the following patient situations to illustrate how a DBT clinician would search for and highlight the valid aspects of a patient's experience within a larger picture of mainly unskillful behaviors and responses. As you read them we ask that you consider what you might be able to find to validate, and how you would communicate that validation to the patient. We will then describe examples of Level 4 (historical/biological validation) and Level 5 (normalization).

Case example

Laura, a 24-year-old single woman was rejected by a male she dated briefly. One night they had an argument over the phone and he hung up and would not answer when she tried to contact him. She got very drunk, went to his home, and banged on the door when he did not answer the bell. He yelled at her from the other side of the closed door to go away. After about 30 minutes of trying to get him to let her in, she went home, called her mother to tell her she was going to kill herself, then cut herself superficially on the arm with a knife and fell asleep.

What aspects of Laura's experience can be validated, and how?

Despite the presence of mostly very disturbing and unskillful behaviors that should not be validated, the DBT clinician would first try to focus on finding the "golden kernel" of valid experience. This might involve validating (a) how distraught Laura must have felt at being rejected by someone in whom she is romantically interested; (b) how out of control of the situation and helpless she feels, which might lead her to have urges to "do something, anything" to get what she feels she needs; (c) how difficult it might be to accept that she cannot have something that she feels she needs. Validation of the pain and the desire to be able to do something to get rid of the pain would constitute a Level 5 validation.

A Level 4 historical validation might have to do with acknowledging that Laura was doing the best she could to help herself manage extreme distress, and that she had not yet developed more skillful ways of dealing with rejection and feeling helpless. Laura may have learned this type of behavior from growing up with an alcoholic parent who locked herself in her bedroom. In the past, throwing tantrums, not taking no for an answer, or making threats may have resulted in getting the response she wanted and therefore were reinforced. Thus, although these behaviors are currently unskillful and not effective for her, they make sense given her history.

Case example

Sam, a 27-year-old single man, who has difficulty keeping a regular job because he got into frequent interpersonal conflicts, works as a freelance journalist and frequently requires financial support from his parents to meet living expenses. His work is sporadic and he periodically gets into situations in which he has no money for food or rent, is in danger of being evicted, and feels suicidal because he feels too ashamed to ask his mother for money. Despite the fact that this has happened more than once, he refuses to seek regular employment. He feels that it is beneath him to work for anyone other than himself, that it would make him feel too demoralized and would interfere with pursuing his interest to work for himself as a journalist. He was offered a good-paying full-time position that he promptly turned down.

In this case, a Level 4 validation would consist of acknowledging Sam's desire to be independently employed and his sense of humiliation and difficulty that he experiences working for someone else. Also, the clinician would highlight the self-validation and increased sense of self-esteem that he experiences by working as a freelance journalist. A Level 5 validation would focus on the understanding of how difficult it is to experience shame – anyone would want to avoid it. The clinician can reflect to Sam that he is caught between two experiences that induce shame in himself: working for someone other than himself and needing financial support from his family.

Validation and change

Although we have discussed validation as being related to acceptance, it is also relevant to change. Ignoring the need for change is a form of invalidation in that it does not take the problems and negative consequences of the patient's destructive behaviors seriously. Furthermore, it can send the message that the therapist either does not care enough (e.g., does not want to do the "hard work" of change or wants the patient to stay suffering) or does not view the patient as capable of change. This can lead to hopelessness and desperation on the patient's part. Thus, acceptance and validation are combined with change strategies. The balance of change with acceptance is one of the most important aspects of the dialectical approach and is solidly based in the Zen/mindfulness perspective. Change is achieved through the tension and resolution of the essential conflict between acceptance of individuals as they are right now and demanding that they need to change.

Dialectic synthesis

The dialectical stance encourages a synthesis of either/or thinking into a yes/and perspective – directly addressing the dichotomous thinking that is characteristic of individuals with BPD and which often leads to maladaptive behaviors [7]. As an example of how this might translate at the level of clinical intervention, let us consider the example of a patient threatening to kill herself when her clinician informs her of an upcoming vacation. In DBT, the clinician would validate the patient's distress about the clinician going away, and also validate the patient's desire or need for the clinician to not leave. It is also valid for the clinician to need and want to take a vacation without being afraid of the patient's suicidality. Viewing the situation from a yes/and perspective (both individuals have valid, yet opposing needs) instead of from an either/or view (the patient is wrong for "threatening" the clinician, or the clinician is wrong for leaving the suicidal patient) allows for a dialectical synthesis of the opposing needs.

Change: Theory and techniques

Another prominent theoretical orientation that contributes to maintaining a dialectic stance (balancing acceptance and change) is that of social and behavioral learning theory. Learning theory underlies the "change" strategies and interventions of DBT. There are some basic learning theory concepts that are central to the DBT theoretical and psychotherapeutic approach that will help clinicians understand the approach to change that DBT takes.

Conditioning

Behaviors are understood to be maintained through either classical or operant conditioning.

Classical conditioning

Classical (or respondent) conditioning is illustrated by the well-known Pavlov's dog paradigm [8], in which a dog is presented with a bowl of dog food at the same time that a bell is sounded. The dog salivates when the food (an unconditioned stimulus, i.e., no learning is required to obtain this response) is presented. After a number of times of receiving the food at the same time as the ringing of the bell (conditioned stimulus), the dog learns to associate the sound of the bell with the presentation of food. The dog will then salivate when the bell is sounded, in the absence of the food. Thus, in this paradigm, the food is the unconditioned stimulus, the bell is the conditioned stimulus, and the salivation is the response (i.e., behavior). The sound of the bell stimulates the behavior, even when the "real" stimulus, the food, is absent.

The classical conditioning model helps us understand the origin of current maladaptive behaviors that have no clear trigger in the present but that have been conditioned by past experiences. Particularly in BPD patients, who have a high incidence of past trauma, their current self-destructive or unskillful behaviors are often prompted by conditioned stimuli in the current situation that have become associated with an unconditioned stimuli from the past. For example, one patient had an intense fear reaction when she was walking down the street. Upon exploration, we realized that the smell of bread baking was wafting out of a window while she was passing by. This odor reminded her of visiting a grandmother who was very emotionally abusive toward her. Thus, the abuse and the aroma of baking bread were paired and the aroma became a conditioned stimulus that triggered the fear reaction (the behavior), in the absence of the abuse (unconditioned stimulus).

Understanding the conditioned stimulus/behavioral connection helps us to validate a behavior that, on the face of it, seems to have no clear trigger (no valid reason) in the present. In addition, we can intervene by working to loosen the connection between the conditioned and unconditioned stimulus (through exposure to the conditioned stimulus in the absence of the unconditioned stimulus).

Operant conditioning

The model of operant conditioning [9] illustrates how maladaptive behaviors are maintained through positive or negative reinforcement. In this paradigm, a stimulus provokes a behavior, which is then followed by a consequence that rewards (positive reinforcement), removes an aversive aspect of experience (negative reinforcement), or punishes. It is important to note that punishment and negative reinforcement are quite different. Negative reinforcement strengthens a behavioral response by removing an aversive condition while punishment is designed to reduce a behavior by administering a negative consequence. Any consequence that results in an increase in a target behavior is called a reinforcer. Thus, for example, for individuals with BPD who engage in nonsuicidal self harm behaviors such as superficial cutting, the cutting behavior is (negatively) reinforced (and therefore has an increased likelihood of continuing) because it quickly results in the reduction of intense emotional and physical discomfort (the elimination of or decrease in an aversive state).

Understanding the role of reinforcement (operant conditioning) in maintaining maladaptive behaviors contributes to the ability to both validate and change these behaviors. Both clinician and patient can observe the connection of the behavior with the reinforcement without judgment, and can learn to intervene by "managing contingencies," through the removal of reinforcers.

Operant conditioning also describes the importance of the frequency of reinforcement in maintaining behaviors, that is, reinforcement schedules [10]. Some behaviors are reinforced in a continual manner, such that every time a behavior is performed, reinforcement is received. For example, when a dog is given a biscuit each time he gives his owner his paw, this is continuous reinforcement. If the reinforcement is suddenly discontinued, the dog will soon learn that the biscuit has stopped coming and he is more likely to stop giving his owner his paw. However, if the owner were to switch to giving the biscuit intermittently, with no predictable pattern, the dog maintains the reinforced behavior in the absence of the biscuit for a much longer time than if he had been continually reinforced.

Behaviors that have been developed within an intermittent reinforcement schedule are difficult to eradicate. Unfortunately, the types of maladaptive self-harm and dysregulated behaviors we are targeting with our patients are usually a product of such an intermittent reinforcement schedule. As described in the biosocial theory (Chapter 4), unskillful behaviors such as temper tantrums are intermittently reinforced by sometimes (unpredictably) eliciting a validating response from a usually invalidating caregiver.

While learning principles are prominent in all forms of CBT, some forms of CBT emphasize the importance of, and therefore focus on, the role of cognitions rather than behavior. For example, the CBT developed and adapted by Beck et al. [11] and further adapted for suicidal individuals [12] emphasizes the importance of distorted cognitions. Exposing and examining these faulty cognitions then become an important focus of the treatment. Correcting them is believed to be the pathway to change. Alternatively, DBT places a greater emphasis on emotion and behavior. Given the behavioral perspective, DBT defines cognition as behavior. DBT focuses on understanding which reinforcers maintain a maladaptive behavior and attempts to loosen the links that lead to the behavior through a variety of means. This is not to say that DBT never examines distorted cognitions nor that Beck's CBT never examines behavioral reinforcers. Instead, different types of CBT vary in their approach to problems as do the variety of psychodynamically oriented psychotherapies.

Summary

Dialectical synthesis of acceptance and change is at the core of the DBT psychotherapeutic approach to understanding and treating BPD. DBT assumptions regarding patients and the process of conducting psychotherapy are directly informed by the dialectic, and assign equal amount of responsibility for the patient's improvement to the DBT clinician, the patient, and the treatment approach itself. The focus on mindfulness allows clinicians to cultivate a stance of total acceptance of patients as they currently are functioning and behaving. Explicit validation strategies provide a therapeutic intervention for active acceptance of the patient. Learning principles provide a nonjudgmental understanding of how unskillful patterns are learned, as well as an understanding of how they can be unlearned and replaced by new, more skillful patterns. Behavioral change interventions are based on models of classical and operant conditioning. Clinicians strive to push relentlessly for change, albeit within the context of an accepting, nonjudgmental, and validating therapeutic relationship.

References

1. Linehan, M.M. (1993) *Skills Training Manual for Treating Borderline Personality Disorder*, Guilford Press, New York.
2. Linehan, M.M. (1993) *Cognitive Behavioral Treatment of Borderline Personality Disorder*, Guilford Press, New York, pp. 106–120.
3. Cialdini, R.B., Vincent, J.E., Lewis, S.K., et al. (1975) Reciprocal concessions procedure for inducing compliance: The door-in-the-face technique. *Journal of Personality and Social Psychology*, 31, 206–215.
4. Freedman, J.L., Fraser, S.C. (1966) Compliance without pressure: The foot-in-the-door technique. *Journal of Personality and Social Psychology*, 4, 195–202.
5. Robins, C.J. (2002) Zen principles and mindfulness practice in dialectical behavior therapy. *Cognitive Behavioral Practice*, 9, 50–57.
6. Kabat-Zinn, J. (1994) *Wherever you go there you are*, Hyperion, New York.
7. Linehan, M.M. (1997) Validation and psychotherapy, in *Empathy Reconsidered: New Directions in Psychotherapy* (eds A. Bohart and L. Greenberg), American Psychological Association, Washington, DC.
8. Pavlov, I.P. (1927) *Conditioned Reflexes*, Oxford University Press, London.
9. Skinner, B.F. (1938) *The Behavior of Organisms: An Experimental Analysis*, Appleton-Century, New York.
10. Pryor, K. (1985) Reinforcement: Better than rewards, in *Don't Shoot the Dog: How to Improve Yourself and Others Through Behavioral Training*, Bantam Books, New York, pp. 1–34.
11. Beck, A.T., Freeman, A., Davis, D.D. (2003) *Cognitive Therapy of Personality Disorders* (2nd ed.), Guilford Press, New York, pp. 187–215.
12. Wenzel, A., Brown, G.K., Beck, A.T. (2006) *Cognitive Therapy for Suicidal Patients: Scientific and Clinical Applications*, American Psychiatric Publishing, Inc., Washington, DC.

Chapter 7

The ABC's of DBT – overview of the treatment

In this chapter, we provide an overview of the basic framework of a DBT treatment.

> **Key points**
> - DBT has four stages of treatment
> - The four DBT treatment modes: Individual therapy, group skills training, between-session skills coaching, and DBT supervision team
> - How DBT is a modification of CBT

Stages of treatment

DBT has several stages of treatment based upon the problems that need to be addressed. One stage is completed before moving to the next. However, there are times when patients move from a later stage back to an earlier stage depending on their problems at the moment. It is important to note that DBT has a hierarchy of target problems to be addressed and, while the treatment agenda is collaborative, certain problems are addressed in a particular order and this is described prior to the initiation of treatment but is not negotiable. For example, any self-harm behaviors are discussed first and foremost in each session if they are present. We will discuss other aspects of the hierarchy in Chapters 7 and 8.

At the outset, the first phase of work with a patient is called Pretreatment and Orientation. In this phase, the commitment to the treatment is developed and the model and requirements are described. This is the phase in which patient and therapist agree to work together and establish the conditions under which the treatment will proceed (see Chapter 8).

Once complete (the pretreatment stage can take a few sessions), the treatment enters Stage 1. Stage 1 specifically targets the reduction of life-threatening behavior, and is therefore the most researched and of particular interest to clinicians who treat the chronic

---

The Dialectical Behavior Therapy Primer: How DBT Can Inform Clinical Practice, First Edition.
Beth S. Brodsky and Barbara Stanley.
© 2013 John Wiley & Sons, Ltd. Published 2013 by John Wiley & Sons, Ltd.

suicidality of BPD patients on an outpatient basis. Within the context of treating self-injury, other behavioral, interpersonal, cognitive, and emotional difficulties are also addressed. These include behaviors that interfere with the therapy and interpersonal difficulties. This phase of treatment can take about 12 months. The interventions that comprise Stage 1 DBT therapy will be the main focus of the second section of this book.

Once a patient has control over self-harm behaviors, the patient can decide to enter into Stage 2. The main target of Stage 2 in DBT is to increase the capacity for nontraumatic emotional experiencing, and to address the ways in which PTSD symptoms are interfering with quality of life goals such as social and vocational functioning. Since many individuals with BPD have a history of childhood abuse [1, 2], Stage 2 DBT introduces exposure-based procedures to treat the residue of childhood trauma [3]. Capacity of control over engaging in self-harm and a commitment to refrain from self-harm behaviors should be fully assessed before transitioning into Stage 2 where the primary focus is on emotional exposure and experiencing. A manualized prolonged exposure (PE) DBT intervention has been designed and is being researched by Melanie Harned [4]. Because PTSD symptoms and the inability to experience emotion can be an obstacle to reducing self-harm behaviors, the PE intervention has been introduced as an adjunct to Stage 1 DBT in which life-threatening behaviors are still the primary target. Preliminary results [4] indicate that even patients who are still in Stage 1 DBT are able to tolerate emotional exposure to PTSD if they have acquired emotion regulation skills. Since the PE protocol is in the early stages of dissemination, and Stage 2 DBT is not fully manualized, we will not be reviewing Stage 2 interventions in this book.

Other quality of life issues, such as self-actualization in social and vocational arenas, become the target of treatment during Stage 3. Finally, Stage 4 treatment focuses on increasing joy and a sense freedom, and of completeness and connectedness.

Overview of DBT treatment (Stage 1)

DBT aims to provide increased support for patients to remain safe on an outpatient basis, as well as support for the clinician working with the chronically suicidal outpatient. This is achieved through applying learning principles toward capability and motivation enhancement of both patient and clinician. Patient capability is enhanced through the teaching of adaptive skillful behaviors; motivation through the reinforcement of progress and non-reinforcement of maladaptive behaviors. For the clinician, a DBT consultation team is a source of support and guidance as well as an aid to keep the clinician focused on the treatment goals and format (see Chapter 15).

Overview of DBT components (Stage 2)

DBT consists of three components in which patients participate: individual psychotherapy, group skills training, and between-session skills coaching. The addition of skills training and coaching in DBT derives from a skills deficit perspective. Individuals need not only to understand their maladaptive patterns of behavior but they also have certain deficits that can best be overcome by helping them to develop means of compensation and learning new means of coping and skillful behavior.

Patients often report that they know *why* they "do what they do" but they "do not know what to do instead." Or, if they do know what to do, they do not know how to get themselves to do it. While the first half of this statement may or may not be correct, the second half is almost always true. The addition of the skills training component to the treatment acknowledges this problem by teaching coping strategies and skills in a more explicit manner than is typically done with patients who have personality disorders.

Thus, this approach addresses the need for both understanding maladaptive patterns of thinking and behavior and skill development in treating patients with BPD and other personality disorders. Personality disorders are seen, in part, as deficits in certain skill areas that prevent the person from behaving in an effective manner. For this reason, DBT places a high priority on skills teaching and acquisition. Patients attend DBT skills training group once weekly to learn the concepts of the skills within a supportive environment. Although some role-play and rehearsal of skills takes place in group, the majority of skills acquisition takes place between therapy sessions. Patients are given homework in both their group and individual sessions in order to learn skills through practice. However, in addition to skills training group, patients are encouraged to call their individual DBT clinician for in vivo skills coaching in order to facilitate the learning and using of skills in their day-to-day lives. Individual DBT clinicians are required to make themselves available to their patients between sessions for the purposes of skills coaching. DBT has clearly delineated parameters and a protocol for clinicians to follow (see Chapter 12) in order to be able to make themselves available in an effective way for both patient and clinician.

As can be seen in Figure 7.1, individual therapy and skills training target different aspects of individuals' problems and use different modalities to effect change.

A fourth component of DBT, which does not directly involve the patient yet is a central aspect of the treatment, is a consultation team for DBT clinicians. The consultation team meets regularly in order to provide peer supervisory support to individual clinicians in

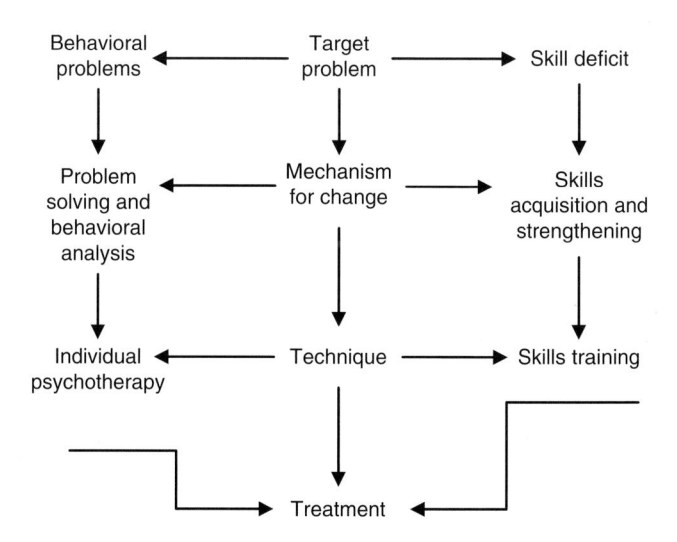

Figure 7.1 Two-pronged approach to treating personality disorders

maintaining a dialectic and validating stance toward their patients. The details of the role of the DBT consultation team and how it works are fully described in Chapter 15. All of these components of the treatment will be described in detail in later chapters. Here is a brief overview of a standard DBT treatment.

Individual therapy

Patients attend at least one, sometimes two, individual therapy sessions of 50–60 minutes each week. These sessions are highly structured. The patient keeps track of the thoughts, feelings, and behaviors that are related to their treatment goals on a diary card, which are reviewed and used by the clinician and patient to collaboratively set an agenda based on the patient's treatment goals. These goals are previously agreed to during a pretreatment phase (described more fully in Chapter 8) in which the clinician and patient commit to a hierarchy of goals. In this hierarchy, the most important goal is the reduction of life-threatening behaviors (suicide attempts, active suicidal ideation, suicidal threats or gestures, and NSSI). The second most important goal is to reduce any behaviors (on the part of the patient or clinician) that interfere with the therapy (therapy-interfering behaviors). Any behaviors that interfere with the patient's quality of life (social and vocational functioning) are addressed third. The clinician uses the agenda to keep the session goal-directed and on track, and balances validation and change interventions throughout the session to make steady progress toward the patient's treatment goals. Clinician and patient collaborate to conduct behavioral chain analyses, and the clinician stays alert to any opportunity to balance this type of change intervention with validating statements. (See Chapter 9 for a full description of how to conduct an individual DBT session.) The clinician also attends to any emotions that might be triggered during the session, and when necessary coaches the patient in using emotion regulation or mindfulness skills to skillfully experience the emotion.

Skills training

The teaching of skillful behaviors with which to replace the maladaptive ones is a major component of capacity enhancement in DBT. Skills training takes place in a weekly skills training group in which skills are taught within a didactic framework, similar to a graduate school seminar, preferably by two coleaders other than the individual clinician. Groups are typically 1.5–2 hours in length and it takes approximately 6 months meeting weekly to review all the skills in the manual. The group serves to introduce and teach the concepts of skills, and it provides an opportunity to interact with other patients who are also learning skills. DBT clinicians utilize the skills training manual written by Linehan [5]. This manual describes the skills and how to teach them, and it contains worksheets and homework assignments to facilitate learning for distribution to group members. In vivo skills coaching is conducted in such a way as to enhance patient capability and motivation.

Skills training is based on learning theory and the group skills leaders utilize behavioral principles such as shaping, modeling, repeated practice, behavioral rehearsal, homework, and reinforcement of socially appropriate behaviors [6]. Behavior change is facilitated by the combination of the direct instruction of information, modeling of behaviors by role models, prompting of specific behaviors, and positive reinforcement of successive approximations toward the desired goal [7]. (See Chapters 10 and 11 for a full description of DBT skills and skills training.)

Between-session phone coaching

A unique feature of DBT is the availability of the clinician between sessions to coach the patient in using skills when they are having trouble using them on their own to cope, especially with self-harm and suicidal urges. When first hearing about this aspect of DBT, clinicians can become frightened that they will be spending a lot of time on the phone. However, as we will fully describe in Chapter 12, DBT provides a protocol that limits between-session phone calls to a brief interaction that targets skills coaching or relationship repair. By providing this type of clinician availability, patients are more likely to use skills and clinicians can actually prevent the amount of time spent fielding crisis calls.

During the early commitment phase of DBT treatment (see Chapter 8), clinicians orient patients to the use of skills coaching with the clinician between sessions. Between-session calls are encouraged in order to enhance patient capacity to use skills and to generalize them in response to real-life situations. Calls are also allowed for the purpose of relationship repair, in order to facilitate patient engagement in treatment. These phone calls are brief and targeted – clinician and patient briefly review the current situation and collaborate to decide on a behavioral plan for coping skillfully. Or, in the case of relationship repair, the patient is invited to communicate a problem between the patient and clinician – either something the clinician did that felt invalidating or to apologize for something the patient did that felt unskillful and interfering of the therapy. When patients do not call for coaching when they need to, the clinician targets this behavior in the individual session. A full description of the protocol and parameters for between-session contact can be found in Chapter 12.

Case illustrating the multiple modalities of a DBT treatment

We present the case of Francine (excerpts reprinted with permission from Chapter 19, pp. 309–313, from The American Psychiatric Publishing, Textbook of Personality Disorders, Edited by John M. Oldham, Andrew E. Skodol, and Donna S. Bender, 2005) [8] to illustrate how the individual session, skills training, and between-session coaching modalities are coordinated in a standard DBT treatment.

Case example

Francine is a highly intelligent 28-year-old woman working as a secretary and studying for her bachelor's degree. She lives with her boyfriend of six years; the two were in couples therapy seeking help in deciding whether or not to get married. Francine was referred by the couples' clinician to individual therapy for the treatment of binge-eating disorder: the patient's obesity and out-of-control binge eating were interfering with the couple's sex life. During the course of individual psychotherapy, it became apparent that the patient was exhibiting symptoms of BPD that were contributing to the primary difficulties in her relationship with her boyfriend. Her binge eating was an impulsive behavior that was often triggered by fears of abandonment, feelings of emptiness, and identity diffusion, and it was a self-soothing mechanism for feelings of uncontrollable rage. The patient was also having difficulties in her relationships with supervisors at work due to a tendency to idealize, and then devalue, those in authority, and to feel exploited and to

(Continued)

> (*Continued*)
> view them with suspicion when under stress. The individual clinician identified the need for the patient to develop more skillful coping mechanisms to replace the binge eating and impaired interpersonal functioning, and referred the patient to DBT. Although the patient was not initially interested in changing her interpersonal behaviors, since she viewed her difficulties with her supervisors as external to herself, she was highly motivated to gain control over her eating and agreed to undergo individual DBT and skills training.
> In individual DBT therapy, Francine and her DBT therapist collaborated on identifying the binge eating as her primary treatment target. Francine started tracking her urges to binge and her binge-eating behaviors on a diary card. She also tracked her interpersonal interactions and her moods in order to see if they were related to her binge eating. When Francine engaged in binge-eating behavior, she and her therapist would conduct a behavioral chain analysis to identify triggers, thoughts, and behaviors that led to urges to binge. During these behavioral analyses, the therapist would identify skills that Francine was learning in the skills training group and work with Francine to figure out how to apply them in these types of situations.
> Francine immediately took to the skills training. She found the mindfulness skills extremely helpful in allowing her to observe and describe urges to binge, which gave her increasing control over her eating behaviors. She learned distress tolerance skills that helped her distract from and also tolerate the feelings of anger and emptiness without resorting to binge eating. She called her individual clinician for skills coaching when she was feeling urges to binge. This helped her by giving her support to try emotion regulation skills, sit with her feelings, and ride out the urges without acting. Calling for coaching also helped her learn how to identify the urges before she acted on them, and gave her a positive experience in asking for help. In addition, her relationships improved. She described it as follows: "Mindfulness skills helped me more clearly distinguish between my thoughts and behaviors in an interpersonal interaction, and what the contribution of the other person was."

How is DBT different from CBT?

From our overview of the theory (Chapter 6) and framework of DBT, it is quite clear that although DBT is a variant of CBT and incorporates many CBT interventions, DBT also represents a distinct approach to treatment. These are some of the main parameters along which DBT can be distinguished from other forms of CBT.

The degree to which DBT targets emotion, behavior, and cognition. Standard CBT highlights the contribution of automatic thoughts and dysfunctional core beliefs in the development of depression and suicidal thinking. CBT for depression, as well as for BPD, maintains a primary focus on cognition and the interventions are aimed at challenging and reframing of distorted interpretations. CBT also incorporates behavioral activation skills for individuals who are depressed. One of the adaptations that DBT makes in applying CBT to BPD is to add a primary focus on targeting emotional dysregulation. As described in Chapter 4, the biosocial theory of BPD highlights emotional dysregulation as the core deficit that underlies the dysregulated behaviors and cognitions of individuals with BPD. DBT also places a greater emphasis on skills acquisition and behavioral change. The DBT skills modules and group skills training are an integral part of the treatment, and all patients learn all of the skills systematically.

Dialectical synthesis. The balance of validation with change, the synthesis of judging experience as good or bad, all or nothing thinking, and the switch from either/or to yes/and thinking constitute DBT's unique overarching philosophical worldview that informs the therapeutic stance and specific interventions and runs throughout the conduct of a standard DBT psychotherapy.

Nonnegotiable hierarchy of treatment goals. For a patient to be in DBT they must agree to address any life-threatening behaviors when they are present. In each DBT individual session, the clinician inquires about the presence of suicidal ideation, urges to self-harm, or any self-destructive behaviors. This insistence on addressing self-harm behaviors and keeping them "on the front burner" is unique and helps the clinician to stay vigilant to suicide risk. The hierarchy of goals will be fully described in Chapter 8.

DBT consultation team. While most psychotherapeutic approaches encourage practicing clinicians to obtain clinical supervision, and to consult with colleagues when struggling with a difficult clinical situation, DBT was the first psychotherapy to build in such consultation and make it a required part of the standard treatment. The DBT team approach to supervision is also unique in terms of format. Team meetings are structured with mindfulness practice and agenda setting, and the emphasis is on supporting the clinician to find dialectic synthesis and the effective balance of validation and change within the therapy (see Chapter 15). Other treatments (e.g., transference-focused psychotherapy (TFP) [8, 9]) have also incorporated this modification into their protocol for treating suicidal borderline patients.

Summary

DBT psychotherapy takes a multipronged treatment approach that includes individual psychotherapy sessions, group skills training, between-session in vivo skills coaching, and a DBT consultation team for clinician support. The balance between acceptance and change and the focus on a dialectical synthesis run consistently throughout all the therapeutic modalities, and always inform the therapeutic stance of the DBT clinician.

References

1. Brodsky, B.S., Cloitre, M., Dulit, R.A. (1995) Relationship of dissociation and childhood abuse in borderline personality disorder. *American Journal of Psychiatry*, 152 (12), 1788–1792.
2. Herman, J.L., Perry, J.C., van der Kolk, B.A. (1989) Childhood trauma in borderline personality disorder. *American Journal Psychiatry*, 146, 490–495.
3. Foa, E.B. (1997) Psychological processes related to recovery from a trauma and an effective treatment for PTSD. *Annals of the New York Academy of Science*, 821, 410–424.
4. Harned, M.S., Korslund, K.E., Foa, E.B., et al. (2012) Treating PTSD in suicidal and self-injuring women with borderline personality disorder: Development and preliminary evaluation of a dialectical behavior therapy prolonged exposure protocol. *Behaviour Research and Therapy*, 50 (6), 381–386.
5. Linehan, M.M. (1993) *Skills Training Manual for Treating Borderline Personality Disorder*, Guilford Press, New York.

6. Stanley, B., Bundy, E., Beberman, R. (2001) Skills training as an adjunctive treatment for personality disorders. *Journal of Psychiatric Practice*, 7 (5), 324–335.
7. Spieglar, M.D., Guevremont, D.C. (1998) *Contemporary Behavior Therapy* (3rd ed.), Brooks/Cole Publishing, Pacific Grove.
8. Levy, K.N., Yeomans, F.E., Diamond, D. (2007) Psychodynamic treatments of self-injury. *Journal of Clinical Psychology*, 63 (11), 1105–1120.
9. Kernberg, O.F., Yeomans, F.E., Clarkin, J.F., et al. (2008) Transference focused psychotherapy: Overview and update. *International Journal of Psychoanalysis*, 89 (3), 601–620.

Part II
Using DBT in clinical practice

Chapter 8

Commitment and goal setting

Top 10 question to be addressed in this chapter:

What can clinicians do to help patients who are extremely sensitive to criticism tolerate change interventions in order to remain in treatment and not leave prematurely?

We will describe and illustrate DBT concepts and techniques that can be used in the beginning stages of treatment to elicit an explicit commitment to treatment and to set clear treatment goals.

Key points

- DBT begins with a "pretreatment" phase in which the patient and therapist discuss the requirements of the treatment, the patient, and the therapist, as well as the obstacles to an effective therapy, and determine whether they will work together.
- DBT is a transparent therapy; the techniques and parameters of the treatment as well as their rationale are discussed openly with the patient. This includes a discussion of the BPD diagnosis.
- Clinicians and patients explicitly set a hierarchy of behaviorally defined treatment goals and forge a commitment to working together toward these goals.
- The reduction of life-threatening behaviors is at the top of the hierarchy and is called a Target 1 goal. The reduction of therapy-interfering behaviors is a Target 2 goal, and the reduction of "quality of life"-interfering behaviors is a Target 3 goal.
- Specific interventions are designed to elicit the commitment – strategies such as getting the "foot in the door," "closing the door in the (patient's) face," playing devil's advocate, and validation.

The Dialectical Behavior Therapy Primer: How DBT Can Inform Clinical Practice, First Edition.
Beth S. Brodsky and Barbara Stanley.
© 2013 John Wiley & Sons, Ltd. Published 2013 by John Wiley & Sons, Ltd.

Case example

A common scenario for a DBT clinician is receiving a call from a colleague referring a "difficult and hopeless (to treat) borderline" patient who engages in self harm behaviors including low-lethality suicide attempts and threats. This individual has been in many psychotherapy treatments, has had a number of hospitalizations, has been on numerous medication trials, and nothing seems to have helped, or improvement is limited. In the current therapy, the clinician reports that the patient is adamant about what is "in" or "out of bounds" as subject for discussion in sessions. In particular, she refused to discuss her self-injury reporting that it "works," it was not her primary problem and that "It's her therapy and her therapist has no right to tell her what to discuss or not discuss." The therapy has not progressed. This clinician heard about DBT, told the patient about it, and now the patient is very interested in DBT and feels that it is her "last chance" to get better.

The clinician agrees to a consultation.

Where does a clinician begin to make a difference for such a patient? In DBT, there is the "pretreatment phase" in which the patient and clinician place an explicit emphasis on setting goals and commit to working together to achieve them. Clinicians agree to be as helpful as they can to the patient in staying motivated and focused on achieving goals. Expectations regarding how the work will proceed are established and agreed upon. In the case example, the question of what is out of bounds is addressed at the outset. If the patient were to agree to being in DBT, she would have to agree to make the discussion of self-injury a priority. The rationale for this would be clearly described.

The goal-setting process involves a dialectic synthesis of both collaboration and "insistence" on a hierarchy of goals in which the reduction of self-injury is the top priority of treatment. In this phase, an important intervention focus is eliciting a commitment to making the reduction of suicidal and NSSI the top priority [1]. The overarching principle is that patients and clinicians are entering into an explicit partnership in which clinicians provide guidance for the patients in reaching the goals to which they have committed. The pretreatment phase sets the tone and establishes a firm foundation for treatment engagement and a working collaboration.

Hierarchy of goals: The three S's – staying alive, staying in treatment, and stability

The hierarchy of goals in Stage 1 is listed in Table 8.1. The *primary goal* is the reduction of life-threatening (also called Target 1) behavior. This specifically refers to any suicide attempts, suicidal ideation and/or planning, and NSSI, including self-cutting, burning, and head banging. The reduction of homicidal ideation, or urges, or attempts to harm another person is

Table 8.1 Hierarchy of goals

Target 1 goals: Reduction of life-threatening behaviors
Target 2 goals: Reduction of therapy-interfering behaviors
Target 3 goals: The reduction of "quality of life"-interfering behaviors

also a Target 1 behavior. Additionally, unsafe sexual behaviors or severe food restriction associated with anorexia that is considered life-threatening can be set as Target 1 goals as well. In the adaptation of DBT for the treatment of bulimia nervosa, behaviors such as binge eating, purging, restricting, and laxative use are considered to be Target 1 behaviors [2].

The *second goal in the treatment hierarchy* is the reduction of any behaviors that interfere with the therapy and the therapeutic relationship (also called Target 2 behaviors). This includes lateness, missed sessions (individual and skills group), failure to keep a diary card (described in Chapter 9), and any other behavior on the part of the patient or *clinician* that interferes with the therapy. Examples of therapy-interfering behaviors on the part of the clinician include lateness, not returning phone calls, taking a judgmental stance toward the patient, pushing too quickly for change, and invalidation of the patient. The idea here is to highlight the importance of maintaining the therapeutic relationship and to facilitate the collaboration necessary to accomplish patient goals. It is important to note that therapy-interfering behavior of the clinician is discussed in the same manner as therapy-interfering behavior of the patient. This can be quite a shift for clinicians and they may feel defensive and wish to avoid such discussions. However, the clinician can serve as a positive role model for the patient in expressing their willingness to discuss their own behavior should it be interfering with the treatment. At the same time, this does not mean that the therapists use the session to unburden themselves. So the therapist's repeated lateness need not include an extensive discussion of the recent separation from the spouse resulting in significant childcare problems.

The *third goal* in the hierarchy is to achieve a stable life through the reduction of "quality of life"-interfering behaviors, such as substance use, social problems, and vocational difficulties. Behaviorally defined goals in this category might include temper outbursts, avoidance behaviors, binge spending, and missing school or work, to name a few.

Prioritizing the goal of reducing self-harm behaviors

The first task of the clinician is to establish an agreement with the patient regarding this hierarchy of goals, particularly the primary one of reducing self-injury. The sessions in which this agreement is reached are considered part of the pretreatment phase. Once there is agreement, the clinician uses the hierarchy of goals to structure each individual therapy session. When a patient reports engaging in Target 1 behaviors, they are addressed in session. In the absence of life-threatening behaviors, any therapy-interfering behaviors on the part of the patient or clinician are then targeted. If there are no life-threatening or therapy-interfering behaviors, then the session can revolve around the "quality of life"-interfering behaviors. This hierarchical order of addressing issues is one of the "non-negotiables" in DBT. If a patient does not agree to this hierarchy of treatment goals, treatment does not proceed to Stage I work.

One might think that many patients would balk at this requirement, wanting to discuss in sessions only what they want to bring up, and quit right at this point. Yet, in our experience, this is not the case. When we explain to patients that this hierarchy of goals is adhered to because we want to do everything we can to help our patients stay alive and remain in treatment to get the help they desire, there is little argument. We have yet to have a patient refuse to be in DBT because of this hierarchy of goals.

The hierarchy of goals can provide a guideline for clinicians who, while not adopting the full DBT model, are treating actively suicidal or self-harming patients. The hierarchy provides a road map for staying goal-focused, for monitoring suicidal ideation and behaviors, and for not getting caught up in the "crisis of the week," which may or may not be related to the most pressing treatment goals.

Active clinician stance

In DBT, therapy does not proceed until there is a minimum commitment on the part of the patient to make the reduction of life-threatening behaviors the top priority in treatment and agreement on goals and process are reached. Insistence on this minimum commitment is balanced by emphasizing that the patient is freely choosing to enter into DBT. The approach to forging a commitment reflects a dialectic tension that runs throughout the treatment between clinician direction and patient responsibility. However, the clinician takes an active stance in insisting on having a patient who is showing up to therapy and who has some (minimal level of) willingness to work toward making positive life changes. The clinician is taking a "life worth living" position vis-à-vis the patient and asking the patient to join with this stance.

Such an active, directive stance on the part of the clinician may seem heavy-handed and coercive for clinicians who are trained to maintain a neutral stance. However, individuals with BPD experience great difficulty in setting these goals for themselves. They often believe that suicidal behavior (and NSSI) is a legitimate solution to their suffering, that it is the only validation of their subjective experience of pain, and that they cannot picture not having it as an option. They have trouble knowing what they want for themselves, partly because they do not feel empowered to achieve it. Most of all, they feel worthless, and that they deserve to die. Thus, individuals with BPD need the clinician to take a strong stance in order for them to be able to engage in a meaningful therapy and to work toward a life worth living. Patients have reported to us that in previous therapies when clinicians either did not discuss self-injury routinely or did not take a strong stance in opposition, they ended up feeling that their therapist gave tacit approval to the behavior. As will be illustrated, the commitment process involves a dialectic synthesis between insistence on the hierarchy of goals and encouragement of patients to make these goals their own.

Nonsuicidal self injury is also considered a life-threatening behavior (and merits Target 1 designation) despite the fact that it is performed without intent to die. Empirically, NSSI exists on a continuum of self-destructive behaviors that include actual suicide attempts, in which individuals intentionally self-harm with some intent to die [3] (see Chapter 5 for definitions of suicidal behavior and NSSI). At times, patients cannot clearly distinguish whether there is or is not suicidal intent. Furthermore, behaviors that begin as nonsuicidal can turn into suicidal behaviors. And, individuals who engage in NSSI are at increased risk for suicidal behavior. Finally, ongoing engagement in nonsuicidal self-harm results in a distorted perception of the potential lethality of a given behavior [4], which can lead to accidental high-lethality behaviors.

Phenomenologically, making deliberate (albeit nonsuicidal) self-harm anything less than a top priority goal may send an implicit message that the behavior is, if not acceptable, then perhaps tolerable. Since this type of behavior is often conducted in secret, in a dissociated state of consciousness [5–7], not explicitly asking about and targeting the self-harm exacerbates an already compromised sense of reality. Patients are usually too ashamed to readily report their self-harm behaviors and often present to the clinician in such a manner as to ward off direct inquiry about it. Even so, patients usually experience the clinician's lack of inquiry as a sign that the clinician does not really care.

Patients often present with a "cover story" in which they minimize their behaviors or feelings, in an attempt to appear more competent than they really are and to push the clinician away from discovering their vulnerabilities. The hierarchy of goals and the prioritization of targeting self-harm behaviors reduce inadvertent ignoring of these behaviors and give the clinician a road map to prevent being pushed away from the patient and buying into a cover story. This allows the patient to trust that the clinician is genuinely concerned, and ultimately become more forthcoming about what is really going on.

Taking a more active stance in the way we have described, through explicit goal setting and prioritization of life-threatening behaviors, can be incorporated into a non-DBT psychotherapy and can, thereby, increase patient (and clinician) engagement in and efficacy of the treatment.

Commitment to treatment

We present the following case to illustrate the interventions used to elicit treatment commitment.

Case example

Kim is a 28-year-old single white woman living with two roommates. She came to outpatient DBT treatment from a day program she attended for three months following hospitalization for a suicide attempt. The suicide attempt consisted of a serious overdose of her roommate's sleeping pills, which she took impulsively after an argument with her boyfriend. She lost consciousness, was found by her roommate, and was taken to the ER where her stomach was pumped. She regained consciousness after a few hours.

Kim was taking writing courses and looking for an office job. After graduating from college she worked as an administrative assistant at a financial firm for about two years until she became depressed and angry and would either not show up to work or get into altercations with coworkers. As she described it, "I stopped going to work because I felt as if my boss was deliberately trying to give me a hard time." She was referred to DBT because she had been diagnosed with BPD and was intermittently suicidal. She experienced suicidal ideation, would occasionally engage in NSSI consisting of making cuts on her inner arm without intent to die, her mood fluctuated from depression to anger to feelings of emptiness, and she had interpersonal difficulties due to increased guardedness and suspiciousness when she was under stress. She reported a severe history of repeated sexual abuse at the hands of her stepfather between the ages of 8 and 12. When drunk, he would come into her room at night and frighten her into having intercourse and remaining quiet about it. This abuse ended when her mother and stepfather divorced. Kim suspected that her mother knew about it although when confronted she denied any knowledge of the abuse. This resulted in an inability to trust her own perceptions, as well as a very conflicted relationship with her mother, whom she perceived as unprotective, weak, and needing of protection herself. Kim entered DBT with reluctance. She wanted help with dealing with her history of abuse but did not want to discuss her suicidal behavior and ideation.

Commitment strategies

Foot-in-the-door/door-in-the-face

The therapeutic strategies to elicit commitment incorporate cognitive–behavioral techniques for motivation enhancement, as well as compliance enhancement techniques based on the social psychological concepts of "foot-in-the-door," "door-in-the-face" [1, 8, 9].

Foot in the door

In order to enhance commitment to treatment and the treatment goals, DBT therapists get their "foot in the door" by emphasizing how DBT is a highly effective treatment for the patient and by heightening the patient's interest in trying something new. The original social psychological concept of getting the "foot in the door" refers to the phenomenon that individuals who agree to a small request are more likely to agree to a larger request [8, 9]. Getting the "foot in the door" is a central technique in sales and marketing. Thus, in DBT, therapists "sell the commitment" by presenting the aspects of DBT that would most likely appeal to the patient – such as how the treatment is designed to address the particular issues of the patient and how the therapist is available between session as a skills coach to help the patient feel supported in learning more skillful behaviors. The goal is to stimulate interest and a willingness to "sign on" and work hard in therapy.

Door in the face

In our experience, patients often present as eager and willing to try DBT. They have been told that DBT is the treatment for them and they are willing to sign on without even hearing the details. Therefore, commitment strategies are just as necessary when the patient comes in professing an eagerness to change. Rather than having to get the foot in the door, a more common theme of the commitment phase is illustrated by the patient who is very quick to agree to the goal of reducing self-injury. Once the foot is effectively in the door, and it has been established that the reduction of life-threatening behaviors is the primary goal of treatment, clinicians switch gears and employ the "door-in-the-face" strategy of playing devil's advocate. This might take the form of questioning whether this is an appropriate time for patients to enter treatment. After all, as much as their chronic suicidality is problematic for them, they have been this way for a very long time. Self-harm behaviors, as disturbing as they are, are an effective short-term solution for managing unbearable pain. What makes them think they are ready to give this behavior up? And why now? Patients are encouraged to convince the clinician that they feel ready to proceed. In this manner, clinicians encourage patients to take responsibility for choosing to be in treatment at this time, to accept these goals as their own. This strategy also serves the purpose of what Linehan calls "selling the commitment" [10]. Patients should be encouraged to provide counterarguments to the doubts that will undoubtedly arise as therapy proceeds.

Review of the BPD diagnosis

One of the ways that DBT clinicians interest their patients in treatment is by explicitly educating them about BPD (or whatever the primary diagnosis may be) and the potential usefulness of this treatment approach for their problems. Since DBT was originally designed to treat BPD, this involves psychoeducation regarding the BPD diagnosis by reviewing the diagnostic criteria and encouraging patients to consider which characteristics seem to describe their experience. Clinicians then describe how treatment will target exactly the types of problems the patient is experiencing.

Open discussion of the BPD diagnosis, especially during the first few sessions, may run counter to standard clinical training [11]. Standard therapeutic approaches do not encourage this level of transparency, especially in the case of BPD, a diagnosis that carries such stigma (see Chapter 4). Clinicians assume that patients will have a strong negative reaction upon receiving such a diagnosis, and that this would interfere with building an alliance. Indeed, some patients do balk at the diagnosis, and the clinician can validate their disappointment at receiving a label that carries such a stigma. In our experience, some patients will say at this moment "But I don't want to have BPD" with the implication that because they do not want the diagnosis, they do not have it. This is a golden opportunity to discuss the concept of "radical acceptance," accepting fully and deeply that which is, and how the route to getting to no longer have the diagnosis is by accepting the diagnosis. Furthermore, some patients agree to the symptoms and problem behaviors but have disdain for the name because they have had experiences in which BPD is discussed in a very disparaging manner.

More often, though, patients feel reassured and drawn in by having a name for what they are experiencing, and a therapy designed to address their specific difficulties. A matter-of-fact, didactic approach communicates respect for the patient and sets the tone for a collaborative effort between clinician and patient to take an objective look at the patient's difficulties and find solutions. Reviewing the BPD criteria and encouraging patients to provide extensive examples of how they experience particular symptoms is also an elegant method of history taking in which the clinician can, in the course of a natural conversation, become familiar with the patient's emotional and behavioral profile. Clinicians who are not conducting full DBT can nevertheless incorporate this type of psychoeducation and transparency into psychotherapeutic treatments with their BPD patients.

Reviewing BPD criteria with Kim in the first session

> **Case example**
>
> CLINICIAN: Have any of your previous clinicians given you a diagnosis?
> KIM: Yes, I have been told that I have Bipolar II.
> CLINICIAN: Did anyone ever mention or did you ever hear the term borderline personality disorder?
> KIM: (getting visibly upset) No, I don't have borderline! Being borderline means being angry all of the time, demanding, manipulative, unreasonable, and no one wants to have anything to do with you. That's not me. I don't want to have that label!
> CLINICIAN: I can totally understand why you wouldn't want to be labeled, and especially if it means being an angry person that no one wants anything to do with. Kim, maybe it would help if we didn't call it borderline, since that name carries such a stigma. What if we call it something else, such as emotion dysregulation disorder, or even Quantity X? Let's not get stuck on what we call it – let's take a look to see if DBT may be a good treatment for you. DBT is a treatment that was designed to help people who have difficulties regulating their emotions and behaviors. Besides, I don't agree that having BPD means all of those terrible things. It is a psychiatric disorder like any other that causes pain and suffering and requires treatment. Let's review the criteria together and see if it is helpful in describing the types of difficulties you experience.
>
> Kim agreed, and we reviewed the nine *DSM IV* criteria for BPD one by one. She endorsed seven of the nine criteria, but was clear that she did not experience chronic emptiness, nor did she experience behavioral impulsivity other than self-injury. She did not abuse drugs or alcohol, did not binge eat or spend, and did not engage in dangerous sexual behaviors.
>
> Upon reviewing the diagnosis, Kim was actually relieved to hear that there was a name for what she had been experiencing all of her life, and expressed some frustration that it had taken so long for someone to figure out that this was her problem. She was encouraged by the fact that others also experience these problems.

Describing BPD as a disorder of dysregulation

Another way to discuss the BPD diagnosis is to present it as a disorder of dysregulation. Linehan has reconceptualized BPD as a disorder of dysregulation in five areas of functioning [12]. These include dysregulation of self, cognition, behavior, emotions, and interpersonal functioning. In reviewing the criteria for BPD with the patient, it is useful to demonstrate how the nine *DSM* criteria (see Chapter 4) can be seen as dimensions of these five areas of dysregulation. Thus, emptiness and identity diffusion are related to self-dysregulation. Paranoid ideation and dissociative states are examples of cognitive dysregulation. Recurrent suicidal behavior and behavioral impulsivity such as spending, eating, or substance use binges are areas of behavioral dysregulation. Affective instability and intense anger are manifestations of emotional dysregulation. Fear of abandonment and idealization/devaluation are aspects of interpersonal dysregulation. Patients can more easily relate to the idea that many of the difficulties they experience can be due to difficulties in regulating their emotions, behaviors, thoughts, and interactions with others. For some, this approach can make them feel more validated, less pathologized, and more open to treatment.

Psychoeducation to the etiology of BPD

Part of the pretreatment protocol involves the review of the biosocial theory of the etiology of BPD [12] (see Chapter 4). This promotes the commitment to treatment in a number of ways. First, patients often feel extremely validated by the biosocial theory. The concept resonates with their experience that they seem to have an inborn temperament that might be different from those around them, and that their primary caregivers in childhood did not sufficiently validate their emotional experience.

Second, the biosocial theory places the development of unskillful behaviors within the nonjudgmental context of learning theory, which helps make sense of these behaviors and begins the process of teaching the patient to self-validate. By examining the ways in which unskillful behaviors may have been positively reinforced in their early environment,

---

Case example

PATIENT: I hate myself for losing my temper like that – I am so out of control. There is no reason for me to behave that way – my girlfriend didn't deserve it. I am such an idiot and she isn't going to want to be with me if I can't stop it. I can't stand feeling this way.

CLINICIAN: I bet there is a good reason that you became so angry and if we figure out what it is perhaps you might be better able to control your reaction in the future. Do you remember what happened that might have triggered your temper outburst?

PATIENT: Well my girlfriend was trying on a dress for a wedding that we are going to attend, and I thought it looked really good on her but she didn't trust my judgment so she texted a photo to three other friends to get their opinions.

CLINICIAN: How did that make you feel?

PATIENT: I became really upset because she wasn't taking my feelings seriously. I wasn't getting through to her so I started to raise my voice and attack her for not being able to make a decision without consulting all of her friends.

CLINICIAN: Maybe at the moment you thought that by raising your voice and losing your temper you would get through to her. Has that been your experience in the past?

PATIENT: Well I do think my parents didn't understand that I was upset about something until I started yelling and throwing a fit.

CLINICIAN: So then it would make sense that you learned that a temper tantrum could actually be effective in getting your parents to understand what you were feeling. Your "out of control" behavior was rewarded. Now it's a learned behavior and it makes sense that you still try to get your feelings validated in that way, even though it is no longer working for you.

PATIENT: I never really thought about it that way. But I still need to figure out how to control it.

CLINICIAN: Yes and it is easier to try to unlearn this behavior when you stop condemning yourself for it. You can learn to validate yourself that you have been doing the best you can to get what you need, while at the same time trying to learn more effective, skillful ways to do so.

patients can be encouraged to understand and validate the reasons they are unskillful rather than negatively judge themselves. For example, consider this intervention when a patient reports having engaged in self-injury that followed a temper tantrum. She reports feeling shame about having temper tantrums that are disruptive to her relationships with significant others.

The patient may be more likely to tackle learning more skillful behaviors once she can accept the valid reasons for these behaviors and take a nonjudgmental stance toward them. The idea that the clinician is sharing this theory in an open manner sets the tone for a working alliance in which the clinician and patient are equal partners. Clinicians clearly do not have a hidden agenda and do not withhold their thinking from the patient throughout the course of treatment.

Reviewing the biosocial theory with Kim

> **Case example**
>
> The clinician spent some time in the first session reviewing the biosocial theory with Kim. She responded by stating that she had often felt that her emotional reactions were much more intense than those of her friends and family, and that people were always telling her to calm down, that she was overreacting, and that there was no reason to react as strongly as she did. This had made her doubt her emotional responses and left her feeling confused and angry. She could begin to see that some of her destructive behaviors were attempts to obtain an understanding response from her caregivers. She reported the sense that her angry outbursts finally resulted in having her feelings taken more seriously. The idea that these behaviors could have been positively reinforced gave her a new perspective that she had not previously considered.

Validation strategies in the commitment phase

Because the commitment process is about making agreements to work toward change, validation strategies are necessary to balance the emphasis on change with an equal focus on acknowledgment and acceptance of how difficult change can be. The six levels of validation [13], and validation strategies, are described comprehensively in Chapter 6. For the purposes of goal setting and making agreements at the outset of treatment, the following types of validation are particularly useful: staying awake/alert; accurate reflection; stating the unspoken; historical–biological validation; and validation of the pain that the patient is experiencing and the difficulty in making changes. In some ways, the biosocial theory is all about historical/biological validation – understanding the patient's current dysfunctional behaviors within the context of their predisposition to emotional dysregulation, as well as the historical transaction between their inborn temperament and the invalidating environment.

Balancing validation with change in the commitment phase with Kim

> **Case example**
>
> The main challenge was to obtain Kim's commitment to the goal of reducing self-injury. From her perspective, the self-injury was not problematic.
>
> CLINICIAN: Let's talk about what we are going to be doing together. I know that you have been struggling with suicidal thoughts and behaviors in the past and I think it is vital to work on decreasing them.
>
> KIM: Well, I don't think that's a problem for me anymore – that overdose was stupid and I won't do anything like that again. I want to talk about the sexual abuse I experienced when I was a kid – that is what is getting in the way of everything, making me feel bad, and causing problems in my relationships.
>
> CLINICIAN: I can really understand that. I'm sure that your past is getting in the way and causing a lot of emotional pain for you. I definitely want to help you with that. I am concerned, though, that talking about the abuse will bring up a lot of difficult emotions for you. I want to make sure that you have control over any self-destructive behaviors so that we can explore those feelings without triggering suicidal thoughts and behaviors.
>
> KIM: (getting agitated) You don't get it. Having to live with the horrible feelings and memories is just too much to bear and suicide feels like the only way out for me sometimes.
>
> CLINICIAN: You feel that I don't understand how difficult the abuse was for you because I am suggesting that we make the reduction of the suicidal urges a goal in our work together, right?
>
> KIM: Right! Working on overcoming my abuse will help me feel less suicidal.
>
> CLINICIAN: Kim, I do need to spend more time understanding what happened to you and how it is affecting you now. I definitely want to hear more about your experience and your pain about what happened. I can only try to imagine what it must have been like to be a little girl, so out of control and helpless, and alone with what was being done to you. I also want to make sure you stay alive. Exploring your memories of abuse could increase your suicidal urges, and it is risky to do this without having some skills in place for coping with the feelings that will arise. If you agree to learn skills to control suicidal urges, I promise I will focus on understanding and helping you with your painful feelings and memories.

The use of validation strategies over a number of sessions allowed Kim to feel that the clinician understood the disruption that her trauma history caused her in all areas of her life, despite the insistence on focusing on reduction of her self-injury. Kim and the therapist eventually made a commitment to work together to reduce her self-injury. They identified consistent attendance as a second goal of treatment. Finding employment would be a quality of life goal that they would work toward in the absence of self-injury or therapy-interfering behavior. While Kim agreed to focus on reduction of self-injury as the primary goal, the clinician agreed to balance this with understanding that the suicidal feelings and self-injury were validations of Kim's pain.

Kim's desire to focus on the trauma rather than on self-destructive behaviors is a common scenario faced by the clinician in Stage 1 DBT treatment, in which reduction of life-threatening behavior is the primary goal. Another concern that is often voiced by patients is that they never felt understood by their previous clinicians, and therefore discontinued treatment after only a few months. From a DBT perspective, this may be conceptualized as a result of an overemphasis on change, and not enough validation, on the part of the clinician.

In addition, patients often assume that the therapy will soon turn into a situation in which clinicians impose their own goals onto patients, and that neither the therapy nor the goals of the treatment will be their own. To quote another patient, Roni, during her first DBT pretreatment session: "I'm suspicious that the cognitive behavioral approach will result in my being brainwashed into giving up on things I really believe in." Validation strategies are crucial to address these concerns, during the pretreatment phase as well as throughout treatment.

Case example

In Roni's case, she (based on her previous therapy experience) expected the clinician to insist on her taking daily showers, and other hygiene-related activities as an initial goal of treatment. Not only did Roni NOT want to set this goal for herself, she really resented what felt like an imposition and judgment on the part of her previous clinicians. During the commitment process, the DBT clinician validated the idea that the goals of therapy should be related to what Roni wanted for herself and asked Roni to describe what *she* wanted to work toward in therapy. It turned out that Roni's primary goal for herself was to meet a man and enter into a fulfilling romantic relationship. The clinician agreed that this was an important quality of life goal that she would be very willing to work on with Roni. She then pointed out that perhaps daily showers and good hygiene practices would be useful steps toward this goal. Roni agreed, and became very interested in tracking these behaviors on her diary card.

Thus, the validation of Roni's goals for herself, and her participation in the goal-setting process, allowed her to choose for herself a goal that originally felt imposed upon her.

Door in the face

Case example

Nadia was hospitalized twice for suicidal ideation and nonsuicidal self-cutting behaviors. She had never been in outpatient therapy, but stated in her first pretreatment session that she was concerned that her cutting behaviors had gotten worse over the past year and that she was terrified that she would cut herself too deeply one day and accidently kill herself. She very much wanted to give herself the chance to live a good life, and was very excited to begin therapy. The clinician was very encouraging, but realized that most of the commitment work would need to involve the "door in the face" strategies. She began to gently anticipate with Nadia how it would feel to come to therapy every week and talk about difficult feelings and to fight urges to cut herself by using new, skillful behaviors. Nadia agreed that it would be difficult and could anticipate that there might be times when she would not want to come to session or not call for coaching. But she insisted that she owed it to herself to do this, that she could not go on harming herself, and she very much wanted to feel better about herself. Her desire to have a family one day was an incentive for her to stop her self-harm behaviors.

The clinician encourages the patient to clearly state the reasons they are willing to tolerate the distress of therapy and working toward change. Also, the clinician will need to remind the patient of these reasons and revisit this conversation at those times in the treatment when commitment and motivation are flagging.

Orientation to treatment

The pretreatment commitment phase includes an orientation to the way in which therapy will work. This orientation can be conducted as part of the "door in the face" aspect of the commitment process. Learning new behaviors and skills will require a lot of hard work. In DBT, patients are expected to attend both individual and group skills training sessions regularly and on time, as well as to complete weekly diary cards, and group skills homework assignments. They are asked to contact the clinician between sessions for skills coaching. This requires learning how to ask for help effectively, and willingness to try new, unfamiliar behaviors, refrain from the old tried and true unskillful behaviors, and tolerate higher levels of distress. (The orientation regarding guidelines for between-session contact is described fully in Chapter 12.) Again, the clinician encourages patients to think seriously about and formulate a clear idea as to why they would be willing to take on the work.

Anticipating the difficulty of stopping unskillful behaviors is helpful in enhancing motivation to work toward that goal. The clinician can acknowledge the distress associated with the behaviors, but also emphasizes their effectiveness in reducing what the patient believes to be, and experiences as, unbearable pain. Clinicians gently anticipate how difficult it will be for patients to stop the behaviors. As patients agree to the goal of reducing self-injury, clinicians agree to help patients tolerate the pain and, in a standard DBT, promises to be available to coach them in learning new skills for managing their emotions and behaviors.

Hammering out the commitment – agreements

Patient agreements

There is no limit to how many sessions the pretreatment phase may take. The commitment strategies should encourage a process by which the patient takes responsibility for making the commitment to work with the clinician on these goals. Therapy should not proceed until the patient makes a "minimum commitment" to the hierarchy of goals. The commitment phase must establish that the goals are agreed to by the patient, not that the clinician is imposing these goals.

Reduction of self-injury. At a very minimum at the beginning of treatment, the patient must agree to work with the clinician toward the reduction and ultimate elimination of suicidal and NSSI. The patient is agreeing to make this the number one goal of treatment, one that takes priority over every other treatment goal.

Attendance. Patients are asked to agree to the expectation that they will make every effort to attend weekly individual and group skills sessions. They are also expected to call in advance in the event of absence or lateness. Patients agree to target missed sessions and lateness as "therapy-interfering behavior" that is addressed in session in the absence of Target 1 behaviors.

Termination. DBT has only one formal termination rule. Patients who miss 4 weeks in a row of scheduled therapy sessions, either individual or group, are out of therapy. Although this rule was developed as a research requirement, Linehan has adapted it as a useful clinical guide to reduce the phenomenon of drifting out of treatment. And, being terminated from treatment does not mean that the patient is barred from reentering. This reentry typically involves an extensive commitment discussion (and some time away from treatment) about how to ensure that the same thing does not happen again. Although the patient can choose to terminate treatment at any time, she is expected to come to session and discuss the proposed termination with her individual clinician.

Clinician agreements

Whether or not these are made explicitly to the patient during the commitment phase, the following are agreements that clinicians are implicitly making when they agree to accept a patient for DBT treatment. Many of these agreements are not unique to DBT, but are informed by DBT assumptions. DBT places more emphasis on the fact that the clinician is also making a commitment than many other treatments do. The therapist agreements are described explicitly to the patient.

Clinicians agree to make every reasonable effort to conduct therapy that is competent and helpful to the patient. Clinicians *cannot* solve the patients' problems and prevent them from using unskillful behaviors or even from killing themselves. Clinicians *can* be a guide, can encourage and teach patients to use new, skillful behaviors.

Clinicians make an agreement to obey ethical guidelines and professional ethics codes. They agree to respect the patient, and to maintain confidentiality. Clinicians agree to do their best to refrain from therapy-interfering behavior, by maintaining a balanced, validating, nonjudgmental therapeutic stance. Toward this end, clinicians also agree to seek consultation when necessary. It is customary to inform the patient that the clinician meets weekly with a consultation team. The patient needs to know that the patient will get help when needed, but will also seek help in a professional manner that maintains confidentiality.

Attendance. Clinicians will be available for all scheduled sessions, and will make every reasonable effort to reschedule a session that they have to miss. DBT clinicians explicitly agree to be available between sessions for skills coaching. The guidelines for this type of availability are described in detail in Chapter 12, and are reviewed clearly with patients during the pretreatment sessions.

Maintaining a dialectic stance. Clinicians also agree to constantly strive to maintain a balance between change and validation. They can also anticipate making mistakes in pushing for change too quickly, and should commit to taking responsibility for these mistakes as therapy-interfering.

Availability for between-session contact. As part of the initial agreements that are made, the clinician describes the between-session skills coaching, which is an integral part of DBT treatment. The parameters of the clinician's availability (see Chapter 12) are described. The clinician agrees to be available in this way, and also elicits an agreement from the patient to both utilize this availability to work effectively toward treatment goals and to observe the parameters.

Termination. The clinician makes the agreement to do his or her best to protect the patient from unilateral termination, but also makes as explicit as possible the conditions under which the clinician may choose to end the treatment. These might include not working toward goals, or not observing clinician's limits.

Summary

DBT offers techniques and interventions to establish a firm foundation in the initial phase of psychotherapy aimed at (a) increasing the likelihood of strong therapeutic engagement on the part of both patient and clinician and (b) making clear progress toward the reduction of self-harm behaviors in individuals with BPD. In DBT, a pretreatment phase is dedicated to a dialectic process of commitment and goal setting. Both the process and the content of the goal-setting process are informed by DBT assumptions and stance, emphasizing dialectic synthesis. The outcome of the pretreatment phase is that both patient and clinician commit to working together to achieve a hierarchy of goals.

The hierarchy of treatment goals is the reduction of (a) life-threatening behaviors, (b) therapy-interfering behaviors, and (c) "quality of life"-interfering behaviors. Secondary goals include targeting areas of dysregulation and skills deficit. As treatment proceeds, these goals will be operationalized in behavioral terms and will provide a focus, a framework for each session and for the overall direction of therapy.

There are many times throughout the course of therapy when patients appear to lose interest or motivation in working toward the goal that they originally committed to. In these cases, clinicians remind patients of the commitments they made. The commitment phase is revisited as many times as necessary to keep the therapy on track toward the goal of reducing self-injury. As Linehan states, commitment is a behavior that can be elicited, learned, and reinforced. Patients will need reminding [1].

The pretreatment commitment strategies allow the clinician to actively engage patients in the goal-setting process. They create a foundation for continued motivation enhancement so that the clinician can encourage the patient to address these goals throughout the treatment.

Some of the DBT commitment strategies that are portable to a non-DBT psychotherapy include explicit goal setting using the hierarchy of goals, prioritization of the elimination of life-threatening behaviors as a treatment goal (when they are present), fostering of a collaborative partnership between therapist and patient in working toward these goals, transparent psychoeducation to the BPD (or other primary) diagnosis, and orientation of the patient regarding what to expect in treatment.

References

1. Linehan, M.M. (1993) *Cognitive Behavioral Treatment of Borderline Personality Disorder*, Guilford Press, New York, pp. 286–289.
2. Wisniewski, L., Safer, D., Chen, E. (2007) Dialectical behavior therapy and eating disorders, in *DBT for Clinical Practice* (eds L. Dimeff and R. Koerner), Guilford Press, New York, pp. 174–221.

3. Muehlenkamp, J.J. (2005) Self-injurious behavior as a separate clinical syndrome. *American Journal of Orthopsychiatry*, 75 (2), 324–333.
4. Stanley, B., Gameroff, M.J., Michalsen, V., et al. (2001) Are suicide attempters who self-mutilate a unique population? *American Journal of Psychiatry*, 158, 427–432.
5. Herman, J.L., Perry, J.C., van der Kolk, B.A. (1989) Childhood trauma in borderline personality disorder. *American Journal of Psychiatry*, 146, 490–495.
6. Suyemoto, K.L. (1998) The functions of self-mutilation. *Clinical Psychology Review*, 18 (5), 531–554.
7. Brodsky, B.S., Cloitre, M., Dulit, R.A. (1995) Relationship of dissociation and childhood abuse in borderline personality disorder. *American Journal of Psychiatry*, 152 (12), 1788–1792.
8. Cialdini, R.B., Vincent, J.E., Lewis, S.K., et al. (1975) Reciprocal concessions procedure for inducing compliance: The door-in-the-face technique. *Journal of Personality and Social Psychology*, 31, 206–215.
9. Freedman, J.L., Fraser, S.C. (1966) Compliance without pressure: The foot-in-the-door technique. *Journal of Personality and Social Psychology*, 4, 195–202.
10. Robins, C.J. (2002) Zen principles and mindfulness practice in dialectical behavior therapy. *Cognitive Behavioral Practice*, 9, 50–57.
11. Lequesne, E.R., Hersh, R.G. (2004) Disclosure of a diagnosis of borderline personality disorder. *Journal of Psychiatric Practice*, 10 (3), 170–176.
12. Linehan, M.M. (1993) *Cognitive Behavior Therapy for Borderline Personality Disorder*, Guilford Press, New York, pp. 10–12.
13. Linehan, M.M. (1997) Validation and Psychotherapy. In A. Bohart & L. Greenberg (Eds.), *Empathy Reconsidered: New Directions in Psychotherapy*, American Psychological Association, Washington, D.C.

Chapter 9

The DBT tool kit: The essential DBT strategies and what happens in the individual session

Top 10 questions to be addressed in this chapter:

How do clinicians help patients manage their chronic suicidal ideation, threats, and gestures in an outpatient setting?

Are there effective therapeutic techniques for directly treating non-suicidal self-injury and other destructive behaviors?

"I don't know why I cut myself, it just happened." This statement is heard over and over from patients as they begin to work in DBT on eliminating their self-injury. In order to make therapeutic progress, this behavior has to move from being a mystery to being considered understandable and, in fact, becoming understood. In this chapter, we describe in detail the therapeutic interventions used to target treatment goals in an individual DBT session. Here we focus on the targeting and treatment of suicidal behaviors and NSSI. However, the interventions are the same for targeting therapy-interfering and "quality of life"-interfering behaviors, which will be more fully described in Chapter 17.

Key points
- The basic tools in a DBT session: Diary card; agenda setting; chain analysis; in-session behavior; and skill rehearsal
- Establishing session structure by using a diary card to set the agenda
- Choosing a behavioral target using the diary card
- Conducting a behavioral analysis to target suicidal or other unskillful behavior
- Balancing validation and change and finding dialectical synthesis
- Keeping the patient engaged – active therapist stance and dialectical strategies

So, the foundation for treatment has been laid, and the goals and commitments are in place. The patient has agreed that the first order of business is to reduce and eventually eliminate life-threatening behavior. The clinician has agreed to support the patient in achieving her goals. How exactly do we approach this ambitious and crucial goal? In this chapter, we describe the nuts and bolts of conducting individual DBT sessions. Step by step, we will illustrate how DBT applies strategies of validation and change to systematically work toward the elimination of self harm behaviors through understanding the role that they serve and the development of effective skills for managing painful feelings and destructive impulses. In this chapter, we describe how the individual therapy session is structured and the behavioral techniques that are applied in the sessions. In addition to these individual sessions, patients attend a weekly group (described in Chapter 10) where relevant skills are taught.

Establishing session structure

The structure of sessions is provided by the hierarchy of goals inherent in the treatment, the use of a diary card, collaborative agenda setting, balancing change with acceptance, and two forms of chain analysis – (a) behavioral analysis where the links leading to a problem behavior are determined and (b) solution analysis in which alternatives (e.g., skills that can be utilized) are generated for various points along the chain to break the links. These tools provide the clinician with a road map so as not to lose focus on goals within the session, and to not be responding to the "crisis of the week" without making long-range progress on goals.

The diary card

In working with patients who have BPD, it is important to track their problems over time between sessions because patients often experience difficulty recalling their mood fluctuations, their self harm behaviors, and the situations that provoked them. To help with this recall, patients are asked to maintain a daily record of target behaviors (problems that are being actively addressed in treatment, e.g., NSSI, suicide ideation and behavior), level of distress, and use of skills that are being taught in the skills group, on a diary card [1, 2]. A diary card is a modified version of a behavioral, thought and mood diary, a common tool in many cognitive behavioral therapies for the treatment of depression, anxiety, and eating disorders [3, 4]. The diary card serves a number of purposes. Diary keeping, generally, is a standard cognitive–behavioral technique that facilitates awareness of (and ultimately modification of and control over) thoughts, feelings, and behaviors. If the card is kept properly, on a daily basis, it provides a fairly accurate account of the patient's emotional and behavioral experiences throughout the course of the week. Otherwise, trying to retrospectively reconstruct a meaningful picture of a subjective mood state is a challenge for the most even-tempered individual but particularly for individuals with BPD who often experience their current state as their only subjective experience. Given the mood lability and state dependency that is so common among individuals with BPD, it is nearly impossible for them to be able to provide an accurate retrospective report of how they were feeling on a given day over the course of the week. In other words, they are likely to think they had a bad week if they are currently distressed and, conversely, not recall the negative events they experienced in the past week if they are not feeling dysregulated at the time of the session.

What is a diary card?

In DBT, the standard diary card consists of a grid that contains seven rows for the days of the week, and numerous columns for the recording of target feelings, thoughts, and behaviors. We present a sample template for a diary card in Table 9.1. Numerous versions of the diary card have been developed over the past 10 years. In addition to those developed by Linehan [1, 2] and Koerner [11], five versions of the diary card developed by individuals who have been in DBT can be found and downloaded from the website www.dbtselfhelp.com.

Patients are expected to fill the card out on a daily basis, recording and rating the extent to which they experienced thoughts, feelings, and urges, or engaged in actual behaviors. Standard targets to be recorded on the diary card include alcohol and substance use, daily medication use (both prescribed and over the counter), ratings of suicidal ideation, levels of subjective misery, urges to self-injure, and whether or not they engaged in a self harm behaviors. The therapist and patient can identify other life-threatening (reckless driving, starting physical fights, homicidal ideation, unprotected sex, deliberate abstinence from life-saving medication, etc.) and/or quality of life behaviors (binge eating, binge spending, harmful avoidance behaviors, starting arguments, lateness) to track. Additionally, they often expand the list of subjective emotions to include anger, anxiety, sadness, boredom, shame, mania, depression, agitation, and joy. Patients are asked to rate their feelings, suicidal thoughts, and urges to self-injure on a scale that ranges from 0 to 5.

A second grid is designed to assist patients in keeping track of the skills they are using on a daily basis (see Table 9.2). Each skill that is taught in skills training (see Chapter 11) is listed, and when the skill is used is noted as well as whether it helped. They also indicate whether or not they thought about skills but did not use them. This is particularly important because it focuses the therapeutic dyad on what is standing in the way of using strategies that may be helpful in coping.

The diary card facilitates learning how to observe and report internal experience and become more familiar with a broader range of emotional experience. The black/white extremes in which individuals with BPD can view the world is often reflected initially in scores of either 0 or the highest value on their scale, with nothing intermediate. Thus, they are either enraged or not angry at all, panicked or not fearful or anxious at all. The clinician uses the diary card to gently question whether these extreme values can, in fact, be graded and differentiated, and, thus, facilitates the process of educating patients in the recognition of lower to mid-range levels of emotional experience. They can learn to identify that they might be annoyed rather than rageful, or anxious rather than panicked.

This is particularly useful in terms of assessing suicidal ideation. As BPD patients often live with chronic suicidal ideation, monitoring the levels of ideation rather than its presence or absence, can be a more meaningful approach to risk assessment. For example, when a patient rates suicidal ideation as level "3" on a given day, the therapist can inquire into what a "3" means for the patient. What types of thoughts did the patient have? How long did they last? Did they come and go or were they constantly present throughout the day? Did the patient consider a method and/or a plan? Was there any intent to act on the thoughts? The parameters of frequency, intensity, active versus passive intent, and presence or absence of planning can all contribute to a patient's rating. Once the therapist and patient clarify the parameters that contribute to a given rating, there is more awareness about level of intensity and intent.

Table 9.1 Sample diary card

Day	Alcohol no.	OTC drugs	Prescription drugs	Street drugs	Misery (0–5)	Suicidal ideation (0–5)	Self-harm urges (0–5)	Self-harm actions (Y/N)
Monday								
Tuesday								
Wednesday								
Thursday								
Friday								
Saturday								
Sunday								

Table 9.2 Sample template of skills diary card

Wise mind	Monday	Tuesday	Wednesday	Thursday	Friday	Saturday	Sunday
Observe	Monday	Tuesday	Wednesday	Thursday	Friday	Saturday	Sunday
Describe	Monday	Tuesday	Wednesday	Thursday	Friday	Saturday	Sunday
Nonjudgment	Monday	Tuesday	Wednesday	Thursday	Friday	Saturday	Sunday
One-mindful	Monday	Tuesday	Wednesday	Thursday	Friday	Saturday	Sunday
Effectiveness	Monday	Tuesday	Wednesday	Thursday	Friday	Saturday	Sunday
Interpersonal skills	Monday	Tuesday	Wednesday	Thursday	Friday	Saturday	Sunday
Mastery	Monday	Tuesday	Wednesday	Thursday	Friday	Saturday	Sunday
Positive experiences	Monday	Tuesday	Wednesday	Thursday	Friday	Saturday	Sunday
Opposite action	Monday	Tuesday	Wednesday	Thursday	Friday	Saturday	Sunday
Distract	Monday	Tuesday	Wednesday	Thursday	Friday	Saturday	Sunday
Self-soothe	Monday	Tuesday	Wednesday	Thursday	Friday	Saturday	Sunday
Improve	Monday	Tuesday	Wednesday	Thursday	Friday	Saturday	Sunday
Pros and cons	Monday	Tuesday	Wednesday	Thursday	Friday	Saturday	Sunday
Radical acceptance	Monday	Tuesday	Wednesday	Thursday	Friday	Saturday	Sunday

Instructions: Circle the days you worked on each skill.

> **Case example**
>
> Toni typically rated suicide ideation as either 0 or 5 (highest rating). Upon questioning, she rated 5 when she had any ideation at all, even if she had no intent to act on it. Over time, she learned to rate thoughts of wanting to die as a 1, and through further explorations of her actual ideation, she learned that Level 5 indicated that there was active intent to act on her thoughts. This distinction was very important because the type of therapeutic intervention indicated varied depending on the severity of ideation. So for a rating of 1, increased focus of effective skills use was appropriate while a rating of 5 dictated increasing monitoring on the part of the clinician and Toni.

Balancing validation with change regarding the diary card

At times, patients arrive at the individual session without a completed diary card. This is considered to be behavior that interferes with the effective progress of therapy (Target 2) and, therefore, needs to be discussed after either addressing any life-threatening behaviors or upon determining that there are none that week. Because a diary card is necessary for establishing the session agenda, it has to be completed prior to setting the agenda for the day's session. Patients can complete the record on their own or with the clinician at the beginning of the session. The clinician should investigate the obstacles that interfered with completing the diary card. For example, did they completely forget about it? Did they think about it and make a willful decision not to do it? Did they think about it and put it off until later? Did they think it is a useless exercise? Were they afraid that recording something made it more real or that thinking about their day at the end of the day would make them more upset? Each of these three obstacles requires a different set of problem solving and provides an opportunity for teaching new skillful behavior.

Targeting a missed diary card can easily trigger feelings of being blamed and criticized. Therefore, while stressing its importance and problem solving about how to get it done, and done properly, the clinician must also validate the patient regarding the difficulty and/or unpleasantness of the task of completing a diary card. Addressing a missed diary card, as with any other target behavior, is performed in a matter-of-fact, collaborative, nonjudgmental manner, setting the therapy-interfering behavior up as an objective problem that the patient and clinician collaborate on, as partners together, to solve.

Addressing a missing or incomplete diary card is similar to addressing lateness to a session. However, clinicians who are just beginning to work with a diary card and are not familiar with (or are not convinced about) its usefulness, may feel uncomfortable with the idea of targeting the behavior, especially when they are anxious about possible suicidality or self-injury and want to make sure they have time to adequately address risk assessment. Clinicians may also anticipate (and want to avoid) a negative response from the patient, who may feel judged and criticized by clinician's queries regarding the missing diary card. It can also feel heavy-handed to clinicians not used to working with this type of structure to "force" a patient to do something. Yet the diary card, and the agenda that is created around it, is an essential tool for an effective treatment.

The hierarchy of goals helps here [5] (see Chapter 8). It has already been agreed upon that suicide risk reduction and addressing life-threatening behaviors always precedes discussion of therapy-interfering behavior. Validation strategies [6] are also necessary whenever the clinician identifies an area for change. Validation strategies can inform the approach the clinician takes in addressing the issue, so that problem solving is conducted in a straightforward manner, while highlighting the valid aspects of the patient's behavior. Validation strategies that can be used to address a missing or incomplete diary card include appreciation of the difficulty in conducting this task (Level 5 validation – see Chapter 6) or feelings of not wanting to do it. The clinician might state: "I understand that it is difficult and that you don't want to do it, but it is important to do so that we can work most effectively toward your goals." It is striking how this simple sort of validation helps to avoid an adversarial and argumentative interaction.

Setting the agenda collaboratively

Clinician and patient review the diary card together and use it to collaboratively create an agenda for the session. The agenda is based on the hierarchy of goals that was agreed to in the commitment phase of therapy [5]. This means that life-threatening behaviors, when present, are first on the agenda. As we have reviewed, these include any acts of NSSI, suicide attempts, as well as spikes in suicidal ideation, particularly suicidal ideation with intent and planning. Therapy-interfering behaviors are second, and quality of life-interfering behaviors are third (see Chapter 17). Setting an agenda based on the patient's treatment goals helps keep each session, and over the long run the entire treatment, goal-focused.

If the patient engaged in self-injury, a chain analysis (described later) is necessary. In the absence of self-destructive behavior, any therapy-interfering behavior is also highlighted and can be subject to a chain analysis. In the absence of either self-injury or therapy-interfering behavior, the patient can choose a quality-of-life issue to address in the session.

When setting the agenda, the most life-threatening behavior must be addressed first. Thus, if a patient has engaged in nonsuicidal self-harm, but also reports suicidal ideation with intent to act, the therapist will place the suicidal ideation on the top of the agenda.

Chain analysis

When self harm, or any other target behaviors, have been present over the course of the week, a key therapeutic tool, "chain analysis," is utilized in order to explore in detail the events, feelings, cognitions, and behaviors that led up to a target behavior. There are three terms used to describe this central change intervention in the DBT individual session. A chain analysis may also be referred to as a "behavioral analysis" [6]. When the therapist weaves skills (i.e., alternative courses of action, ways of thinking and behaving) into the chain in order to help the patient break the links in the chain, this is termed as conducting a "solution analysis" [7]. We will be using the term "chain analysis" throughout.

In DBT, a chain analysis can be considered an aversive consequence of the Target 1 behavior since it is painstaking and can sometimes be upsetting and shame-provoking to revisit a self-harm episode in detail. If there is no life-threatening behavior, but there is either therapy-interfering or "quality of life"-interfering behavior, then a chain analysis is recommended but optional (see Chapter 12 for a chain of therapy-interfering behavior). The chain analysis is a central technique in most behavioral therapies [8], and is the principle strategy for change employed in DBT as well. It is an incredibly powerful tool. And, while most therapeutic approaches, including psychodynamic psychotherapy, use some form of this kind of narrative, it is the exquisite detail of the chain analysis and the fact that it is written that enhances its utility. Furthermore, the dialectical approach to chain analysis is unique to DBT, and will be described and illustrated in detail. It serves as an antidote to a frequent statement made by new patients about their NSSI when the therapist begins to try to understand the antecedents: "I don't know why I did it, it just happened. I can't possibly talk about what led up to it." Through behavioral analysis, the therapist can work with the patient in a nonjudgmental manner and invite the patient to be inquisitive together to see if there is something more to the behavior than "it just happened."

Balancing validation and change regarding the chain analysis

There are numerous steps involved in conducting a chain analysis, which requires an excruciatingly detailed review of an episode of self harm or other target behaviors. As you may imagine, such a review of unskillful behavior, in order to identify areas of change, can be an extremely aversive experience, one viewed by patients as a judgmental, critical review of the mistakes they made. In the majority of cases, patients are very reluctant to engage in this analysis and insist that the incident is over and there is no point in dredging up the pain and negative feeling state that was present at the time. A chain analysis is the antithesis of their usual mode of coping, which is to avoid feeling the pain at all costs. Therefore, at each step, the clinician needs to be attentive to any opportunity to validate patients. It is important to validate the difficulty of engaging in such a process, while at the same time presenting confidence in the analysis as one of the most effective therapeutic tools. The clinician might state: "I wish there were an easier way, but I have found this approach to be the most useful one. Let's proceed slowly, and I'll be here to support you in experiencing whatever difficult emotions come up. Although it is understandable that you don't want to experience those painful feelings, they will come back anyway and we need to help you develop skills for tolerating and ultimately changing them." The clinician remains vigilant to patients' experiences during the chain analysis and addresses emotional reactions as they emerge.

Mechanism of conducting a chain analysis

It is important to take notes during a chain analysis. The exact behavior, and the date it was engaged in, is recorded. It is helpful to actually sit side by side during this exercise so both the patient and clinician can see the links in the chain as they are written. It increases active participation by both of them in the process. This orientation engenders a spirit of nonjudgmental discovery whereby the therapeutic dyad are detectives together looking for links in the chain that resulted in the problem behavior. Clinician and patient then proceed to identify the vulnerability in the patient or environment, the precipitating event(s), the thoughts, feelings, and actions that lead to the behavior, and the consequences of the behavior.

Identifying the target behavior

The first step in conducting a chain analysis is to identify the target behavior to be analyzed. Obvious life-threatening behaviors include suicide attempts (overdose, wrist-cutting, etc.), and NSSI behaviors. Thoughts such as suicidal ideation and urges to self-injure can also be operationalized as behaviors to target in an analysis. Therapy-interfering behaviors such as lateness, failure to do homework or diary card, missed sessions, and not observing the clinician's limits [9] (see Chapter 8) are also subject to analysis. Other "quality of life"-interfering behaviors to analyze include substance use, binge/restrictive eating, social and vocational difficulties, and interpersonal problems.

Identifying the consequences of the behavior

The positive consequences of the self-destructive behavior for the patient, such as immediate relief from unbearable emotional pain, are highlighted and validated. Consequences of a given behavior can be either within the individual or in the environment. They can be short term and immediate, or longer term. A reinforcing environmental consequence of nonsuicidal self-cutting, for example, might be increased care-giving and concern from others. A short-term reinforcing consequence within the individual may be an intense emotional and physical release from unbearable pain. Longer-term negative consequences within the individual might be regret and feelings of deep shame. A longer-term aversive consequence in the environment would be loss of relationships because people often tire of and are frightened of hearing about repeated suicidal threats.

Understanding and highlighting consequences is a powerful clinical intervention that serves a number of purposes. Understanding positive consequences has a validating effect by making sense of and somewhat normalizing the behavior by placing it in the context of being "effective" in achieving a "positive" outcome. Identifying consequences in the environment allows for contingency management as part of a solution.

Distinguishing between immediate and longer-term consequences serves several functions as well. Patients can begin to cultivate an awareness of longer range consequences that may help them tolerate distress rather than yield to destructive escapist behaviors in the short term. A thorough understanding of short-term versus long-term consequences is also very informative for the clinician in devising effective behavioral plans and instrumental reinforcement interventions. Short-term consequences of unskillful behaviors are often rewarding. Examples of these might be immediate relief from unbearable emotional pain, escape, getting a nurturing response, or self-validation. Long-term consequences are more likely to be aversive – shame, regret, losing relationships. A very important example for patients is the instance where the patient's boyfriend becomes very attentive when the patient threatens suicide (short-term consequence) but ends up breaking up with the patient because the repeated suicide threats feel overwhelming and too burdensome (long-term consequence). In the immediacy of a situation, patients tend to sacrifice long-term consequences for short-term gains.

> ### Case example
>
> A patient once described how she lost her opportunity to work with a beloved clinician who was treating her for anorexia nervosa because she was not able to maintain the minimum weight that he set as a condition for treatment with him. Both the clinician and the patient believed that the patient's strong attachment to the clinician would be a strong incentive for her to maintain her weight, and the threat of losing him as a clinician would be a deterrent for her restricting behavior. Not only was she unable to stop restricting, she was distraught because he inaccurately interpreted her inability to maintain the weight as an indication that she did not care about her relationship with him. Furthermore, because she had a great deal of difficulty knowing what her internal state was (e.g., angry, embarrassed, anxious), she began to wonder whether or not she did care about the relationship with her therapist. She thought she did, but could she be wrong? In conducting a chain analysis of her restrictive behavior, it became apparent that the threat of losing her therapy with the clinician, while a strong and distressing consequence, was too long term and did not equip her with coping mechanisms to manage her emotional distress in the short term.

Thus, effective behavioral plans must include support and planning for managing immediate consequences in addition to built-in longer-term reinforcers.

Validation of the positive consequences of even the most unskillful behaviors can help set a nonjudgmental tone for the most difficult phase of the chain analysis. The patient and clinician collaborate in reconstructing the series of events (thoughts, feelings, actions, and environmental events) that lead to the self-injury. The clinician asks for as much detail as possible, and, as therapy progresses, weaves solutions or alternative skillful behaviors the patient might have used, into the thread of the analysis. When first including solutions into the behavioral analysis, the therapist will likely have to be the one to provide alternatives. As the treatment moves forward and patients learn skills in skills training, they can take a much more active role in suggesting what can have been done instead. This, as previously mentioned, is solution analysis.

Identifying the precipitants

One of the main functions of the chain analysis is to increase the patient's awareness of the precipitants of a targeted behavior (e.g., suicide attempt). As mentioned, it is quite common for patients at the start of treatment to insist that there are no precipitants, that it is impossible for them to identify any, or that things happen too quickly to understand the progression. From their experience, the feelings come on instantaneously, out of the blue, as in a panic attack. Sometimes they are not aware of anything preceding an impulsive or self-destructive act, and only become aware of their experience in the midst of, or directly after, the action itself. Additionally, patients often dismiss any suggestions of a prompting event because they have experienced those types of events many times before without engaging in a destructive behavior. When the patient is unaware, the simple retelling of the events that preceded the behavior, without any judgment that the events were or were not connected to the behavior, elucidates the possible connections. In this way, the therapist and patient do not engage in a tug of war about what did or did not lead to the behavior.

Identifying the vulnerability

This is where the concept of vulnerability is helpful. Any particular event may not necessarily lead to an impulsive or destructive behavior because by itself it is not enough to trigger a series of emotions, thoughts, urges, and behaviors. The vulnerability, which may exist within the individual, or within the environment, increases the individual's susceptibility to and interacts with a given prompting event, increasing the likelihood of a problem at a given point in time. Examples of vulnerabilities that exist within the individual include an episode of depression or hypomania, insomnia, premenstrual syndrome, and physical illness. Vulnerabilities that are environmentally determined may be a stressful deadline (such as finals week in school), a dysfunction in the home environment, financial pressures, an anniversary, or some other reminder of a stressful event or past trauma. Thus, identifying a particular vulnerability that may be more active or present in a given situation, and that make individuals more susceptible to a given trigger, can help them develop an ability to become familiar with, recognize, and predict their own patterns for engaging in unskillful behaviors. With greater predictability and recognition comes increased control over impulsivity and freedom to choose a more skillful course of action.

Identifying the trigger

As stated, patients usually are unaware of the event that triggers the chain of thoughts, feelings, and behaviors that culminate in a self-destructive act. And indeed, sometimes they are difficult to pinpoint. However, often the reason the triggers are not clear is because patients dismiss and invalidate their response to an event, thinking that they should not get upset over something so inconsequential. Triggers usually become clear as the episode is dissected in detail during the course of the analysis, with the clinician paying attention and validating that what seems like nonevents actually count as possible triggers. Another reason it is difficult to identify triggers is because there are many steps between a trigger and the event, and these steps need to be identified in order to connect one to the other.

Case example

In a chain analysis of an episode in which Felice unexpectedly banged her head against the wall, she reported that everything was "going fine" on Saturday with her boyfriend. She started getting annoyed when he did not want to go bike riding and wanted to stay home and watch TV, but she did not think too much of it – at least he still wanted to hang out with her. Then his friend came over and the two of them started talking about something that did not include her. At that point, she had the idea that she should probably leave, and she told her boyfriend she was going to leave since they were not including her. He told her not to be silly, of course they were, and so she stayed. She became increasingly upset and started to feel that it was her own fault – she wanted so much to be with him that she allowed herself to settle for just being in the same room with him. She left, sat on the steps in his apartment building, and started banging her head against the wall.

In retrospect, it became clear that the trigger of this episode was the initial disappointment of her boyfriend wanting to watch TV instead of engaging in an activity with her. And, she had actually been aware that this had annoyed her. However, she quickly dismissed this idea – why should his wanting to watch TV cause her to bang her head against the wall?

Method of inquiry

Where do you start the analysis? If the trigger is not readily apparent, or if the starting point of the episode is not clear from the review of the diary card, it helps to ask the patient to think back and to identify the first awareness she had that something was wrong. What was that first awareness? Was it a thought, a feeling, a physical sensation, an event (any type of environmental stimulus, an aroma, a sight, something she saw), or a behavior? What did she do, think, feel, or what happened next? Obtain as much detail as possible regarding the sequence of actions, cognitions (interpretations), feelings (subjective phenomenological, physiological sensations), and events. Do not assume that you understand how one step in the chain connects to the next. Break each step down to its smallest component. For example, patients often state that they were feeling depressed, and then started thinking about wanting to harm themselves. On the face of it, this can make some sense. However, many individuals feel depressed but do not ever have suicidal ideation or thoughts of self-harm. Rather than assume you understand how the depression led to suicidal ideation, be extremely curious about it. Inquire as to what the depressed feelings were. There is at least one step between depressed feelings and suicidal ideation – feelings of hopelessness. But this step, when explored in a chain analysis, can be broken down into a number of small steps, and between each step is an opportunity to use a skill to break the chain leading to self-injury. If patients cannot identify a starting point, therapists can suggest working backward from the problem behavior to the events just prior to the behavior, then the ones that preceded those events, and so forth.

Case example

Ellen was feeling lonely and asked her boyfriend to come over. He was out with his friends and did not want to leave them to come to see her that night, but he promised to spend the next day with her. Ellen felt depressed when she got off the phone. She felt sad, started thinking, "I will never be able to get what I want in relationships, there is something wrong with me because I need so much and no one can ever do enough for me, I hate myself and I will never be able to change, I may as well give up and kill myself." She then decided to take an overdose of her prescribed medication.

Weaving skills into the chain analysis: Solution analysis

> **Case example**
>
> During the chain analysis, the clinician began identifying steps along the chain in which more skillful behavior could be introduced. First, she highlighted some of Ellen's interpretations: "There is something wrong with me, I'll never be able to change," "I will never be able to get what I want in relationships," and suggested that Ellen use cognitive restructuring to consider other interpretations. Could she use distress tolerance skills to get through the night by herself and find out that she did not absolutely need her boyfriend? Mindfulness skills might help her to observe the moment and not project too far into the future based on how she was feeling at this moment. Emotion regulation skills might help her also identify that she was angry at her boyfriend, and to validate that anger even if she also understood and could validate his desire to be with his friends.

Illustration of an individual therapy session

We present the following diary card (Table 9.3) to illustrate the steps involved in conducting a typical individual DBT session. The session consists of a review of the diary card, noticing patterns of behavior, reviewing the skills used during the week, and setting the agenda based on the hierarchy of goals and the diary card review. Once the agenda is set, a chain analysis is conducted if the patient engaged in any life-threatening behaviors. The clinician maintains a nonjudgmental stance, remains attentive to in-session affect, balances the emphasis on problem solving and change with validation, and works toward the synthesis of opposite poles of experience.

> **Case example**
>
> Alice came on time for her session and handed the clinician her diary card from the previous week. On Saturday evening, she drank two mixed alcoholic drinks and on Wednesday evening she drank four mixed drinks and got drunk from that. Thursday she took Tylenol for a headache. She used no street drugs all week. She had passive suicidal ideation almost every day during the week, and on Thursday these thoughts intensified. She had significant levels of misery almost every day and these feelings intensified on Wednesday and Thursday. Thursday was her most difficult day – her suicide ideation was high and her urges to self-injure were extreme, and she engaged in nonsuicidal self-cutting behavior that day. She made no suicide attempts, and she engaged in binge-eating behaviors on Sunday, Monday, Wednesday, and Thursday. The clinician and patient agreed that the first item on the agenda was to do a behavioral analysis of the cutting. This chain analysis would include targeting the suicidal ideation as well. The clinician asked her if there was anything else she wanted to address in the session. She said that she was thinking about quitting her job and wanted to talk about it. They agreed to try to save some time after the chain analysis to at least begin to address this issue.

Table 9.3 Alice's diary card with a self-injury episode

Date	Alcohol	OTC meds	Prescription meds	Street drugs	Misery (0–5)	Suicidal ideation (0–5)	NSSI urges (0–5)	NSSI actions (Y/N)	Eating binges (Y/N)
Monday	0	0	Took them	None	3	1	0	N	Y
Tuesday	0	0	Took them	None	3	1	0	N	N
Wednesday	4 drinks	0	Took them	None	4	2	0	N	Y
Thursday	0	Tylenol	Took them	None	5	4	5	Y	Y
Friday	0	0	Took them	None	3	1	0	N	N
Saturday	2 drinks	0	Took them	None	2	0	0	N	N
Sunday	0	0	Took them	None	3	2	0	N	Y

Without the hierarchy of goals in place, the clinician might be tempted to begin with Alice's job situation. After all, quitting a job is a big decision that Alice might make impulsively and could have serious negative consequences. However, DBT insists on making SIB the first priority in treatment for a number of reasons. First, not addressing self-injury sends an unspoken message that it is not as important as whatever other immediate crisis situation that may arise. Secondly, the lives of BPD individuals are often quite chaotic and therapy could easily consist of putting out the fire of the week instead of making systematic progress on reducing self-injury. Finally, stability in vocational functioning can only really be achieved if an individual develops the skills necessary to tolerate distress without becoming suicidal or self-injurious. And, importantly, most behaviors like the job situation for this patient end up being part of a chain and get discussed during the chain analysis.

In addition to guiding the agenda, the diary card is useful in providing a framework for inquiry in the chain analysis. Let's examine Alice's diary card and see how the clinician would proceed with obtaining the necessary details in order to pursue a productive line of inquiry into the cutting behavior.

First of all, when there is significant suicidal ideation, the clinician should first address the nature of the suicidal ideation. Alice reported Level 4 suicidal ideation (on a scale of 0–5) on Thursday. The clinician asks Alice to detail her thought processes. Alice described that she was having thoughts of overdosing on her prescription medication for a few hours, and even went so far as to take the bottles out and put them on her desk. After a few hours, she put them back in the medicine cabinet. The clinician notices that suicide ideation and misery were accompanied by the use of Tylenol, which was to treat a hangover headache. The clinician hypothesizes that drinking alcohol, getting drunk the night before, and being hung over may have left Alice emotionally vulnerable the following day. What led to the drinking the day before? Alice describes that she drank in order to cope with misery of the day before, which was triggered by a comment her boyfriend made. She also engaged in binge eating to deal with the misery. This led to her feeling even worse the next day, more emotionally vulnerable, and less able to fight urges to cut herself. On Saturday and Sunday, there was a similar pattern and relationship between drinking one day and increased misery the next.

Diary card record of skills used

Let's look at the back of Alice's diary card (Table 9.4) in which she indicated which skills she used during the week.

Alice used mindfulness and distress tolerance skills during the week. The clinician wanted more details about when she used them and whether Alice felt they were helpful to her. Alice described how she practiced mindfulness as part of her skills group homework assignment. On the days that she indicated, she spent two minutes observing and describing, without judgment, the experience of petting her cat. She used the distress tolerance skills of distracting most days this week, which she mostly found helpful. She also thought about and used the skills on Wednesday night after she had the upsetting conversation with her boyfriend. She had tried to call a friend to get help in dealing with her upset feelings, but her friend didn't pick up the phone. She was discouraged that she tried to use skills but they did not help her.

Table 9.4 Alice's diary card record of skills used

Wise mind	Monday	Tuesday	Wednesday	Thursday	Friday	Saturday	Sunday
Observe	(Monday)	(Tuesday)	(Wednesday)	Thursday	(Friday)	(Saturday)	Sunday
Describe	(Monday)	(Tuesday)	(Wednesday)	Thursday	(Friday)	(Saturday)	Sunday
Nonjudgment	Monday	Tuesday	Wednesday	Thursday	Friday	Saturday	Sunday
One-mindful	Monday	Tuesday	Wednesday	Thursday	Friday	Saturday	Sunday
Effectiveness	Monday	Tuesday	Wednesday	Thursday	Friday	Saturday	Sunday
Interpersonal skills	Monday	Tuesday	Wednesday	Thursday	Friday	Saturday	Sunday
Mastery	Monday	Tuesday	Wednesday	Thursday	Friday	Saturday	Sunday
Positive experiences	Monday	Tuesday	Wednesday	Thursday	Friday	Saturday	Sunday
Opposite action	Monday	Tuesday	Wednesday	Thursday	Friday	Saturday	Sunday
Distract	(Monday)	(Tuesday)	(Wednesday)	Thursday	(Friday)	(Saturday)	Sunday
Self-soothe	Monday	Tuesday	Wednesday	Thursday	Friday	Saturday	Sunday
Improve	Monday	Tuesday	Wednesday	Thursday	Friday	Saturday	Sunday
Pros and cons	Monday	Tuesday	Wednesday	Thursday	Friday	Saturday	Sunday
Radical acceptance	Monday	Tuesday	Wednesday	Thursday	Friday	Saturday	Sunday

Instructions: Circle the days you worked on each skill.

The clinician praised her for practicing mindfulness and for thinking about using distress tolerance skills, even if they did not completely prevent her from engaging in the unskillful behaviors of binge eating and drinking alcohol. The fact that Alice thought about and tried a new skill represents a change in behavior, a shift from the automatic reactions she may have had in the past. The clinician points out that if she was able to stop and think about using a skill, she was actually using mindfulness. She was observing and describing that she was feeling upset and needed to problem solve. Through highlighting and praising any skillful behaviors, the clinician encourages a synthesis of an "all or nothing" view of skillfulness/unskillfulness. Even though Alice ended up binge eating, drinking, and even self-injuring the next day, it does not mean she was not skillful at all. She demonstrated that she is, in fact, learning new, more effective ways of behaving. As she continues to apply skills, they will become easier to use and more helpful to her. Once she is able to step back and think about using skills, she will be able to increase her ability to problem solve, tolerate distress, and find the right skill at the right time that will eventually replace an unskillful behavior.

After reviewing the diary card and skills used, the clinician begins the chain analysis of the episode of self-injury that Alice recorded on her diary card. The details and hypotheses generated by the review of the diary card provide a guide for inquiry during the chain analysis. The clinician decides to begin the analysis with Alice's conversation with her boyfriend. The thoughts and feelings that were triggered by this conversation led to feelings of misery, which led to binge eating and drinking, which led to a headache, increased emotional vulnerability, and suicidal ideation the following day, which led to more binge eating and, finally, self-cutting.

During the analysis, the clinician asks for as much detail as possible in order to get a sequence of thoughts, feelings, physical sensations, urges, behaviors, and events. At the same time, the clinician monitors the patient's affect and if necessary stops the analysis in order to address any feelings that have arisen. The clinician weaves solutions into the chain analysis, balances the inquiry with validating comments, and encourages the patient to be nonjudgmental.

Case example

Alice's behavioral analysis

MAJOR PROBLEM BEHAVIOR:	Cutting myself.
VULNERABILITY FACTORS:	I had a hangover headache, had four drinks the night before, work has been stressful.
PRECIPITATING EVENT IN THE ENVIRONMENT:	Argument with my boyfriend.
ANALYSIS OF EVENTS:	Wednesday, I was feeling stressed out at work to begin with. I was looking forward to seeing my boyfriend for dinner.
EVENT:	boyfriend called and told me that he was sorry that he didn't feel like coming out to dinner as we had planned. He said he was too tired.
(CLINICIAN:	What happened next?)
BEHAVIOR:	I started screaming at him, told him to go fuck himself, and hung up the phone.

(What were your thoughts or feelings? What was your interpretation of why he was canceling?)

COGNITION:	I thought – if he really loved me he would want to come out with me and wouldn't be too tired.
FEELING:	I felt disappointed and angry.
EVENT:	He called me back to try to apologize and explained that he wasn't feeling well.
BEHAVIOR:	I yelled at him again and told him to just forget it. (Did you not believe him?)
COGNITION:	Right, I thought that if he really wanted to he could figure out how to come out with me.
EVENT:	He got angry with me when I said forget it and he hung up the phone.
FEELINGS:	I felt frustrated, angry, was crying at my desk. I started to feel guilty about yelling at him, but I also was still so angry, I started getting very confused and didn't know which feeling was right – should I feel angry or understanding?
BEHAVIOR:	I called my best friend to see if she could help me sort out my feelings, but she wasn't around.
BEHAVIOR:	I left work and went home.
BODY SENSATION:	I was feeling empty and agitated, I needed to calm down but I didn't know how.
BEHAVIOR:	I got home and started eating whatever was in my cabinet – a lot of cereal.
EVENT:	My friend called and asked if I wanted to go out.
BEHAVIOR:	We went out to a bar and I had four drinks.
BEHAVIOR:	Got drunk.
EVENT:	Woke up with a hangover.
FEELINGS:	Felt miserable. Kept wanting to call my boyfriend but didn't know what to say, was hoping he would call but he didn't. I was feeling more and more guilty about yelling at him and felt ashamed of my behavior. I started to fear that he would leave me and that I would never be able to keep a boyfriend. I started to hate myself and feel hopeless about ever being able to change.
BODY SENSATION:	My head felt as if it were going to explode.
COGNITION:	It was still morning and I started to think that cutting would be the only way to make it stop. I thought to myself, why not just go ahead and do it, otherwise I'll be fighting urges all day.

Consequences of cutting myself – in self.

SHORT-TERM:	Immediate relief of the intense feeling of pressure in my head, validation of how upset I was (positive), punishment relieved guilt.
LONG-TERM:	Shame, self-hate, feeling like a loser, feeling hopeless about being able to get better (negative).

Consequences of cutting myself – in the environment.

SHORT-TERM:	boyfriend apologized when he found out that I cut myself (positive consequence)
LONG-TERM:	Having to do this chain analysis in therapy, guilty that boyfriend feels responsible for my cutting.

Different solutions

Emotion regulation skills. Observe and describe my interpretations, mindfulness of the current emotion, don't necessarily act on my feelings, just watch them. Self-validation. Opposite action to call boyfriend and apologize. Avoid avoiding. Let go of unnecessary guilt.

Use some *mindfulness skills* to challenge my expectation that I'll be feeling the urge to cut the whole day. Just because I feel the urge now doesn't mean I'll be feeling it later. Try to find wise mind by observing and describing my emotions nonjudgmentally.

Distress tolerance skills. Try some other substitute actions once the urge to cut is present – ice water, breathing, exercise. Is there any other way to get relief from the confusion and pain? Do a pros and cons analysis, try to remember how disappointed I feel after I cut myself. Radical acceptance.

In this case, Alice and her therapist were able to get a coherent, detailed sequence of the events, thoughts, feelings, body sensations, and behaviors that led up to the target behavior. Some patients have the capacity to recall, observe, and describe their experience early on in the treatment and will be able to engage in a fruitful chain analysis from the start. However, in most cases, there is a learning curve (on the part of both patient and clinician) to be able to reach an adequate level of detail in a sequence that makes sense. The chain analysis is usually a work in progress, a behavior itself that is shaped over time by repetition, rehearsal, and practice.

At the beginning of a DBT, the chain analysis is mainly directed by the therapist, who is very actively inquiring into and eliciting the steps on the chain from the patient. Over time, the therapist learns how to inquire more pointedly into the steps that take place between one point and another. And, over time, and with repetition, rehearsal, and practice, patients become increasingly aware of the triggers, thoughts, feelings, behaviors, and body sensations that lead to unskillful behaviors, and become more actively engaged in identifying the steps on, and weaving the skills into, the chain. Sometimes, in the middle and later stages of a DBT, patients can prepare chain analyses on their own and bring them into the session to review with their therapists. The more detail obtained, the greater the ability to conduct a solution analysis, targeting skills to a particular point on the chain.

Some of the most common obstacles to conducting a chain analysis are having the patient claim that they have no memory for the details of the target episode, or a flat unwillingness to engage in the process of the chain analysis. Or, the patient may be willing to engage but then quickly becomes emotionally dysregulated. This can be a response to self-invalidation that is often triggered by a recap of unskillful behavior, or to feeling invalidated or criticized by the clinician during solution analysis. These roadblocks, if not skillfully addressed, can lead to paralysis in treatment or even treatment dropout. The therapy can become overly focused on the process of therapy itself in lieu of working toward the patient's target goals.

Clinical strategies for getting "unstuck"

Conducting a chain analysis is one example of a change intervention that requires the clinician to maintain a dialectic stance and to strive for dialectic synthesis. We have emphasized the role of validation and illustrated how the clinician learns to automatically search for and highlight the valid when the patient is indicating a lack of receptiveness to problem solving and other change interventions. However, in addition to validation, Linehan offers what she terms as "stylistic" and "dialectic" strategies designed to keep both clinician and patient engaged and moving forward in treatment. We will give a brief review of these strategies here [10, 11]. These strategies are not only intended for conducting a chain analysis – rather they are strategies that are to be utilized throughout the individual psychotherapy session to encourage movement and avoid therapeutic impasse.

Stylistic strategies

We have acknowledged the challenges faced by clinicians to stay engaged with their BPD patients owing to anxiety about suicidal behaviors, and feelings that they are targets of undeserved hostility. Resentment can arise when clinicians mistakenly misinterpret suicidal communications and behaviors as deliberate attempts by patients to evoke concern, and to obtain attention and a caregiving response. We have also emphasized how the relatively inactive therapeutic stance (therapeutic neutrality and long silences) of TAU is often intolerable to BPD patients. An active therapist stance encourages transparency and often mitigates hostility and mistrust.

DBT offers unique strategies to aid clinicians in grabbing the attention of their BPD patients and keeping them deeply engaged and moving forward. Reciprocal and irreverent strategies help the clinician maintain the dialectic balance necessary to keep a patient from getting stuck. *Reciprocal communications* refer to when clinicians listen to and take patients extremely seriously, take what they say at face value without interpretation, and impart sympathy and empathy for their plight. Reciprocal communication might also involve having a clinician directly answer a personal question using self-involving self-disclosure within the clinician's personal limits (see Chapter 12). These types of communication foster the therapeutic alliance, a collaborative spirit, transparency, and trust.

Yet, sole emphasis on reciprocal strategies can also lead to therapeutic impasse. As the book *Stop Walking on Egg Shells* [12] portrays, people are often afraid to give honest feedback to BPD individuals because they fear the intensity of the reaction. And yet, this type of feedback is necessary for them to change and achieve what they want and need in their relationships and their lives. Thus, not giving feedback serves to perpetuate ineffective coping. At times, the DBT clinician needs to balance reciprocal communications with an irreverent style that emphasizes change. *Irreverence* in DBT is saying something completely unexpected, or offbeat, sometimes using humor. An irreverent communication usually takes the patient off guard, and can help them see something from another point of view. Sometimes, it involves giving honest feedback, which Linehan terms as "plunging in where angels fear to tread." Or, irreverence can take the form of reframing a situation in an unorthodox manner. An example of this might be telling a patient who abuses substances that completely honesty is not expected with respect to substance use. Such a response will take the patient off guard and thwart their usual modus operandi of hiding and minimizing problem behaviors including substance use. The patient will no longer need to constantly try to prove themselves, and the clinician will not be in the position of constantly challenging the patient's dishonesty. They can move on to more effectively target the substance use itself. If used carefully and skillfully, irreverence can create an opening for resuming forward movement.

Dialectic strategies and irreverent communications

Dialectic strategies can be used within the individual session to keep the patient engaged, a little off balance, and moving forward. They are also helpful in situations when therapist and patient are stuck. For example, it is often the case that a patient might feel extremely misunderstood and react negatively when a therapist recommends the use of skills. In such a case, the therapist might decide to "enter the paradox" which involves highlighting the extreme ends of the situation and present them to the patient to resolve. Thus, when Patty's therapist expressed her concern that Patty is missing too many days from work and suggested that they problem solve together to help her use skills to get to work, Patty became extremely upset and accused the therapist of not understanding how sick she is because she was asking her to do something she cannot possibly do. The therapist entered the paradox by responding, "I suppose I am asking too much from you. I also don't want to give up on you by believing that you are not able to get to work."

Although the use of *metaphor* is not unique to DBT, much emphasis is placed on using analogies, anecdotes, stories, myths, and metaphors to illustrate a point and make it more emotionally accessible. Metaphors and stories create images that are easy for the patient to remember and to refer to. Framing a change intervention within a metaphoric image can also soften the impact and provide a validating balance. Linehan's metaphor for the concept of radical acceptance (see Chapter 11) is "learning to love the dandelions" in the garden. Another metaphor that we like to use for addressing therapy-interfering behavior or to encourage patient responsibility is "I am throwing a life preserver out to you as you are drowning in the water – you have to grab onto it." To a patient who is constantly being triggered to self-harm within her abusive romantic relationship we might say, "You want me to give you an asbestos suit so that you can live in a burning house."

"Playing devil's advocate" is used during the commitment phase of treatment (see Chapter 9) but can also be employed at any point in the session to draw out skillful behavior. The clinician takes the extreme opposite (unskillful) position from the patient in order to encourage the patient to argue for the more skillful position, toward ultimate dialectic synthesis. This strategy is also used to challenge distorted beliefs about interpersonal interactions and emotions (see Chapter 9). For example, a belief that "all negative emotions are destructive" is stated in an extreme form in order to stimulate a more thoughtful synthesis such as "Negative emotions are not destructive in and of themselves, sometimes they are helpful (e.g., fear can get people to act to remove themselves from a dangerous situation), and sometimes lead to destructive behaviors."

When a patient is in a more emotionally dysregulated state of mind and says something provocative or in an exaggerated manner, she is usually expecting to be challenged. Through the use of the strategy of "extending," the clinician throws the patient off by doing the opposite, by taking her more seriously than she is taking herself. This often has the effect of "calling the patient's bluff" and having the patient backtrack and indicate that she is not as serious as all that. An example of this is when a patient threatens to quit her job unless her supervisor accommodates her scheduling request. The clinician becomes alarmed and takes the threat to quit very seriously, and indicates that the session must focus on preparing for when the patient no longer can afford to come to therapy, or to pay her rent. Unless the patient is very serious about quitting her job, she will most likely acknowledge that she was exaggerating and that she has no intention of quitting. At this point the clinician can work with the patient to use skills regarding her job situation.

"Making lemonade out of lemons" is an irreverent and dialectic response to a patient who is expressing distress about a bad situation. The clinician, instead of responding with a reciprocal communication of empathy or sympathy, might decide to say something about how this situation presents a wonderful opportunity to use skills. An example of this might be if a patient loses a bad job or experiences a breakup of an abusive relationship. The patient might be focused on the loss, while the clinician responds by congratulating the patient for her good luck in that she no longer has that stressful situation to deal with.

This may have the effect of jolting the patient out of an emotional state into a state of mind in which she is more able to engage in problem solving.

These dialectic strategies are designed to "activate wise mind" in the patient. Wise mind is the state of mind in which an individual can be both emotional and logical at the same time, to be emotionally engaged in a regulated manner. DBT proposes that individuals with BPD experience three distinct states of mind – wise mind, reasonable mind, and emotion mind [2]. Reasonable mind is the state of mind in which an individual is emotionally cut off and overly reliant on their intellect and logic. When in reasonable mind, there is little access to emotional experiencing and therefore a vulnerability to be quickly triggered into a state of emotion mind, in which emotions are dysregulated and the ability to reason is impaired. Wise mind is the dialectic synthesis of the two extreme states of mind. This concept of the three states of mind is more fully described in Chapter 11. The basic idea here is that within an individual session with a patient, progress is often impeded when the patient is either in an overly emotional state of mind or an overly reasonable, logical state of mind. In order to fully engage in the therapeutic endeavor, a balance between these two extreme states of mind needs to be found. The clinician uses dialectic strategies to jolt a patient out of the overly reasonable, intellectualized position, or to retrieve them from a state of emotional dysregulation. The challenge is to balance reciprocal and irreverent communications in order to most effectively activate wise mind. These strategies give the clinician guidance in preventing a negative countertransference response and in maintaining a wise mind therapeutic stance, which facilitates treatment engagement in the clinician. When patient and clinician are both in wise mind, therapy can move forward.

Summary

An individual DBT psychotherapy session has a particular structure. There is an outline for each session that gets filled in by the therapist and patient by agenda setting and chain analyses which can include skill rehearsal. The patient uses a diary card to keep track of thoughts, feelings, and behaviors that are related to their treatment goals. This diary card is reviewed by clinician and patient at the beginning of a session to collaboratively create an agenda for the session. If the patient engaged in any life-threatening behaviors during the week (including NSSI or active suicidal ideation), this becomes the first item on the agenda. Behavioral analyses are used to explore the episode of self-harm behavior in depth, and to generate solutions to the problem behavior.

Chain analysis is a useful tool for gaining understanding into the emotional and behavioral events that lead to an unwanted behavior, and for generating specific solutions. It is also built in to treatment as an aversive consequence of the maladaptive behavior. The expectation of spending a good portion of the next therapy session involved in a painstaking analysis of a self-injurious act often serves as a deterrent.

Within the structure there is also flexibility. In conducting a chain analysis, the clinician is attentive to the emotions that arise as a painful behavioral episode is recalled in detail. The clinician must attend to affect and if necessary stop the chain analysis in order to teach or coach the patient in using skills in vivo to manage their emotional response.

The chain analysis is a change intervention, and therefore the clinician is vigilant to validating the difficulty of the chain analysis process, as well as to any other aspect of the patient's experience that can be validated.

Over time, the balance of structure and flexibility within the individual DBT session provides a road map that allows the clinician and patient to work systematically toward the achievement of the patient's treatment goals. Agenda setting, using the hierarchy of goals and diary card, helps prevent sessions from getting derailed by the emotional crisis of the moment. Repeating chain analyses over time increases awareness of the patients' vulnerabilities and the triggers that lead to unskillful behaviors, as well as of the skillful behaviors they use to replace them. The collaborative nature of the sessions, as well as ongoing validation and positive reinforcement for skillful behavior, keeps both clinician and patient engaged in the therapeutic work. Stylistic and dialectic strategies are used to challenge and engage the patient on an emotional level, and transcend therapeutic impasse.

We have presented the essential DBT tools as they are used in a full standard DBT individual psychotherapy session. However, any and all of these "tools" can be incorporated by clinicians without adopting the full DBT model. In particular, we provide suggested activities for practicing the use of a diary card, agenda setting, and learning how to conduct a chain analysis.

Suggested activity for agenda setting

A patient comes into session 15 minutes late. Her diary card is partially completed. She immediately launches into expressing distress about a school paper deadline and her inability to work on the paper. She wants your help to figure out how to get her paper done, or whether she should ask her professor for an extension. Upon reviewing the diary card, the therapist notices that the patient engaged in NSSI during the week – she cut herself superficially on her forearm.

How would the therapist go about structuring the session? What are the Target 1, Target 2, and Target 3 goals and which would the therapist place on the agenda? How might the therapist counter any opposition from the patient about placing emphasis on a Target 1 rather than a Target 3 goal?

Suggested activity for learning chain analysis

A patient reports that she had a spike in suicidal ideation during the week in which she engaged in some planning and had some intent to act, but did not. She did, however, call her mother and threaten to kill herself. Although she is not currently suicidal, the therapist and patient agree to do a chain analysis to find out what led to the spike in ideation and her threat to her mother. Using a patient that you know well who might engage in this type of behavior, try to identify what the environmental triggers might be for a spike in ideation for that patient. What might be an ongoing vulnerability to that type of trigger? What are the short- and long-range consequences of threatening suicide for that patient? What are some of the thoughts or interpretations that lead to increased suicidal thinking?

References

1. Linehan, M.M. (1993) *Cognitive Behavior Therapy for Borderline Personality Disorder*, Guilford Press, New York, pp. 184–186.
2. Linehan, M.M. (1993) *Skills Training Manual for Treating Borderline Personality Disorder*, Guilford Press, New York, p. 32.
3. Burns, D.D. (1999) *The Feeling Good Handbook*, Plume Publishing, New York.
4. Fairburn, C.G. (2008) *Cognitive Behavioral Therapy and Eating Disorders*, Guilford Press, New York.
5. Linehan, M.M. (1993) *Cognitive Behavior Therapy for Borderline Personality Disorder*, Guilford Press, New York, pp. 174–176.
6. Linehan, M.M. (1993) *Cognitive Behavior Therapy for Borderline Personality Disorder*, Guilford Press, New York, pp. 254–264.
7. Linehan, M.M. (1993) *Cognitive Behavior Therapy for Borderline Personality Disorder*, Guilford Press, New York, pp. 275–281.
8. Wexler, D. (2001) *The PRISM Workbook*, W.W. Norton & Co., New York.
9. Linehan, M.M. (1993) *Cognitive Behavior Therapy for Borderline Personality Disorder*, Guilford Press, New York, pp. 319–328.
10. Linehan, M.M. (1993) *Cognitive Behavior Therapy for Borderline Personality Disorder*, Guilford Press, New York, pp. 371–398.
11. Koerner, K. (2012) *Doing Dialectical Behavior Therapy. A Practical Guide*, Guilford Press, New York, pp. 148–152.
12. Mason, P., Krieger, R. (2010) *Stop Walking on Eggshells: Taking Your Life Back When Someone You Care About Has Borderline Personality Disorder* (2nd ed.), New Harbinger Publications, Oakland.

Chapter 10

Skills training: The rationale and structure

Skills training is an integral component of DBT and complements work done in individual DBT sessions. A *Skills Training Manual* for clinicians with handouts for patients was written by Linehan [1]. Patients who enter DBT attend both individual sessions and group skills training sessions on a weekly basis. Skills training groups are sometimes used as adjuncts to other forms of therapy for patients not in DBT, on inpatient units, and day hospital programs as "stand-alone" interventions. In DBT, the importance of skills training is based on the concept that patients have deficits and that they need to learn new ways of coping that they have not, heretofore, learned or been able to apply when needed. In this chapter, we provide guidelines for incorporating skills training into a clinical psychotherapy practice.

> **Key points**
> - Rationale for skills training; skills deficits and the concept of "emotional dyslexia"
> - How is skills training conducted
> - Using DBT skills training as a "stand-alone" intervention

The skills deficit model

A major distinction between the cognitive behavioral (DBT) and psychodynamic approaches is that DBT does not focus on understanding the unconscious conflict underlying symptoms and behavior. The focus, instead, is on identification of skills deficits that prevent effective behavior. For example, lack of skills in tolerating negative emotion might lead to impulsive, maladaptive behaviors. Examples of skills deficits include the inability to soothe oneself in healthy and adaptive ways, a lack of means to act assertively and appropriately in interpersonal interactions, and a tendency to act impulsively and not restrain acting until the options and consequences are fully considered.

The Dialectical Behavior Therapy Primer: How DBT Can Inform Clinical Practice, First Edition.
Beth S. Brodsky and Barbara Stanley.
© 2013 John Wiley & Sons, Ltd. Published 2013 by John Wiley & Sons, Ltd.

Deficit compensation takes place through skills training, which involves a much more didactic approach than is taken in psychodynamic or supportive psychotherapy. Skills training directly helps patients develop alternative strategies for behaving and coping without necessitating a full understanding of the underlying dynamics.

A criticism of this approach has been that symptom substitution will result without full understanding and resolution of the underlying conflict. However, there is little evidence to support this, and preliminary data suggests that it is not the case. In Linehan's RCT comparing DBT to TBE in the community [2], the majority of the experts in the community were practicing psychodynamic psychotherapy with the BPD study participants. In a recent study [3], the DBT group demonstrated more intrapsychic change over the course of treatment than did the participants in the TBE treatment group.

Etiology of skills deficits

How do skills deficits occur? There are several possibilities. One reason for deficits in skills relates to the way in which skills are normally taught to young children. It may be that some of the basic building blocks for skills acquisition are missing in some people and that the way in which emotion regulation and interpersonal skills are normally taught to children are too "advanced" for a subset of the population. In other words, the underpinnings on which skills are built are just presumed to be present. An analogy can be drawn to teaching children with dyslexia to read. Children with dyslexia need to be taught to learn to read "beneath" the level where children without this disability begin to learn reading. Trying to teach dyslexics at the same entry level as others is like building a house without a foundation or like teaching them a foreign language by beginning at the 200 level instead of the introductory level. What is introductory for them is "more introductory" than children without dyslexia. So we could say that individuals with BPD and other forms of severe emotion dysregulation have "emotional dyslexia" in which basic self-soothing techniques, knowledge of emotions, and capacity to interact effectively need to be taught at a very basic level that is not needed for others without emotion dysregulation.

Alternatively, Liberman et al. [4] suggest that deficits in social skills stem from a lack of appropriate role models, the deterioration in social functioning that often accompanies the onset of psychiatric illness, environmental trauma, and shifts in the social environment that render certain skills less effective. Additionally, dispositional emotional vulnerability can make it difficult to acquire skills since effective learning requires concentration and focus, both of which are nearly impossible under conditions of emotional dysregulation.

Lack of skills knowledge and dispositional factors are not the only reason for skills deficits. Individuals may know how to act skillfully but lack proficiency due to inadequate practice, lack of motivation, and/or inability to accurately determine the context within which to use a skill [5]. Therefore, skills training must include teaching not only of skills content, but also increasing the proficiency of skillful behavior through rehearsal and practice, increasing the ability to discriminate the conditions under which skills must be applied, as well as addressing issues of motivation to use skills.

Rationale for skills training

DBT skills training is based on the premise that individuals cannot change simply through understanding their problematic patterns of thinking and behaviors, they must explicitly learn new skills and ways of coping. Skills training in DBT consists of psychoeducation toward the development of coping skills. Linehan has suggested that it may be the most important and effective ingredient in DBT. Skills training is used as a helpful adjunct to individual psychotherapy and psychopharmacology whether the patient is in DBT individual therapy or not. Skills training provides (a) enhancement of coping skills for tolerating painful emotions and distressing events; (b) improvement in capacity to regulate emotions and refrain from using self-destructive behaviors; (c) increased capability to deal with interpersonal interactions more effectively; and (d) improved capacity in being "mindful" (i.e., being in the present and, thereby, not worrying and becoming dysregulated thinking about the past or future) and refraining from being judgmental.

Skills training complements psychotherapy through the direct teaching of coping skills, acquisition, and practice. This direct teaching is necessary to augment the understanding gained through individual psychotherapy, but the insight provided by psychotherapy helps to enhance the application of new skills in place of ingrained and maladaptive behaviors. A major component of skillful behavior is recognizing patterns of maladaptive behaviors, the stressors that trigger them, and the need for more skillful behavior in these situations. In particular, individual psychotherapy can contribute to motivation enhancement, which is necessary to support and promote behavioral change. Thus, skills training is best applied within a context of an ongoing individual psychotherapy in which these patterns and triggers can be recognized and understood.

Principles of skills training

Skills training is based on learning theory and utilizes behavioral principles: shaping; modeling; repeated practice and rehearsal; generalization; and reinforcement. Behavioral change is facilitated by the combination of direct instruction, modeling, positive reinforcement of successive approximations to the desired goal, coaching, and practice.

The first step in the process of skills training is assessment of the skill deficit. Once the specific deficit has been identified, appropriate skills to correct the deficit are selected and training is implemented. In DBT, skills deficits in BPD are conceptualized as deficits in the ability to regulate emotions, behaviors, interpersonal interactions, and cognitive processes. Emotional dysregulation is considered to be the primary area of deficit that drives the dysregulation in the other areas of functioning.

The components of skills training consist of direct instruction, modeling, rehearsal, behavioral shaping, and generalization. In direct instruction, the individual receives the required knowledge to utilize the skill. Then, the skill can be modeled by the skills trainer [5]. Modeling is a powerful tool that allows the patient to observe how to perform the skill as well as to observe the favorable consequences that result from using the skill.

The teaching of skills also consists of prompting, reminding, or coaching the patient to perform a behavior. This is followed by behavioral shaping, in which components of behavior that are successively closer approximations of the target behavior are reinforced.

In order to generalize the skillful behavior into more naturalistic settings, homework is assigned to augment the rehearsal of the skill outside of the training session. In vivo skills coaching (when the patient is in a situation where skills are needed and calls upon the clinician to help apply the relevant skills) encourages the integration of a particular skill into the patient's skills repertoire as a replacement for maladaptive behavior.

Skills training in DBT

While skills training takes place in three of the four DBT modalities – the skills training group, the individual psychotherapy session, and between-session skills coaching calls – we focus here on the skills training group because it is the primary modality for the dissemination of direct instruction in skills, as well as in behavioral rehearsal through role-play, modeling, and the assignment of homework. Between-session coaching and individual sessions rely on group skills training for the teaching of the basic skills. Coaching and individual therapy help the patient learn when and how to apply the skills that have been taught in the group. However, instruction can also take place within the individual psychotherapy session when indicated. The individual therapist will augment behavioral rehearsal with role-play and homework assignments that are specifically targeting the patient's primary and secondary treatment goals. Reinforcement, behavioral shaping, and motivation enhancement to use skills take place primarily within the context of the relationship between the patient and the individual clinician, both within session and through in vivo coaching via between-session phone contact.

The format of the skills training group

The DBT skills training group serves to introduce and teach skills and provide an opportunity to interact with other patients who are also learning skills. Clinicians might understandably have anxiety about assembling a group of highly emotionally reactive individuals together in one room. Similarly, patients can be reluctant about becoming part of a group. One of two reactions is frequently voiced by patients: (a) "Everyone will be better off than me and it will make me feel worse." (b) "Everyone is in worse shape than I am and it will make me think worse of myself to be around them." This reluctance can be handled by discussing how the group is more like a class and that students in any given class are at all different levels and each one gets valuable information. Furthermore, as we will describe in detail, the group instruction is highly structured and conducted in such a way as to discourage personal emotional processing. Patients are oriented to the didactic nature of the group and group skills trainers are responsible for keeping the group focused on skills acquisition.

We have seen that, although some patients are extremely socially anxious and are loathe to attend a group, the group format is the optimal modality for DBT skills training. When at all possible, we encourage and support our reluctant patients to give the group a try, although we will conduct individual skills training if it is the only way to proceed. We find that the group setting allows patients to feel less alone and less judged about having to learn skills. They take heart to learn that there are other people out there "just like me" and they experience a sense of peer support in learning the skills. Often, patients are much more open to the idea that skills can work, and more willing to try them, when encouraged or inspired by a peer in the group. Patients are also much more likely to be supportive and nonjudgmental toward their peers in the group, and then encouraged to take a similar stance toward themselves. In addition, the group "class" format is designed to effectively impart the information the patients need about skills and how to learn them, so that the individual therapy time can be more devoted to helping the patients learn how to actually apply the skills to their life circumstances.

The *Skills Training Manual* (1993) describes skills divided into four modules and how to teach them, and contains worksheets and homework assignments to facilitate learning. The four modules of skills target four areas of dysregulation of BPD: mindfulness, distress tolerance, interpersonal effectiveness, and emotion regulation skills. As of this writing, an updated version of the original 1993 skills manual is in press. We refer the reader to these skills manuals for the most detailed description of the skills and how to teach them. In the next chapter, we provide an overview of the skills that are taught.

General guidelines for skills training

Before the four modules are presented, patients are oriented to the idea that unskillful behavior is the result of a number of factors. Lack of knowledge is only one reason for unskillful behavior. Often, individuals have the capacity for, but not necessarily access to, skillful behavior, due to emotional, cognitive, or situational factors. Patients are oriented to the idea that skillful behavior must occur within all contexts, regardless of emotional state or environmental factors.

Guidelines for running a skills training group

Establishing a group

To cover all the skills in the skills manual requires weekly meetings over a six-month period. Patients are asked to make a commitment to remain in the group for at least six months. Some patients choose to do two six-month cycles in order to reinforce and expand on what they learned in the first cycle. Standard DBT was developed within a research setting, and we have found that certain modifications are sometimes made to adapt DBT skills groups to a private practice or busy clinic or inpatient settings. In standard DBT, a DBT skills training group is led by two DBT group leaders. While this is optimal, it is not always feasible in some settings. In general, we recommend having 6–10 patients in a group at any one time. But, again, this can vary depending on the demands of the setting. DBT, as originally developed, admits patients to the group at the end of any of the four modules, although we know of groups where patients are admitted mid-module in order to engage patients when their interest and motivation is at a peak.

Initial consultation and orientation

When a patient is referred to DBT skills group, we arrange an individual consultation session in order to evaluate the areas of skills deficit, as well as orient them to the group. We explain that a DBT skills group is more similar to a class than to a psychotherapy group. The focus is on learning skills together, and group members are discouraged from bringing in personal stories, and also discouraged from sharing their feelings about other members within the group setting. Since each group member is required to be in individual psychotherapy, we make sure that their individual therapist is on board with motivating, reinforcing, and supporting the patient to utilize the skills. During this evaluation, we orient them to the four skills modules and to what they can expect when they first attend the group. We let them know that they will be entering a group already in progress, that each member has had the experience of entering the group "in progress," and encourage them to ask questions and tolerate feeling a bit confused for a few sessions.

Homogeneous versus heterogeneous groups

Group leaders vary in terms of how homogeneous or heterogeneous they want groups to be in terms of gender, diagnosis, level of functioning, and age. For example, since many individuals with BPD are women with histories of sexual abuse or assault, some clinicians choose to run all-female groups. We recognize the value of offering homogeneous groups, and when we are referring our patients to DBT skills groups, we try to find groups that are the best fit for them in terms of age and level of functioning, in order to improve the chances of success. However, we also have had positive experiences running heterogeneous groups. Group members find common ground in learning the skills. When differences between members become an issue, we utilize it as an opportunity to encourage practice in being effective, and using radical acceptance and other skills to tolerate a group member that is triggering uncomfortable feelings.

Format for skills groups

Groups run for 1.5–2 hours typically and are divided into three phases. Each group starts with a brief mindfulness exercise. After the exercise, the skills trainer leads a discussion encouraging group members to share their experience with the exercise. The trainer highlights certain aspects of the experience for didactic purposes, such as noticing and reframing judgments, or encouraging patients to notice how they were being mindful even when they thought they were not. The trainer looks for opportunities to point out how much more everyone noticed about their experience due to mindfulness and to identify how the quality of mindfulness is different from the usual state of "mindlessness."

The second stage of the group is devoted to reviewing the homework assignment from the previous week. The skills trainer invites group members to share their homework. While members are encouraged to use personal experiences in doing their homework, the skills trainer moderates the homework review with an eye on limiting the amount of personal sharing and keeping it skill focused. When group members come without completed homework assignments, the skills trainer spends some time engaging the patient and the group in nonjudgmental problem solving around how to overcome the obstacles to doing the homework.

After mindfulness and homework review, a new skill is taught and homework is assigned to practice the new skill. In teaching the new skill, the trainer employs the strategies of modeling, self-disclosure, and role-play to enhance skills acquisition. For example, the skills trainer will complete and share her own homework assignment to model skills practice and rehearsal. As indicated earlier, self-involving self-disclosure is often necessary to facilitate willingness to learn a skill (such as radical acceptance; see Chapter 11). The group setting creates an environmental support for skillful behavior by providing support, structure, and accountability.

Keeping the group emotionally contained

Certain rules and procedures are in place to maintain a structured environment that is conducive to skills acquisition. These rules include guidelines for confidentiality, expectations for attendance and timeliness, and for contact outside of the group (if the patients decide they want it) that will protect the integrity of the group and a feeling of safety for each group member.

Discussion of self-harm behaviors is discouraged within the group, in order to avoid triggering the other group members. Personal self-revelation is not encouraged, and personal examples are limited to how they relate to learning skills. Although patients complain about this, and clinicians often feel uncomfortable "ignoring the elephant in the room," there is a strong rationale for this. First of all, there is a lot of content to cover in each group. If patients discuss the problems they are grappling with, the topics that are supposed to be covered will not get discussed. Also, patients, as much as they may want to share their personal problems, particularly if they are upset at that moment, and receive support and attention at the moment, often feel overly exposed after they have revealed themselves to the group in this way. This can result in feeling triggered and dysregulated a few hours after the group, and possibly not showing up for the next group. Group members are also affected by hearing intense emotional details, and leave the group feeling triggered and dysregulated. Therefore, the group process is only attended to when a negative process threatens to destroy the group. Even then, the process is addressed only to the extent necessary to be able to resume focus on skills training.

Reinforcement of skills training in individual therapy

In DBT, skills training group sessions are separate from individual treatment and ideally are run by a skills training leader who is not the individual psychotherapist (although in private practice this is not always possible). The individual treatment, however, is integral to the individual's ability to apply these skills in everyday life.

Individual therapy can help increase patient awareness of the need for skills to replace maladaptive behavior. The ego-syntonic nature of the difficulties experienced by BPD patients interferes with their ability to recognize their problems. Patients often externalize their problems and experience them as stemming from the events in their environment and from the significant relationships in their lives. They do not immediately recognize the need for or reason to change their own behaviors, and often feel criticized and react with hostility and resistance when they are asked to do so. The individual therapy session is the place where the dialectic balance between validation and change can facilitate a willingness to accept the need for skills.

Individual therapy can assist in identifying areas of skill deficit as well as improving skill discrimination. Through repeated behavioral analysis of the behavioral, emotional, and interpersonal difficulties that arise in the patient's life, the individual therapist recognizes maladaptive patterns of behavior and identifies the areas in which skills can replace them. Within the context of the behavioral analyses, opportunities for increased skillfulness are identified and weaved into the behavioral chain.

Most importantly, individual therapy can enhance motivation to change behavior. The individual DBT therapist constantly supports and cheerleads the patient's efforts to try new skillful behaviors. The therapist also validates the difficulty of learning new behaviors, provides in vivo skills coaching for skill rehearsal and generalization, and enhances the positive consequences of engaging in new, skillful behaviors.

DBT skills groups as "stand-alone" treatment

There has been some controversy about whether DBT skills training alone is effective or needs to be done in the context of full-scale DBT. Initially, it was felt that skills alone were not effective. However, there are more recent indications that skills taught in a group format, by themselves, may be effective [6]. Furthermore, DBT skills groups have been conducted as stand-alone interventions for many years now and patients seem to find these groups very helpful. Typically, stand-alone skills groups are conducted in one of three settings: on inpatient units; in day hospital programs; and in outpatient settings (e.g., private practice) where the patients are in individual treatment that is not DBT. In all circumstances, the skills training clinician does not assume primary responsibility for the patient. This is particularly important for at least two reasons: patients referred to DBT skills are typically multiproblemed, and managing them in a group setting alone is not tenable; and the format of skills groups is not designed to monitor clinical conditions. They are, for the most part, interactive/didactic. Discussion focuses on issues understanding and applying the skills, not monitoring and improving the patient's immediate clinical state. So, for example, patients may be fighting urges to self-injure at the time that they are in the group and, because of the nature of the group, this would not be revealed. Nor should it be. Of course, if patients reveal that they are dangerously and imminently suicidal, clinicians, irrespective of their roles, must intervene to save their lives. This would be very difficult to manage if skills trainers had to handle this on their own.

Orientation module for skills training for patients not in individual DBT

In order to maximize the effectiveness of skills training if patients are not in individual DBT, skills training must be put into context. If they are not, patients can be left not knowing why they are being taught skills, and when or how to apply them. Therefore, we recommend that stand-alone skills groups include an orientation component that can be done either individually or in a group setting. The orientation includes (a) the role of the skills trainer (i.e., what the skills trainer can and cannot do) and the rationale for using skills training as an adjunct to other forms of treatment; (b) an explanation of the biosocial theory; (c) the rationale for developing new skills (i.e., skills deficit model) and the goals of skills training; and (d) how to do a behavioral chain analysis including the difference between a chain analysis with and without solution analysis.

Summary

Skills training is a central change intervention in DBT. Ideally, skills are taught didactically within a group format, where patients learn the basic concepts of mindfulness, distress tolerance, interpersonal effectiveness, and emotion regulation. Support for incorporating the skills into one's behavioral repertoire takes place within the group, as well as in the individual DBT psychotherapy session and in between-session skills coaching interactions. Social learning and behavioral principles are utilized to teach skills and shape skillful behaviors. We have described how to conduct a group both within standard DBT and as a "stand-alone" intervention.

References

1. Linehan, M.M. (1993) *Skills Training Manual for Treating Borderline Personality Disorder*, Guilford Press, New York.
2. Linehan, M.M., Comtois, K.A., Murray, A.M., et al. (2006) Two-year randomized controlled trial and follow-up of dialectical behavior therapy vs. therapy by experts for suicidal behaviors and borderline personality disorder. *Archives of General Psychiatry*, 63 (7), 757–766.
3. Bedics, J.D., Atkins, D.C., Comtois, K.A., et al. (2012) Treatment differences in the therapeutic relationship and introject during a 2-year randomized controlled trial of dialectical behavior therapy versus nonbehavioral psychotherapy experts for borderline personality disorder. *Journal of Consulting and Clinical Psychology*, 80 (1), 66–77.
4. Liberman, R.B., Mueser, K.T., Wallace, C.J. (1986) Social skills training for schizophrenic individuals at risk for relapse. *American Journal of Psychiatry*, 143, 523–526.
5. Speiglar, M.D., Guervrement, D.C. (1998) *Contemporary Behavior Therapy* (3rd ed.), Brooks/Cole Publishing, Pacific Grove.
6. Neacsiu, A.D., Rizvi, S.L., Linehan, M.M. (2010) Dialectical behavior therapy skills use as a mediator and outcome of treatment for borderline personality disorder. *Behaviour Research and Therapy*, 48 (9), 832–839.

Chapter 11

Skills training: The four skill modules

DBT skills focus on enhancing sets of skills: (1) mindfulness skills; (2) distress tolerance; (3) interpersonal effectiveness; and (4) emotion regulation. In this chapter, we provide an overview of the DBT skills modules.

> **Key points**
>
> Four DBT skills modules are described:
> - Mindfulness
> - Distress Tolerance
> - Interpersonal Effectiveness
> - Emotion Regulation

The four skills modules and order of modules

DBT skills training consists of four skills modules designed to help individuals with BPD and with severe emotion dysregulation generally. As mentioned in the previous chapter, it takes approximately six months to cover all skills, all four modules, if the group meets once weekly. The mindfulness module is typically repeated after the distress tolerance module, the interpersonal effectiveness module, and the emotion regulation module.

As they gain experience with running skills groups, clinicians develop their own sense of the order in which modules should be taught. The mindfulness module is always taught first because these skills serve as the basis for learning all other skills. In our experience, distress tolerance skills give patients a lot of "bang for the buck" because they are very accessible and patients get quick feedback about their helpfulness. So we typically tackle the distress tolerance module after the mindfulness module. Both the interpersonal effectiveness and emotion regulation modules are quite lengthy and a case can be made for presenting either of them first. Emotion regulation is the heart of the problem that patients have to address and, therefore, it makes sense to teach this module next. On the other

---

The Dialectical Behavior Therapy Primer: How DBT Can Inform Clinical Practice, First Edition.
Beth S. Brodsky and Barbara Stanley
© 2013 John Wiley & Sons, Ltd. Published 2013 by John Wiley & Sons, Ltd.

hand, patients with emotion dysregulation virtually always have problems in relationships; they often come to treatment having lost many relationships and with their current relationships in a precarious state. Thus, a case can be made for addressing interpersonal effectiveness after distress tolerance. Furthermore, the emotion regulation module contains some complex concepts that can be difficult for patients to readily grasp. With these considerations in mind, we have opted for the following order: Mindfulness; Distress tolerance; Mindfulness; Interpersonal Effectiveness; Mindfulness; Emotion regulation.

Mindfulness skills

Mindfulness skills are taught to help patients learn to be in the present in a nonjudgmental way and to refrain from acting impulsively. These skills are based on Buddhist principles. Patients are taught techniques for focusing their thoughts and attention on the present and coupling awareness with a nonjudgmental attitude. Cognitive control is enhanced by learning to observe and describe current emotions and experiences without judgment. Mindfulness involves being fully attentive to the task at hand without being distracted or preoccupied by intervening thoughts or ideas.

The mindfulness skills represent the core area of skills training in that they increase awareness of the present moment. They increase the ability of the patients to step back from their experience and gain enough perspective to recognize when they are being unskillful and when they need to try to utilize a new skill. All of the skills require this type of awareness.

Although the concept of mindfulness training may seem abstract, we find that patients easily take to the idea and are able to utilize the techniques quite readily. Mindfulness training consists of:

1 identifying the three states of mind;
2 what is needed to be mindful, in DBT parlance, the "what" skills;
3 how to be mindful, the "how" skills.

Three states of mind

Linehan presents a model that consists of three states of mind: emotion mind, reasonable mind, and wise mind. According to the DBT model, individuals with severe emotion dysregulation tend to shift between these three distinct states of mind. Emotion mind describes the state of mind in which individuals are completely consumed by their emotions. Their thoughts and actions are dominated by their emotional state and there is little capacity for finding perspective on the larger context of the situation. When in emotion mind, individuals tend to be extremely emotionally reactive without thought to the consequences. The experience of the emotion feels out of control and dysregulated.

At first glance, reasonable mind sounds like a state of mind in which decision-making would be sound. However, while individuals are able to problem solve and have access to logical thought processes when in reasonable mind, they are completely cut off from their emotions. Thus, although they might not be emotionally reactive or impulsive, they may be experiencing a feeling of inner "deadness" or disconnection from themselves and their experience.

Patients are taught that some of their difficulties stem from spending much of their time in either one or the other of these extreme states of mind. They either experience their emotions in an all-consuming way, or they are completely cut off from their emotions. In fact, each extreme state of mind results in a drastic switch from one to the other. For example, feeling extremely emotional can become so distressing that the individual copes by flipping into an emotionally cut off state of mind (reasonable mind). Conversely, feeling emotionally cut off can become distressing and unsustainable, leaving an individual vulnerable to being easily triggered into the emotion mind state. The constant shifting between one extreme state of mind and the other contributes to a fragmented sense of self, and a compartmentalization of emotional and cognitive processes.

Therefore, mindfulness practice encourages the cultivation of a third state of mind, called "wise mind," in which individuals can experience emotions while at the same time have access to cognitive control. Wise mind is described as a state of mind that is greater than the sum of the two other states of mind. From the state of wise mind, individuals can use emotional experiences to guide them in knowing what they need, while have access to cognitive control that will guide them in acting skillfully (or skillfully refraining from acting) upon their emotional wisdom.

Patients are encouraged to pay attention to when they are in the various states of mind, and are especially guided to learn how to identify how it feels to be in wise mind and what types of activities or situations promote their ability to experience wise mind.

What is needed to be mindful

The mindfulness module also provides instruction on the building blocks that lead to the experience of "wise mind." Patients are taught the "what" skills of mindfulness – what you do to be mindful. Individuals can observe, describe and participate. The "observe" skill consists of a pre-verbal shift in perception that allows an individual to step back and notice the experience. One way to describe this perceptual shift is to imagine the experience of noticing the shift of foreground and background while gazing at an M.C. Escher print.

Once the perceptual shift takes place, you can then "describe" it. This consists of finding words to describe the experience. Thus, you can contain the experience, and find some perspective, by stepping back and observing and describing what is happening. For example, instead of being completely consumed by an emotion or a ruminative thought process, you can step back and say, "I am having this feeling or thought."

The "what" skill of "participate" has to do with being completely in the moment with whatever activity you are engaged in. Thus, instead of doing one thing but thinking about something else, you are bringing your mind and your entire being – emotions, thinking, and physical being – into the present and allowing yourself to become completely involved (at one) with the task at hand. Sometimes we use examples of engaging in creative activities such as playing an instrument to illustrate this point.

How to be mindful

In order to be mindful, patients need to learn how to observe, describe, and participate in a particular manner. The quality of the experience becomes mindful if patients learn how to observe, describe, and participate in a "one-mindful," "non-judgmental," and "effective" way.

Mindfulness is about increasing awareness of the present moment. Therefore, it is important to practice bringing attention into the present and training the mind to attend to one thing at a time. In teaching "one-mindfulness," we do mindfulness exercises together in which everyone chooses a particular aspect of the present situation to pay attention to, then observes when the attention drifts to something else, and then practices gently returning the attention back to the chosen target. We liken the exercise to that of doing repetitions with a dumbbell in order to build a bicep muscle. With repetition, the mind develops the strength to notice when attention is drifting and the ability to redirect attention to the chosen aspect of the present. Learning how to observe when attention drifts already increases your awareness, and bringing your attention back to a chosen target in the present strengthens cognitive control.

Another aspect of experience that distinguishes mindfulness from "mindlessness" is a nonjudgmental stance. In order to increase awareness, patients need to learn how to refrain from imposing judgment on our experience. A mindful stance necessitates experiencing things as they are, not as how they "should" be, or how people want them to be. Although patients will argue that judgments are necessary, it is usually possible to convince them that we don't need them as much as we think we do. By learning to observe our judgments, they begin to see that they are unnecessarily imposing judgment on experience much of the time, and that in doing so they cause themselves needless distress. Mindfulness practice allows individuals to learn how to observe and describe experience in a non-judgmental, and more accurate, fashion. In teaching "non-judgmental" thinking, patients are, for example, encouraged to look at a relatively neutral stimulus (choose something to look at in the office, such as a painting on the wall or a piece of furniture, a rug) and practice observing and describing it without judgment, or to notice the judgmental observations (ugly, beautiful, cheap-looking) and reframe them without judgment. Refraining from positive judgment is just as important as controlling the negative judgments, because positive judgments reflect attachment to things having to be a certain way, rather than learning how to view and accept things as they are without needing it to be good or bad.

Mindfulness practice is all about learning how to be effective. Increasing awareness helps individuals to find perspective and keep an eye on the ball regarding how to be as skillful as possible in attaining goals. We encourage patients to refrain from "cutting off their nose to spite their faces." A patient who got into an argument with a cab driver on her way to therapy presented an example of this. She requested that he turn down the air conditioning because it was too cold for her. When he refused to do so, she started screaming at him. He pulled over and called the police. The whole incident caused her to miss her therapy session. In the behavioral analysis in the next session, the issue of being effective came up. The patient was able to see that even though she was entitled to have the air conditioning turned down, it was not worth having the police get involved and having to pay for a cab ride for a therapy session that she missed.

It is very easy to get caught up in being "right," and being right does not necessarily result in being skillful. Effectiveness is learning how to focus on being skillful, which sometimes is not the same as being right. Patients often interpret this to mean that they are being told to "sell out." In teaching "effectiveness," we talk about choosing their battles and finding a dialectic synthesis between being right and being effective.

Finding the middle ground

Walking the middle path, an aspect of teaching mindfulness in DBT was developed by Miller et al. [1] in their adaptation of DBT for adolescents. This skill can also be used with adults. Because dialectical synthesis is at the core of DBT, finding the middle ground is natural to address. One example of this skill is to find the synthesis between reasonable mind and emotion mind. Similarly, this skill focuses patients on accepting what they have in their lives at present while having a desire to have something else in their lives.

Mindfulness readings

We recommend readings to patients to help them cultivate a mindfulness practice. These include inspirational books by Tibetan Buddhist writers such as Hanh [2.3] and Chodron [4, 5]. Dr. Jon Kabat-Zinn, who has developed a mindfulness-based practice for stress reduction, also has published a number of books with suggestions for mindfulness practice [6, 7].

Distress tolerance skills

The second set of skills focus on improving the capacity to tolerate distress. Distress tolerance skills focus on how to live through a crisis situation without trying to change it (when it cannot be changed) and without engaging in destructive behavior. This module addresses behavioral dyscontrol and consists of two sub-modules: (a) crisis survival strategies and (b) acceptance of reality (i.e., things as they are) strategies.

Crisis survival strategies

Crisis survival skills offer hands-on behavioral alternatives to maladaptive coping patterns and include techniques for distracting and self-soothing and guidelines for improving the moment and for learning how to stop and consider the consequences of unskillful behaviors through pros and cons analysis. At first glance, crisis survival skills might seem very simplistic and too obvious to even mention. Yet, we have learned that as simple as they seem, patients have trouble thinking about doing these things for themselves, or knowing when to do them. They need reminding and encouragement. Furthermore, although these strategies are called "crisis survival" strategies, many patients find them helpful when situations are not at the level of a crisis.

There are several crisis survival strategies:

1 Distraction
2 Self-soothing
3 Changing body chemistry/sensations (the TIP skills)
4 Improving the moment (without changing the reality circumstances)
5 Considering the pros and cons of alternative actions

Skillful distraction

Most patients come to DBT therapy with the ability to distract themselves. The challenge is to distinguish between skillful distractions and unskillful avoidance behaviors. Basically, if the behavior is effective and not causing a problem in functioning, it is probably a skillful distraction. Unskillful avoidance behaviors usually have more negative and destructive consequences. Timing is also a parameter for determining whether distraction is skillful or not. If people are distracting themselves when they need to be dealing with something, this is an example of unskillful avoidance behavior.

The DBT guidelines for skillful distractions are given the acronym ACCEPTS, which stands for: engage in Activities (e.g., exercise, watching television), use Comparisons to put the current situation and emotional state in perspective, Contribute to others and society, do activities to induce other Emotions to change the current emotion, Push away, which is to willfully not think about the distressing situation, distract with simple Thoughts (e.g., count to 10, repeat the words of a song or poem), use other Sensations to distract (e.g., take a hot shower, hold ice in hand). These are fairly straightforward and fully described in Linehan's manual [8].

Recommending the use of comparisons to distract from distress needs to be framed in a way so as not to encourage self-invalidation, or to not encourage negative comparisons which may lead to feeling worse. Contributing is a distraction skill that is often extremely effective but not one that patients often consider doing on their own. Examples of contributing could be as simple as calling to listen to and support a friend in need, or can involve some type of volunteer work. Other physical sensations are especially helpful in fighting urges to self-injure in that they are designed to provide some relief from the physiological tension that arises from negative emotions. They include holding ice, submerging one's face in ice water, taking a very hot or cold shower, snapping a rubber band around the wrist, intense aerobic exercise, and relaxation exercises.

Self-soothing

Self-soothing consists of using one or more of the five senses to create a sense of calm. The patient can choose to gaze at a piece of art or a nature landscape, use aromatherapy, listen to music, light a candle, stroke an animal, or another soothing tactile surface, squeeze a stress ball, or enjoy a pleasing taste sensation. Certain barriers to using self-soothe skills arise in that patients often feel undeserving of soothing and when in crisis are more prone to self-punishment. Alternatively, patients can be willful, insisting that others soothe them, and resentful about having to do it for themselves.

Changing body chemistry

This distress tolerance strategy has been added as a skill [9] and is not included in the *Skills Training Manual* [8]. This strategy is termed the "TIP" skills: Change the body (particularly the face) Temperature, Intense exercise, and Progressive relaxation and paced breathing. This is a very powerful intervention for patients to use to change their emotional and physical state quickly. All three of the strategies accomplish this. Changing the body temperature can be done by either splashing cold water on the face or holding an ice pack on the face. Intense exercise, of course, changes bodily and emotional states very quickly, as does progressive relaxation, a basic tool of CBT, and paced breathing.

Improving the moment

Tolerating distress often requires the recognition and acceptance that a certain situation is not going to change. The only option is to accept and improve the moment that individuals are in, not the moment they wish they were in or that they "should" be in. Once they open their minds to this concept, DBT offers skills outlined by the acronym IMPROVE, which stands for using Imagery, finding Meaning, using Prayer, Relaxation, being One mindful in the moment, taking a skillful Vacation, and Encouragement.

To illustrate these skills, we use an example such as waiting to hear from a doctor after taking a diagnostic test. If the test results are due back in three days and the person is extremely worried about the result, the IMPROVE skills can help her tolerate the distress of waiting. By being in the moment and deciding to improve it, one can find meaning in the distress, can pray for strength to get through the waiting period, can be "one in the moment" and remind oneself that there is not any bad news yet, can take a break from the situation, and treat oneself to a small getaway (perhaps to a spa, a hike in the woods, or spending a few hours in an art gallery or museum), or can cheerlead oneself that, whatever the news is, it can be handled. All of these options are more helpful in tolerating the distress of waiting than catastrophizing about the worst-case scenario.

Pros and cons analysis

A pros and cons analysis is useful in carving out space between an urge and an action or consideration of alternatives, a space within which to think past the immediate consequences and create more awareness in the moment of the long-range consequences. This is particularly useful when contemplating self-destructive behaviors. Destructive behaviors such as self-injury, gambling, binge/purge, substance use, are maladaptive coping mechanisms that often have a short-term positive consequence because they provide an immediate escape from distress. However, the long-term consequences interfere with building a sense of control, mastery, and a life worth living, as well as physical well-being. A pros and cons analysis consists of thinking through the pros and cons of acting on a destructive urge, as well as the pros and cons of not acting on the urge and tolerating the distress instead. A pros and cons analysis is best written out ahead of time, either in a psychotherapy session or as a homework assignment. Table 11.1 is an example of a pros and cons analysis of engaging in nonsuicidal self-injurious cutting behavior.

This analysis reveals that there are quite a few pros to engaging in the unskillful behavior. This is helpful in terms of self-validation that this behavior, although shame-provoking,

Table 11.1 Pros and cons analysis of engaging in non-suicidal self-injurious cutting behavior

Pros of cutting	Cons of cutting
Immediate relief from physical tension	Scars – don't like them and have to hide
Stops my thoughts from racing	I feel ashamed of myself
Proof that I am in pain	I don't learn how to handle my emotions
Pros of not cutting	**Cons of not cutting**
I will feel more in control and better about myself	I will have to feel a lot of pain
I won't have another scar	I don't know when the pain will end

does help to reduce distress, and also validates how difficult it is to try to refrain from engaging in it. This analysis also underlines the need for developing a plan to use other distress tolerance skills for sitting with the pain and not engaging in the cutting behavior. The pros and cons can be used to remind the patient of the long range negative consequences (scars, feeling shame) that can help her maintain motivation to use skills to not cut. Patients are encouraged to have their pros and cons analyses handy to consult when they are feeling the urge to engage in destructive behaviors.

Crisis survival strategies are fairly straightforward and patients are often able, with encouragement and support from their clinician, to quickly incorporate them into their behavioral repertoire when in high urge mode. It is often surprising how effective it is to just review and suggest these simple techniques. Patients often have not been taught these strategies or do not know when to use them.

Acceptance of reality: The concept of radical acceptance

The main barrier to using skills has to do with difficultly recognizing that they are needed, or an unwillingness to try them. In order to make use of crisis survival strategies, patients have to cultivate a willingness to do so. The idea of radical acceptance, based on mindfulness and the ability to see things as they are rather than how they should be, is a central tenet in the distress tolerance module. Radical acceptance is radical because it goes against every fiber of an individual's being to accept a situation that is so painful. Acceptance does not mean approval. It means acknowledging the reality of a situation. Once an individual turns her mind to accepting a situation, she can be willing to use skills to tolerate the pain, without causing the additional suffering that comes from refusing to accept the reality of a situation. To illustrate this concept, we use examples from day-to-day life (such as being stuck on the subway and not knowing when it will start moving again), to larger painful experiences (such as the loss of a relationship). Radical acceptance requires turning the mind to acceptance over and over again.

Radical acceptance is a very difficult concept to convey to patients. They feel the need to fight a situation that seems unacceptable or unfair. Fighting is the only response that makes them feel empowered and in control in a situation that is out of their control. They have trouble seeing that accepting a situation that they cannot change is the more controlled and powerful response. However, it is true that radical acceptance of reality reduces suffering. Continuing to dwell on the fact that this "shouldn't be happening" will increase suffering and preclude the use of other skills. As skills trainers, we often use self-involving self-disclosure of a personal experience in which we needed to radically accept a very difficult reality to illustrate this point.

Interpersonal effectiveness skills

The third skills module focuses on improving interpersonal effectiveness. Interactions are often the triggers for suicidal behavior in individuals with BPD. This is a result of the intense dependency on others for self-definition and emotional control, as well as emotionally driven (and often distorted) interpretations of the intentions of others. Although a common misconception is that individuals with BPD are overly assertive, in reality they often have extreme difficulty in asserting themselves, which leads to resentment and then dysregulated, passive (and sometimes actively) aggressive help-seeking behaviors.

Interpersonal effectiveness skills incorporate assertiveness training techniques, mindfulness, and cognitive restructuring. Patients are encouraged to challenge distorted cognitions related to interpersonal interactions and taught how to identify and stay mindful of their goals within these interactions. They learn techniques for effectively making requests, or for saying "no" to unwanted demands, and learn to balance their objective while maintaining relationships and self-respect (i.e., "everything" should not be sacrificed in order to preserve a relationship). There are three basic components of interpersonal effectiveness training that are derived from aspects of all interactions: the goal of the interaction; the relationship; and feelings about oneself during and following the interaction (i.e., self-respect).

Restructuring cognitions about interpersonal relationships

Individuals with BPD subscribe to extreme, sometimes distorted assumptions regarding what it means to ask for help or to say no to an unwanted request. For example, they think that it is selfish to ask for what they want, or that they believe they cannot bear to ask for something and be refused. They believe that people will leave them if they say no. They insist that they should not have to ask for what they want, that people who are close to them should be able to read their minds and know what they need without being told. Thus, interpersonal skills training includes helping individuals to become more aware of and restructure these dysfunctional beliefs in order to promote more effective help-seeking behavior.

Identifying and prioritizing goals for interpersonal interactions

Once the cognitive restructuring takes place, patients are more open to the idea that they can and should learn how to ask for what they want or say no to what they don't want. However, before they can learn the skills for doing this, they are taught to do the homework of thinking through what they really want to achieve in an interaction with another person. By identifying and prioritizing their goals in advance, they can communicate more clearly and remain more mindful during the interaction.

Patients are taught that there are three types of goals that they may have in relationship to another person. The first goal is to be able to make a request or say no to another person's request. This is called the "objective" goal. The second goal has to do with how the patient wants the other person to think/feel about the patient at the end of interaction. For example, a clinician may reflect, "It may be very important to you that the person cares about you, likes you, or won't get angry with you." This is referred to as the "relationship" goal. The third goal is to maintain "self-respect" in relation to the other person.

Thus, making an effective interpersonal request (or saying no effectively) is a balancing act between getting what one wants, keeping the other person interested, and feeling good about oneself. To increase the likelihood of an effective interpersonal interaction, patients are encouraged to identify each of the three goals that they have in relation to the other person and to prioritize the goals. Ideally, all three goals can be achieved in a given interaction. However, it is very common that an objective goal might conflict with a relationship goal. Or an objective goal or relationship goal might conflict with a self-respect goal. For example, if an objective is to say no to an unwanted request, but the relationship goal is to avoid angering the person, there may be a conflict there. Individuals need to decide which goal is more important – saying no or avoiding the angry response. There is no right or wrong here – the individual is encouraged to be as honest as possible about prioritizing these goals.

Factors to consider when making or refusing a request

In addition to prioritizing goals, patients are taught to review certain factors that might determine how forcefully they make a request or say no to an unwanted request. After all, most interpersonal situations are not black and white, and in order to be skillful one has to consider the grey areas and circumstances that might contribute to effectiveness. This includes a realistic assessment of whether the person is able to give what is wanted or whether the patient is able to give what is being requested. Also important is learning how to find the best time for making the request or saying no, and making sure all the facts are at hand in order to make the request or to say no. The nature of the relationship makes a difference as well – is this person a peer, a supervisee or child, or someone in authority over the patient? Is the person a close friend or acquaintance? Individuals need to consider whether they have the right to ask for or say no to something. Finally, they need to think about whether asking or not asking, or saying yes or no, will result in long-term regret or resentment.

Once individuals are clear about goals and their priorities, and they have considered all of the extenuating circumstances, they are able to proceed with using the following skills to make the request.

Interaction objective skills: How to skillfully ask for something or say no

A very popular interpersonal skill with patients is called by the acronym DEAR MAN. It guides patients through an interaction and helps them be more effective when making a request or refusing a request. DEAR MAN stands for:

D Describe the situation
E Express your feelings about it
A Assert what you want (ask or say no)
R Reinforce for the person why it is in their interest to give you what you want
M Be Mindful
A Appear confident
N Negotiate

The first four steps, the "DEAR," are guidelines for what one does to make a skillful request. First, the individual describes the situation as objectively as possible in order to set the stage for what is being asked for. Then how the person feels about it is expressed, using "I" statements instead of accusatory "you" statements. Then the individual clearly asserts what is wanted. In order to increase the chances of getting what is wanted, the individual reinforces the other person by pointing out how it might be beneficial for that person to go along with the request.

The second three steps, the "MAN," are the guidelines for how to make the request. One of the most common pitfalls that detract from interpersonal effectiveness is the inability to stay on point. The other person might either deliberately or unwittingly try to derail the request by bringing up another topic. In order to be effective, patients have to stay mindful and keep bringing the conversation back to the request. Sometimes this requires being a "broken record" and continuing to repeat the request. It might also mean that any attacks or unwelcome comments might have to be ignored in order to stay on message.

Another important skill is to appear as if you feel confident in making your request. The tone of your voice and your body language should communicate that you feel that you have every right to make this request and expect that the other person will consider it. You may need to cheerlead yourself beforehand in order to cultivate a confident stance.

Finally, if after making a clear request, reinforcing the positive aspects of it, staying mindful and confident, the other person is still not ready to agree to it, and then it may be time to negotiate. This might mean offering a compromise, or "turning the tables" and asking the other person to suggest a solution. You should have a compromise ready beforehand so that you don't impulsively offer something that you are not really comfortable with.

Skills for maintaining relationships

The following skills, with the acronym GIVE, are guidelines for maintaining the relationship when the relationship goal is also a high priority.

G Be Gentle
I Act Interested in the other person
V Validate the other person's point of view
E Use an Easy manner

When patients are in wise mind they can easily understand that they attract more bees with honey than with vinegar. However, interpersonal interactions very quickly trigger patients to enter into an emotion mind state, and, therefore, these guidelines are in place to help them maintain a more effective interpersonal approach. In particular, it is a challenge to be interested in and validating of the other person's point of view when it is different. A dialectic synthesis is necessary to understand that it is a person's right to ask for something, or say no to a request.

Skills for maintaining self-respect

Last but not least, it is important to emerge from an interpersonal interaction with a sense of self-respect. The patient should consider how he wants to feel about himself following a particular interaction. The importance of this is evaluated by the patient and it helps determine the quality of the interaction. The acronym FAST stands for the guidelines for maintaining self-respect:

F Be Fair
A Don't be overly Apologetic
S Stick to your values
T Be Truthful

When we teach self-respect effectiveness, we emphasize the idea that self-respect should not be tied to whether or not the objective goal was achieved. After all, regardless of how skillful individuals are in making a request, the other person's response is not in their control and, therefore, cannot guarantee that they will like it or grant it.

By being fair, individuals ensure that they are not taking advantage of the other person and not provoking guilt in them. Patients are instructed to apologize only when they feel that they have done something wrong. They are also taught to refrain from over apologizing for things that are not their fault. Finally, they are encouraged to not compromise their values to get what they want or to get someone to like them because their self-respect is likely to suffer.

Emotion regulation skills

Ultimately, skillful functioning requires the ability to adequately regulate the emotional experience. The emotion regulation skills module approaches this complex task with a rich set of cognitive, behavioral, and mindfulness techniques. Emotion regulation skills include learning how to use mindfulness to observe and describe emotional states, and how to validate and accept one's emotional reactions. Erroneous assumptions regarding the experiencing of emotions are challenged and restructured. This module includes two ways in which individuals can regulate their emotions: change their emotional responses and reduce vulnerability to negative emotions while increasing the experience of positive emotions.

Challenging emotional myths

The experience of emotional dysregulation leads patients to develop distorted beliefs regarding emotions, beliefs that lead them to wish they did not have any feelings at all and that they could live in reasonable mind all of the time. As in the interpersonal effectiveness module, the emotion regulation skills begin with an exercise to identify and challenge "myths" about emotions, distorted beliefs that contribute to the ongoing cycle of emotional dysregulation. Patients may believe that being emotional equals being out of control, and that all negative emotions are destructive. The main take-home point is that emotions themselves are not bad; rather, it is the dysregulated quality of the emotional experience that is the problem. We often say that we do not want to "throw out the baby with the bathwater" and introduce the idea that emotions themselves are important and serve a survival function. The challenge is to learn how to experience emotions in a controlled way that can contribute to finding wise mind and gaining wisdom about what is needed while acting skillfully. We use the metaphor of taming a wild horse and learning how to take a great ride, controlling and guiding the powerful energy of the horse to get where you want to go.

The function of emotions

One of the goals of emotion regulation training is to help patients develop an appreciation of and respect for their emotions, and ultimately learn to validate their emotional experience. Emotions motivate action and help us communicate, and therefore serve a survival function. Patients learn to identify the survival function for and action urge associated with each emotion. For example, fear allows people to detect danger and motivates them to avoid or run away from a dangerous situation. Guilt helps people realize when they have done something wrong and gives them a chance to improve their behavior. Sadness helps individuals identify a loss or a need for something and motivates them to seek what is needed from others. Anger tells people that someone is threatening their safety or well-being and motivates fight behavior, which could include asserting oneself or one's boundaries, healthy competition, and ambition. When regulated, emotions help us out. When emotions are dysregulated, they can no longer serve their function. Fear becomes panic and can immobilize. Dysregulated guilt prompts people to become self-hating and self-punitive. Anger turns into rage and leads to explosive, destructive behaviors toward others and/or property. Sadness can turn into deep depression and feelings of hopelessness.

Model for observing and describing emotions

Aspects of an emotionally dysregulated experience include the perception that emotions happen for no reason, come out of the blue, and are experienced as a "big undifferentiated blob" of negative emotion. Individuals often are unable to label the specific emotion, what they are feeling and why. They are often unaware of the thoughts that might be driving the emotional experience. Sometimes they are not aware of a feeling at all, only that they are driven to act in a certain way that may cause a problem for them later. The emotional arousal happens extremely quickly and becomes all consuming, taking over awareness of cognitive and behavioral processes.

A model for observing and describing emotions breaks down the emotional experience into several components that can help increase awareness and a sense of control. First, patients are introduced to the idea that some type of prompting event triggers all emotional episodes, even if they are not able to identify it. This idea is reassuring in that patients no longer believe that they are crazy and feeling emotional for no reason. Patients work with their individual therapist to start to identify their emotional triggers.

In this model, the prompting event (trigger) leads to some sort of interpretation, an individual's attempt to make sense of the event. We work with patients to investigate the ways in which an interpretation might be distorted by their past traumatic experiences, automatic thoughts or core beliefs. A distorted interpretation can lead to an emotional reaction that may not seem to be appropriate to the current situation, leading the individual (or those around them) to think that the emotional reaction is "wrong." However, once you learn to identify a distorted interpretation, you can see that the emotional reaction makes complete sense based on the interpretation.

Cognitive restructuring can be applied to distorted interpretations. We approach this task using a balance of validation – "It makes sense that you may have interpreted the event in that way based on your past experiences….," and change – "…but this event is not the same as the past." Patients learn to identify automatic thoughts that lead to distorted interpretations. They can then learn how to "check the facts" and open themselves up to another, possibly more accurate, interpretation, which might then lead to a more regulated emotional response.

The next "chain" in the model is to examine the internal physiological and phenomenological components of the emotional reaction. Body sensations such as cold extremities, rising heat or racing heartbeat, butterflies in the stomach, the sense of feeling a certain way, an action urge, these are all components of the emotion that are not visible from the outside, and, therefore, difficult for the individual to trust or validate. In contrast, the external components include body language, verbal expression, and whatever action that is prompted by the emotion. As a result of years of invalidation and feeling the need to hide emotions, there is sometimes a discrepancy between the internal and external components of the emotional reaction, which adds to the confusion surrounding the emotion and awareness of how one is feeling. The "model of observing and describing emotions" serves to improve awareness of the various components of an emotional reaction: the ability to identify triggers, distorted interpretations, to identify and validate the internal aspects of the experience, and to reduce discrepancies between internal experience and external expression.

Primary and secondary emotions

Another factor contributing to emotional dysregulation is that patients have difficulty accepting their initial emotional experience. When a prompting event triggers an interpretation, which then leads to the experience of a particular emotion, the patient will often judge the emotion and/or invalidate it, and criticize him or herself for having the emotion. The original emotion is called the primary emotion and the emotional reaction the patient has to the primary emotion is thought of as the secondary emotion. Learning to accept the primary emotion goes a long way toward regulating the emotion. Often, the secondary emotion is what turns an emotional experience into a dysregulated experience. Usually, the secondary emotion involves feeling shame or anger at oneself for having the primary emotion. For example, a patient feels anxiety in a social situation. She has trouble accepting her anxiety and becomes angry with herself for feeling anxious. If she could self-validate and allow herself to understand her anxiety, she would not get angry with herself. Managing the primary emotion, the anxiety, would become much easier. The secondary emotion contributes to dysregulation because it has to do with negative self-judgment and emotional self-invalidation. Thus, patients can apply the model for observing and describing emotions to learn to accept and validate the primary emotion, as well as to recognize and prevent a secondary emotional reaction.

Reducing vulnerability to negative emotions

As we saw in Chapter 9, one of the steps in conducting a chain analysis is to identify the vulnerability that interacts with a trigger to lead to a dysregulated behavior. We can prevent an emotionally dysregulated episode by reducing the vulnerabilities. There are certain basic steps that everyone needs to take to stay on an even emotional keel. Individuals with BPD or who struggle with emotional lability often do not naturally incorporate these steps into their daily lives. In the emotion regulation module, we teach patients that when they follow healthy eating habits, make sure to get enough sleep and maintain a regular sleep/wake schedule, exercise, treat physical illness, and avoid mood altering substances, they increase their chances of being emotionally resilient in the face of life stressors. As humans, we are biologically wired to function on a circadian rhythm and our system is more easily regulated when we maintain some type of schedule. This is why it is recommended to introduce newborn babies to a feeding and sleeping schedule, in order to regulate their systems.

Invariably, when we inspect the day-to-day functioning of our patients, we identify a striking lack of schedule. They have difficulty sleeping, often stay up very late and sleep into the afternoon hours. They do not eat regular meals (particularly breakfast) and either restrict and binge or just grab a snack (usually not a healthy one) whenever they feel like it. This leaves them fluctuating between low blood sugar and sporadic sugar spikes, with accompanying feelings of fatigue, spurts of energy, and crashes. They often abuse substances and have difficulty engaging in regular exercise. They also do not consistently engage in self-care around their physical health.

Another crucial component of reducing emotional vulnerability is to experience a sense of mastery and productivity. Therefore, we work with patients to develop mastery by identifying tasks, short-term projects or short-term steps toward longer-term goals, that they can complete every day to help them feel a sense of accomplishment. We have also found that even when patients are masterful, they have a very difficult time acknowledging and self-reinforcing their skillful behaviors. We target this in treatment as well, helping patients cultivate the ability to self-reinforce and recognize their progress. Otherwise, they experience only the stress of working without the rewards, which over time can become demoralizing.

Increasing positive emotions

In addition to decreasing vulnerability to negative emotions, patients need to learn how to increase the amount of and ability to experience positive emotions in their lives. The DBT skills for increasing positive emotions include explicit emphasis on incorporating short-term positive events into life on a daily basis, as well as developing long-term goals that will ultimately generate ongoing positive experiences. This includes working on increasing close interpersonal relationships as well as cultivating long-term personal, perhaps vocational, goals that give life meaning and allow one to feel productive and accomplished.

In teaching skills, we have discovered that although patients crave relief from intense distress and negative emotions, they also have a very difficult time tolerating positive emotional states for a number of reasons. Sometimes it is because they experience the positive emotions in a dysregulated manner that resembles hypomania or even mania, which feels very out of control. But mostly, it is difficult for them to enjoy positive emotions because they feel a sense of vulnerability when they are feeling good. They can't trust that the positive emotion will last very long and they are afraid that they will feel even worse when the positive feelings end if they allow themselves to enjoy it. So, in order to protect themselves from what they fear will be crushing disappointment, they anticipate when it will end, consequently shortening the positive emotional experience. They also believe that they don't deserve to feel happy and this contributes to an inability to fully experience the positive. Thus, we teach patients to apply their mindfulness skills to control this type of negative thinking. Mindfulness can increase the capacity to stay in the moment with a positive feeling, and turn the mind away from worry thoughts about when the positive experience will end.

Mindfulness to the current emotion

Mindfulness practice teaches patients how to become less attached to their experience, to observe it and describe their experience without judgment. Mindfulness helps them enter into wise mind, the state of mind in which they can experience emotions without losing good judgment, while maintaining control over acting impulsively on the action urge that is associated with the emotion. Staying mindful of emotions also helps to not act impulsively to escape the emotional experience. The mindful emotional experience will be tolerable because it will be regulated and will not feel out of control. Being mindful of the emotion promotes acceptance and validation of the emotional experience. When individuals are mindful of emotions, they are able to experience them and gain wisdom from the emotion about how they are feeling, and about what they need.

Thus, DBT skills for applying mindfulness to the current emotion are to observe and describe the emotion, and to experience the emotion as a wave that starts off slowly, reaches a peak, and then subsides. By not acting on an emotion, or not getting stuck in ruminative thoughts about the emotion, emotions can run their natural course. This is called urge surfing. We remind patients that they are not their emotion, and that having a feeling doesn't automatically mean that they must act on it. They can even learn to accept and love their emotion rather than to judge it or invalidate it. The more control patient's gain over experiencing their emotions, the more they can learn to trust them.

Opposite action to emotion

The final emotion regulation skill is called opposite action to emotion and is based on behavioral principles of exposure and habituation. Avoidance of emotion contributes to emotional dysregulation in that there is no opportunity to learn how to face and experience the emotion. Learning how to block the escape from the emotion will lead to habituation and will ultimately result in changing the emotional experience. This involves acting opposite to the action urge. Thus, for example, when anxiety is urging someone to avoid a situation, the idea would be to approach instead of avoid. Approaching anxiety-producing situations reduces the experience of anxiety through habituation. Many people have this experience with performance anxiety around public speaking. By overcoming avoidance and accepting opportunities to speak in public (acting opposite), the fear of public speaking subsides once it is seen that there is no real danger.

Patients are taught to consider acting opposite to fear, shame, guilt, sadness, and anger and given homework assignments to practice. When fear or anxiety is overwhelming and leading to paralysis, opposite action would consist of making a list of small steps to take and then choosing to take the first step on the list. Regarding guilt, patients are taught to evaluate whether their guilt seems justifiable (did they really do something wrong?), or whether they are beating themselves up unjustifiably for something they did that was not wrong. If the guilt is justifiable, the opposite action steps are to apologize, make repairs, make a commitment to not make the same mistake in the future, accept the consequences gracefully, and let it go. If guilt is unjustifiable, opposite action dictates to keep repeating the behavior over and over until it can be done without feeling guilty. The opposite action to sadness is to mobilize rather than to isolate. Mobilization and being around people should alleviate feelings of sadness.

In terms of opposite action to feelings of anger, it is important to clarify that the feelings of anger are valid. Opposite action does not mean invalidation of the angry feelings. However, once a patient has been mindful and validating of her angry feelings toward someone, she may decide that she does not want to feel angry anymore. Engaging in opposite action, perhaps by doing something nice for the person or smiling at them, can help her come out of the anger. She does not have to self-validate by staying angry forever.

Summary

Four skills modules, mindfulness, interpersonal effectiveness, emotion regulation, and distress tolerance, are reviewed in this chapter. These skills with worksheets and handouts are described fully in the *Skills Training Manual* written by Linehan.

References

1. Miller, A., Rathus, J., Linehan, M.M. (2007) *Dialectical Behavior Therapy with Suicidal Adolescents*, Guilford Press, New York.
2. Hanh, T.N. (1976) *The Miracle of Mindfulness: A Manual on Meditation*, Beacon Press, Boston.
3. Hanh, T.N. (2009) *Happiness: Essential Mindfulness Practices*, Parallax Press, Berkeley.
4. Chodron, P. (1994) *Start Where You Are: A Guide to Compassionate Living*, Shambhala Publications, Waldshut-Tiengen.
5. Chodron, P. (2005) *When Things Fall Apart: Heart Advice for Difficult Times*, Shambhala Publications, Germany.
6. Kabat-Zinn, J. (1990) *Full Catastrophe Living: Using the Wisdom of Your Body and Mind to Face Stress, Pain and Illness*, Bantam Dell Press, New York.
7. Kabat-Zinn, J. (2012) *Mindfulness for Beginners: Reclaiming the Present Moment and Your Life*, Sound True, Inc., Canada.
8. Linehan, M.M. (1993) *Skills Training Manual for Treating Borderline Personality Disorder*, Guilford Press, New York.
9. Koerner, K. (2012) *Doing Dialectical Behavior Therapy. A Practical Guide*, Guilford Press, New York.

Chapter 12

Between-session contact and observing limits

Top 10 questions to be addressed in this chapter:

How do practitioners maintain limits when they fear it will trigger suicidal behavior and how do they refrain from inadvertently reinforcing suicidal behavior?

How do clinicians offer availability while placing manageable limits on between-session phone calls and requests for contact? In other words, how can clinicians expand their boundaries when appropriate without stretching them too far and how do clinicians keep from stretching them further and further and then abruptly ending the relationship?

How do clinicians handle emotionally dysregulated patients' angry and frantic requests for help in an effective manner?

Between-session contact between patient and therapist is one of the key features of DBT and enhances generalization and learning of new behaviors and coping skills because it gives the therapist the opportunity to work with the patient "in vivo" when they are most in need of using skills. This aspect of DBT is one reason why clinicians unfamiliar with the treatment believe it to be too burdensome for therapists and choose not to learn it. Clinicians who have not yet learned the treatment may think that DBT clinicians are on the phone with their patients continually. This is a misperception. In fact, clinicians who have learned DBT can find that they spend less but more effective time on the phone with their patients with BPD because DBT provides specific guidelines for when and how to have contact with patients between sessions. These guidelines provide a structure for intersession contact that aims to help patients when they need it (e.g., to refrain from engaging in NSSI or making a suicide attempt) and does not involve endless time on the phone.

The Dialectical Behavior Therapy Primer: How DBT Can Inform Clinical Practice, First Edition.
Beth S. Brodsky and Barbara Stanley.
© 2013 John Wiley & Sons, Ltd. Published 2013 by John Wiley & Sons, Ltd.

> **Key points**
>
> - In DBT, between-session contact between clinician and patients is encouraged for very specific purposes: skills coaching when the patients are struggling, patient reporting of "good" news, and repairing ruptures in the relationship with the clinician. We describe guidelines for brief, focused, and targeted between-session contact.
> - Between-session contact balances effective help-seeking behaviors with autonomous functioning on the part of the patients.
> - Techniques for establishing and maintaining the parameters for between-session contact include understanding the difference between natural and arbitrary limits, encouraging contact prior to engaging in self-injurious and suicidal behaviors, targeting the misuse of between-session contact in session, and gradual weaning from skills coaching.

In vivo skills coaching

In vivo exposure and practice is a core behavior therapy intervention and is used in many behavioral treatments including those for phobias, social anxiety, and obsessive-compulsive disorder. The clinician coaches patients and helps them use skills that enable them to tolerate a real-life fear-inducing situation such as flying, riding in an elevator, or eating in a restaurant that feels unclean [1]. Exposure is also used to treat avoidance behaviors.

Similarly, the DBT clinician plays the role of a skills coach, both within and between sessions, for the purposes of skills generalization. Patients learn skills in therapy, but need assistance in applying them within the context of their day-to-day life outside the consulting room. Between-session contact enables the clinician to have an immediate opportunity to coach the patients in using skillful behaviors at the moment when the patients need it.

Clinician availability for coaching is also aimed at averting crises. Patients are encouraged to contact the therapist to find ways of skillfully managing urges to self-harm or avoid engaging in destructive, impulsive behaviors. Clinicians respond to skills coaching calls for help in noncrisis situations as well, reducing the reinforcement that can result from being available *only* in a suicidal crisis, and expanding the opportunity for increased clinician contact in response to skillful help-seeking behavior.

The value and importance of being available between sessions

One of the most misunderstood aspects of DBT has to do with encouraging patients to seek between-session contact with the clinician for skills coaching, reporting good news, and therapeutic relationship repair. Clinicians not trained in the model often have a strong negative reaction to this aspect of the DBT. There is an assumption that patients will take advantage of this availability and bombard the clinician with constant calls of distress. Clinicians are concerned about being "on call 24/7" and not having a life outside work.

Many object to the practice on the grounds that the encouragement of calls for help induces pathological levels of dependency in the patients.

These concerns, while understandable when taken out of context, are based on a misunderstanding of this powerful change intervention. Clinicians may be skeptical and reluctant to make themselves available in this way when first starting to practice DBT. However, we have come to understand the value of being available at a time when a 5–10-minute skills coaching session can make the difference between skillfulness and self-destructiveness. We have been positively reinforced by the sense of efficacy that results by helping our patients learn to call us before they act impulsively, rather than wait to hear about it after the act, and to successfully intervene in preventing a self-destructive behavior.

Although it may on the surface appear to be an imposition and an extra time commitment to be available in this way, this intervention ultimately saves time by both reducing the number of crises that occur and preventing crises from lasting longer and spiraling more out of control. In addition, as clinicians who have taken on the challenge of working with chronically suicidal and impulsive individuals, we appreciate the fact that we can significantly reduce the amount of time and mental energy expended on worrying about them. Knowing that patients will call for coaching before they act destructively, and having the opportunity to speak with them when they are struggling, provides significant peace of mind and prevents burnout.

Guidelines for between-session interaction with patients must be in place in order to maintain such a therapeutic stance. We will describe the parameters of between-session contact between patients and clinician in DBT and the DBT techniques that balance effective help-seeking behaviors with the encouragement of autonomous functioning. These include: (a) observing natural limits; (b) the "24-hour" rule; (c) the chain analysis of therapy-interfering behavior; (d) encouragement of between-session contact as an appropriate skillful way of asking for help; (e) and graduated "weaning" from skills coaching as the patients incorporate more skillful behaviors.

Although being available for between-session contact might be a DBT intervention you would prefer NOT to incorporate into your psychotherapy practice, consider this. In the course of training non-DBT clinicians, we have heard numerous complaints about frequent between-session phone calls from high-need patients with BPD or other disorders of dysregulated emotional and behavioral functioning, such as eating disorders. In addition, there are all too frequent calls from ERs and frantic friends and family members about the patient's self-harm threats and behaviors. Because between-session contact is not an explicit feature of their therapeutic approach, these clinicians do not have a roadmap for fielding these phone calls. They often find themselves on the phone for extended periods of time, engaged in impromptu counseling sessions or crisis calls that feel emotionally draining and unproductive.

Or, clinicians who refuse to accept or return calls between sessions often face intense anger and resentment on the part of the patient during the session, which can also feel emotionally draining and unproductive. Both the lack of support and the negative feelings that this induces can severely impair therapeutic progress, in addition to increasing the chances that the patient will engage in self-destructive behavior. Such experiences lead to increased resentment and decreased motivation on the part of the clinician. These clinicians have come to appreciate and utilize the DBT guidelines and parameters as a framework for managing between-session contact with these types of patients, even in a non-DBT treatment.

Reporting good news

In addition to skills coaching, patients are permitted to call between sessions to report good news. Although one might think that this can wait until the next session, it is often the case that patients forget the good things that happen during the week and will not remember to report them in session. In addition, having a patient call to report success can serve as a reinforcer for the clinician. Finally, when patients know they can have contact with their therapists when things are going well, the contact they have when they are in crisis is not reinforcing. Patients will not think that the only way they can have contact with their therapist is if they are emotionally or behaviorally dysregulated.

Relationship repair

Between-session phone calls are also encouraged for relationship repair with the clinician. Patients with BPD often have a very difficult time tolerating a perceived rupture in a close relationship. When difficulties arise, between-session contact provides the opportunity to address them quickly in order to reestablish the personal connection necessary for a solid therapeutic alliance. If patients feel angry at their clinician for something that happened in session, they are encouraged to use interpersonal skills (see Chapter 11) to address it skillfully and directly. Or, conversely, if they are feeling guilt or regret for therapy-interfering behavior that was directed at the clinician, they are encouraged to call to repair the relationship.

Waiting until the next session is less desirable since it increases the disruption in the therapeutic relationship. Or, the feelings can be momentarily forgotten but still remain unresolved, leading to building resentment and a later disruption. In the worst-case scenario, these types of disruptions lead to premature termination on the patient's part, resulting in a lost opportunity to maintain the relationship.

Modes of skills training

In session

There are several modes of skills training in DBT. While skills are taught didactically in the skills training group (described in detail in Chapter 10), the individual therapy session and the therapeutic relationship is where patients are given direct guidance on how to incorporate skills into their lives. When conducting a chain analysis (Chapter 9), patients and clinicians engage in problem solving by identifying skills that patients can use in the next crisis situation. In addition, within session, clinicians stay alert to opportunities to coach patients in using a skill right then and there. For example, during the course of a chain analysis, the clinician may notice that the patient is having trouble concentrating and may suggest a mindfulness exercise to bring the patient back to the task at hand. When a patient becomes emotionally aroused in session, feeling extremely anxious or angry for instance, the clinician will observe this and assist the patient in emotional exposure and/or recommend distress tolerance skills. In this manner, in addition to learning skills, patients also begin to learn to recognize when they need to use them.

Between sessions

Thus, the basic guidelines for between-session calls, which should be made explicit to the patients at the outset of treatment, are the following:

1. Calls are for the purpose of skills coaching, reporting good news, or therapeutic relationship repair.
2. Clinicians aim at being very skills-focused.
3. Calls are time limited.
4. The patients need to respect the paging hours of the clinician.
5. The patients must call the clinician before engaging in NSSI and suicidal behavior, otherwise the 24-hour rule, designed to encourage contact PRIOR to self-injury, takes effect in which the patient is not permitted contact with the therapist for 24 hours after a self-injury.
6. Failure to call for coaching when it is needed will be addressed as therapy interfering.
7. Failure of the clinician to be available for between-session coaching is therapy interfering.
8. If the patients are not open to skills coaching when they call, the clinician encourages them to call back at a time when they are interested in skills coaching.
9. The clinician should respond to a request for skills coaching in a timely manner; the amount of time the patients should expect to hear back from the clinician should be made clear.
10. Once patients have left word for the clinician that skills coaching is needed, they are expected to use skills while they are waiting to hear from the clinician.
11. The clinician always assesses the suicide risk of the patient at the outset of an intersession contact to ensure that the patient is not at imminent risk. If the patient is imminently suicidal, the therapist intervenes to reduce the risk irrespective of the purpose of the call. Importantly, if the patient contacts the therapist following a self-injury episode but prior to the 24-hour period following the event, even though the clinician does not offer skills coaching during this time, the therapist still assesses suicidality to make sure that the patient is not at imminent risk.

While becoming accustomed to these parameters, it is common for patients to wonder how seriously distressed they need to be to initiate a phone call. A common misconception among patients (and sometimes clinicians) is that these calls for coaching should only happen when the patient is having urges to engage in self-harm behaviors. However, for a number of reasons, we encourage patients to call whenever they become aware of the need to use skills and their difficulty in doing so, preferably before the urge to act on an impulse gets too high. First, we want the opportunity to intervene as early as possible to prevent unskillful behavior. Second, we want the patient to learn how to identify the need for skills earlier on in the chain, so that they can prevent becoming too emotionally dysregulated in the first place, and prevent self-harm urges from getting too high. Third, once the patient is extremely distressed, it is more difficult to problem solve. And finally, but most importantly, we want to reinforce skillful help-seeking behavior by being available when the patient is NOT in crisis. Clinician availability in times of crisis may reinforce and, thereby, increase the occurrence of crises and crisis calls.

Thus, patients are encouraged to call or page individual clinicians between sessions whenever they require help in implementing skills, including when they are fighting urges to engage in self-destructive (or other unskillful) behaviors. Patients are instructed to try skills on their own prior to contacting the therapist and, with this expectation in mind, the clinician will ask patients what skills they have tried. During these phone contacts, the clinician and patients decide upon a number of skillful ways of handling the current stressful situation. Rather than resulting in constant calling by the patients, the phone skills coaching is conducted in such a way as to make the clinician feel more effective and more motivated to help the patients.

Phone contacts are time-limited, focused, and very targeted – limited to skills coaching and therapeutic relationship repair. If the patient calls but is upset and wants to vent but is not open to problem solving, the clinician indicates in a nonjudgmental manner that the call is to be limited to skills coaching. This approach stands in contrast to descriptions of phone contact that we heard from therapists not practicing DBT in which patients call to express their distress at a current situation and the phone call becomes quite lengthy without a particular focus or goal. This can result in a situation where calls become more frequent and lengthier and the therapist feels resentful but is hesitant to change course for fear that the patient will feel terribly rejected and become enraged or engage in self-harm behavior.

If the patient does not want to discuss what skills to use, the call is ended. If skills coaching is agreed upon, clinician and patient quickly review which skills the patient has already tried, and the clinician cheerleads and helps the patient generate a plan to try new skills. The clinician directly praises the patient for calling and validates the difficulty of asking for help, tolerating the pain and trying a new behavior. These contacts usually do not have to exceed a period of about 10–15 minutes, often result in the prevention of self-injury, and therefore are positively reinforcing for the clinician (if not the patient). If the clinician is skillful in observing these parameters during phone coaching calls, appropriate use of these phone calls is quickly learned and skillful help-seeking behavior is shaped.

Structure of a time-limited phone coaching interaction

A basic format for a 10–15-minute phone coaching session would consist of the following steps:

1 *Reinforce patients for reaching out for help.* Surprisingly, in most cases, it is difficult for patients to take this step and they need reassurance that they are not bothering you. However, even with a patient who calls too easily for help, the clinician can praise the patient for wanting to use skills. ("I'm so glad you called and want to use skills.")

2 *Assess the current emotional state of the patient.* If patients are emotionally dysregulated, the first step is for the clinician to soothe, praise, and validate in order to calm them down enough to proceed with skills coaching. Use a calm, reassuring tone, explain that you want to help and can only do so if they calm down.
3 *Ascertain the reason for the call.* Encourage patients to succinctly describe the current situation. The clinician should evaluate whether the patient is interested in skills coaching or relationship repair. For skills coaching, the clinician should try to get enough detail to be able to know what type of skill to suggest. If the patient is not interested in skills coaching, the clinician should encourage the patient to find some willingness to engage in skills coaching.
4 *Find out whether the patient has tried any skills before calling.* Unless the patient is fairly new to DBT, the clinician should inquire about whether the patient already tried to use skills. In later stages of the treatment, patients will be expected to do so.
5 *Suggest skills.* The clinician can offer a number of skills and ask if the patient feels able to try them. Patient and clinician collaborate on a plan of skillful action. Sometimes, distress tolerance skills are appropriate. At other times, mindfulness, interpersonal effectiveness, and emotion regulations skills are called for. Common skills for the immediate situation are: distraction, self-soothing (including skills for reducing physiological arousal – "other sensations"), improving the moment, pros and cons, using a "DEAR MAN" to effectively communicate with someone else, building mastery, and finding "wise mind" (see Chapter 11).
6 *Cheerlead.* The clinician should encourage and express faith in the patient to follow through on this plan.
7 *Ending the call.* Unless the patient is extremely suicidal and unable to utilize the skills coaching, the call can end. Otherwise, the clinician continues with crisis intervention (see Chapter 13).

Non-DBT therapists often feel that patients with BPD will jump at the opportunity to contact their therapist between sessions and that their lives will be consumed by these calls. Surprisingly, it is more often the case that patients do not naturally take advantage of clinician availability for skills coaching. For example, a study of the use of DBT phone coaching in an eating disorder program found that individuals who engaged in NSSI were much less likely to utilize the phone coaching than were individuals whose main symptoms were eating disorder related [2]. In this study, which was conducted on a population of 17 patients enrolled in a five-day-a-week eating disorder program, only 50% of the patients utilized the phone coaching. Although this small study is not generalizable to outpatient DBT psychotherapy for individuals with BPD, it does provide some preliminary data demonstrating that many patients tend to not use (much less abuse) after-hour availability. Patients are reluctant to call for a number of reasons: (a) they have been told in the past that they are too needy and that their neediness has burned out the caregivers in their lives; (b) at the moment of crisis, they do not think about reaching out for help; (c) they know that if they call, they will be encouraged to tolerate distress in a new, more skillful way and they do not know if it will help them; (d) they invalidate their own pain, and expect the clinician to also invalidate their reason for calling, and so decide that the issue is not important enough to ask for help with; (e) they are afraid to hear that it may be an inconvenient time for the clinician and therefore will feel rejected; (f) they do not necessarily want help with using skills, and they may initially feel that they just want someone to listen to them as they describe their painful state.

Making the phone call is often more difficult than relying on past tried and true (albeit unskillful) behaviors. For this reason, calls for coaching are not merely offered to the patients. They are a principal change intervention in DBT, and the learning of this new, appropriate help-seeking behavior is directly targeted. More often than not, the clinician needs to shape this help-seeking behavior by making an intersession phone call as a homework assignment. Patients are praised for making the call and the difficulty of asking for help in this way is validated. Failure to call for coaching when necessary is targeted as therapy-interfering behavior. Early on, if the patient does not make the call at the agreed upon time, the clinician can reach out and initiate the call. This serves powerful therapeutic goals in that the desired behavior is encouraged and shaped even though the clinician has to initiate it at first and it also lets patients know that they remain on their clinician's radar screen even when they are not in session.

For clinicians who are not adopting the full DBT model, using phone call contact in the way we describe is viable. Clinicians can simply explain the purpose of phone contact and the rationale for adhering to this approach. This will help focus both the patient and the therapist on how a call can be used productively and helps maintain boundaries to phone contact. This approach will ultimately help therapists feel more able to maintain rather than avoid phone contact while moving the therapeutic process along more quickly by helping patients apply skills at the moment they most need them.

Case example

Encouraging Skills Coaching

CLINICIAN (during an individual session with Julie): I have noticed that the past couple of weeks you have been struggling with urges to cut yourself and have not called me for coaching. I would really like to be able to help you when you feel that way instead of finding out when you come in for session that you have cut yourself.

JULIE: Well, I did think about calling you, but I didn't want to bother you.

CLINICIAN: It bothers me more that you ended up cutting yourself. But I can understand that it might take a while for you to believe that I would welcome a phone call for coaching. How about a homework assignment – call me once this week just to let me know how you are doing, whenever you feel like it, not necessarily when you are having a difficult time. Maybe that would be easier for you.

JULIE: Okay, I will try that.

A few days later...

JULIE (calling for coaching): I am calling because I am having urges to overdose on my meds and I remembered that you said you would rather hear from me before I do anything.

CLINICIAN: Absolutely! It's great that you called. I'm sorry you are having urges to overdose. I'm hoping you want to work with me to make sure that you do not do so.

> JULIE: I am really having a hard time concentrating on my schoolwork and I feel like giving up and just killing myself. But maybe you can help me figure out how to get some work done. I have a paper due in a few days and I haven't even started.
>
> CLINICIAN: I would really like to help you with that. What is getting in the way of doing your work?
>
> JULIE: I keep feeling that I am a failure. I can't seem to get started with this paper. Even if I write something, it won't be good. I will never be able to get my degree and get a job.
>
> CLINICIAN: I can see that you are judging yourself, and thinking too far into the future and convincing yourself that you will never get what you want. It makes sense that this will interfere with being able to focus on doing your paper now. Would you be willing to do some mindfulness and staying focused on the present? How about just sitting down at the computer and spending one hour writing down any of your thoughts about this paper, without judgment and without it being in "perfect" form. After that, you can take a break, maybe do something self-soothing.
>
> JULIE: Just one hour! I will never be able to finish my paper on time!
>
> CLINICIAN: Just tonight – one hour. Then you can call me tomorrow and we will continue to take it one step at a time.
>
> JULIE: Okay – I will sit down and do what I can for an hour, then I will bake some cookies and call my mother.
>
> CLINICIAN: Great! Let me know how it goes and call me again if you need more help staying in the moment and nonjudgmental with the paper.
>
> JULIE: Okay.

Often, as in this case, a 5–10-minute consultation is enough to help the patients ride through a brief emotional episode without acting impulsively in a way that would result in long-term negative consequences. The effectiveness of the clinician's intervention lies in being able to help the patient get some perspective, and offer a concrete course of action coupled with a supportive, cheerleading presence so that the individual does not feel alone in taking on the challenge of trying a new behavior and tolerating the distress.

Of course there are those patients who do not appropriately use the phone calls by calling for purposes that are not agreed upon, or by calling more frequently than needed and responding in a demanding or help-rejecting manner. This behavior is targeted matter-of-factly in treatment (Target 2 therapy-interfering behavior) and distress tolerance skills are taught and encouraged.

Conversely, there are patients who only call when they have already begun or completed a self-injurious act. The appropriate balance between constant/inappropriate calling and not calling on time or at all involves a dialectic synthesis toward developing appropriate help-seeking behavior.

Twenty-four-hour rule

The '24-hour rule' [3], built in as an aversive consequence for self-injury, as an encouragement to not engage in self-destructive behavior and to reach out for help prior to engaging in the behavior, states that patients cannot call the clinician for 24 hours after they have engaged in self-injury (any Target 1 behavior). If a patient calls her clinician after the act, the clinician, once ascertaining that the patient is safe from further self-harm, expresses regret that the patient did not contact him before engaging in the behavior and reminds the patient that she can resume contact after a 24-hour period. If the patient seems suicidal, the clinician can proceed with crisis intervention, which means coaching or helping her to get whatever assistance she needs to stay safe. Otherwise, the clinician expresses to the patient that he wishes she would have called sooner to receive skills coaching and support. The clinician then expresses the desire to hear from her as soon as the 24-hour period is over if she needs skills coaching. Thus, patients are encouraged to call before they engage in self-harm behavior, giving the clinician a chance to intervene. The 24-hour rule does not extend to therapy sessions, so that if patients engage in self-harm, they are encouraged to attend a scheduled therapy session within the following 24-hour period.

Enforcing the 24-hour rule can be very difficult for both patients and clinicians, especially clinicians new to DBT. Often patients feel abandoned by the clinician at a time of high need. The clinician may end the call feeling worried about whether the patient's anger will lead to further self-injury. In these cases, there are a number of points to consider: (a) although this intervention may seem harsh, it is effective in shaping help-seeking behavior in the future; (b) the clinician can contact a colleague to review what happened, to get support, and to decide on a course of action if necessary; (c) one of the more confusing aspects of self-injury and suicide attempts in these individuals is that they often feel better after they have acted on these impulses (see Chapter 6). Thus, in many cases, the urge to self-injure is not as strong since they have already engaged in the behavior.

For clinicians who are not practicing the full DBT model, applying the 24-hour rule may be difficult. However, the basic principle of encouraging patients to call prior to engaging in self-injury rather than afterward is an approach that can be used by clinicians generally. Clinicians can explain in a straightforward manner that the goal is to help patients eliminate their self-injury and the most effective way to do so is to contact the therapist prior to the self-injury in order to help the patient not self-injure.

The 24-hour rule is an extremely powerful aversive consequence, and often is not needed more than once with the same patient. Patients quickly learn that they must call before they engage in self-harm, and this promotes therapy-enhancing calls for skills coaching.

Addressing therapy-interfering behavior

In the event that patients do not comply with the guidelines for contacting the clinician between sessions, the behavior is targeted in session as therapy-interfering. Examples of such therapy-interfering behaviors include rejecting every suggestion the therapist makes out of hand, telling the therapist that the skills coaching is making them worse, or hanging up on the therapist.

> ## Case example
>
> CLINICIAN (During the agenda setting in the individual session with Alice): It's great that you didn't engage in any self-harm behaviors this week, Alice. And I am glad that you called me for coaching – did it help you fight the urges?
>
> ALICE: Yes, I ended up using the skills that we talked about over the phone to not cut myself.
>
> CLINICIAN: That is really great. When you use skills after we have spoken on the phone, that is therapy-promoting behavior. I did want to raise the issue of one particular phone message that you left me that I felt was therapy interfering, though.
>
> ALICE: I know, I left that message on your voice mail saying that your coaching wasn't helpful and that I was going to hurt myself anyway.
>
> CLINICIAN: Yes, and although I am so glad that you didn't harm yourself, it was very distressing for me at the time to hear that message, and then I couldn't reach you to find out whether you were okay.
>
> ALICE: I know it was not right to leave that message, and then to not answer your calls, but at the time I was really angry, I felt that you didn't get how bad I was feeling, and I couldn't control myself.
>
> CLINICIAN: So let's do a behavioral analysis and see what was going on and how you could learn to express your anger more skillfully next time. And also then maybe I can better understand how you are feeling at those times and what I can say that might be more helpful. Is there anything else you want to add to the agenda for this session?
>
> ALICE: If we get a chance, I'd like to talk about a fight I had with my mother.
>
> CLINICIAN: Okay, let's try to do both.

In this example, the clinician places a chain analysis of the therapy-interfering behavior, related to an inappropriate between-session phone message left by the patient, on the agenda. Since this is a strong change intervention, and one that can become easily upsetting to the patient and can discourage skillful use of between-session phone calls, the clinician used a lot of validation and nonjudgment in raising the issue. The possibility that the clinician may have been therapy-interfering (by not responding in the most understanding manner) is also alluded to so that the behavioral analysis is presented as an opportunity to identify how both parties could have been more skillful.

Without judgment, assumptions, or interpretations of the patient's anger or sense of entitlement, the clinician initiates a behavioral analysis in the individual therapy session. This analysis is conducted to examine and determine the thoughts, feelings, and events that led to the behavior, and to generate solutions and apply skills to the reduction of this behavior (see Chapter 9 for details regarding conducting a behavioral analysis).

The clinician validates any aspects of the patients' experience that seem valid. Examples of such validation include acknowledging the pain of their distress, or understanding that skills coaching may have been experienced as criticism or being accused of "wrong" behavior. At the same time, this acceptance of pain and difficulty is balanced by a clear emphasis on the fact that the behavior is interfering with the therapy and must change.

When the therapeutic alliance is strong and in place, the clinician can also use Level 6 validation (see Chapter 6) in this situation. This would mean that clinicians would be "radically genuine" with patients about how their unskillful use of between-session contact is making it difficult for the clinician to stay motivated to help. Clinicians state that they do not want this to happen and, therefore, clinicians and patients need to help patients figure out how to not push clinicians away.

Arbitrary versus natural limits

Clinician availability for skills coaching between sessions within these parameters represents the dialectic synthesis between the two opposite poles of intervention – complete availability under any circumstance 24 hours a day versus no availability at all between sessions. The "no availability" extreme on this continuum represents what DBT refers to as an arbitrary therapeutic limit [4]. An arbitrary limit is one that is based on a general theory or belief regarding how things should be in all or most circumstances, rather than on a close examination regarding the specific circumstances of a situation or characteristics of an individual. Many forms of therapy often discourage between-session contact, for example, based on the idea that the "frame" of treatment necessitates that the therapy occur only in the consulting room at the scheduled time [5, 6].

Based on this definition of the frame of therapy, patients' requests for between-session contact may be viewed as pathological in some way. Either the patients are too needy, or they are feeling entitled to more than they should need. Or the patients are not respectful of the frame or boundaries of the treatment. Requests for contact between sessions are, therefore, experienced as burdensome by clinicians and as work that they should not have to do and as possibly counter-therapeutic. In many therapeutic approaches, the parameters of treatment are the same regardless of the individual needs and characteristics of different patients and clinicians.

From a DBT perspective, the sense of burden clinicians experience vis-à-vis their borderline patients stems in part from the arbitrary limits of conventional therapy, rather than from the level of need of the patients. The dialectical assumptions (see Chapter 6) can be useful in reframing the clinician's interpretation of a patient's need for between-session contact, replacing the sense of burden with a therapy-enhancing experience of efficacy.

The symptomatology of BPD challenges the effectiveness of conventional therapeutic boundaries. Individuals with BPD struggle with impulsivity, emotional lability, and mood-dependent behavior. The emotional state of patients at any given point in time, during a therapy session, for instance, is not indicative of their level of functioning between sessions. Their behavioral dysregulation and chronic suicidal ideation often results in revolving-door inpatient hospitalizations [7] that are demoralizing and life-disrupting. These patients require additional support if they are to maintain the minimum level of safety and functioning to sustain their outpatient status. Expecting them to manage their impulses on their own in the time period between sessions leaves them more vulnerable to behaviors that can at best severely set back their progress in building a stable life with a steady occupation and enduring relationships and at worst can result in death. The negative impact of repeated hospitalizations cannot be underestimated – job loss, loss of living situation, interruptions in schooling, and relationship disruptions.

Another example of an arbitrary limit is "technical neutrality." This is a psychoanalytic concept first defined by Anna Freud, meaning that the clinician takes a stance that is equidistant from each of the three "parts" of the psyche as defined by Sigmund Freud – the id, the ego, and the superego [8]. This concept of neutrality seems to have translated into a particular therapeutic stance that prompts clinicians to respect the patients' space and discourages direct inquiry. This is often experienced by the borderline patients as uncaring, which can breed resentment in clinicians who feel that their well-meaning efforts are being willfully misinterpreted. In DBT, a "neutral" stance on the part of the clinician when the patient is in need of a more direct intervention can be considered therapy-interfering behavior on the part of the clinician. So, for example, in DBT, calculated self-involving self-disclosure on the part of the clinician is a stylistic strategy that is encouraged as a form of validation, problem solving, skills training, contingency management, and exposure.

Observing natural limits

Arbitrary limits, and the assumptions that underlie them, can be counterproductive in the treatment of BPD. In DBT, clinicians are encouraged to observe "natural" limits regarding their availability and in the ways they use self-disclosure. Thus, although some type of between-session availability on the part of the clinician is a requirement of DBT, the parameters of this availability are determined by the clinician's natural limits.

Self-disclosure on the part of the clinician is an example of a stylistic strategy encouraged to promote normalization of the patient's experience (Level 5 validation), and which can also encourage problem solving and emotional exposure. The extent to which a clinician is willing to self-disclose, in the service of helping the patient, is subject to natural limits that exist within the clinician in relationship to a particular patient at that moment in time.

DBT clinicians are encouraged to question whether the limits they are observing are arbitrary ones, based on non-DBT assumptions. With the assistance of the consultation team (see more in Chapter 15), clinicians are encouraged to explore and become as aware as possible of their natural limits regarding availability and self-disclosure. Natural limits are to be monitored and communicated clearly to patients.

Natural limits are, by definition, different from one clinician to the next. They can also differ within the same clinician regarding different patients, or within the same clinician across different life circumstances or situations. Some natural limits seem clear – for example, a clinician who tends to be a "night owl" may not mind being available for skills coaching later in the evening, while an "early bird" clinician would. However, more often than not, identifying one's natural limits can be quite challenging, especially when as a clinician you experience your limits differently with different patients. Sometimes this is a trial-and-error process, since clinicians may not be aware of their natural limits until they feel they have been overstepped. Clinicians agree during the commitment phase to make every reasonable effort to help patients. When a patient is experiencing a crisis, or is in extreme pain, the concept of what is reasonable versus what is beyond the clinician's limits may become unclear and confusing.

Physical touch in psychotherapy is another area in which natural limits can be explored. While zero tolerance for any type of sexual contact with patients is a clear limit that must be observed, other forms of nonsexual physical expressions of affection or caring such as an encouraging pat, a handshake, or a supportive hug are interventions that promote warm engagement and are sometimes experienced as helpful to patients. Therapists are encouraged to explore their natural comfort (or discomfort) level with these types of interventions and to proceed with caution while observing their own personal limits. Such exploration might result in the therapist being very clear that they are NOT comfortable with any type of physical touch and that this is a limit that will be observed. However, this determination will be a result of an exploration of one's natural limits rather than on arbitrary boundary setting.

Case example

Eleanor started DBT about three months ago and has worked very hard to get her self-harm behaviors (head banging) under control. She attends individual and group skills training regularly and on time. She has been reluctant to call for coaching. She thinks about calling but feels a sense of shame about needing to ask for help. She also does not want to make herself vulnerable to her therapist in this way. Also, she knows that she will feel very accountable for using skills if she calls for coaching and, therefore, she is ambivalent about putting herself into a situation in which she fears she will not be able to find relief from her urges. After conducting a chain analysis around these thoughts and feelings, Eleanor took the plunge and started to call for coaching, which resulted in successfully using skills to ride through urges without banging her head. At this point in the treatment, she began to ask her therapist for a hug at the end of the session, since she was feeling closer to her therapist and more willing to ask for what she needed and for support. The therapist, at first, thought she was willing to hug her. Over the course of the next few months, it became clear that Eleanor was expecting a hug after each session. The therapist observed in herself a growing discomfort with this and started to feel very put upon by this expectation. It felt especially uncomfortable for the therapist to hug Eleanor on weeks in which Eleanor engaged in her head banging behavior. The therapist was feeling that she was "rewarding" and therefore positively reinforcing the self-harm behavior. The therapist, in consultation with her team, thought carefully about why she was feeling so uncomfortable with the "hugs on demand," and became clearer about her own personal boundaries. Although she was nervous about broaching this with Eleanor, she also knew that in order to maintain a positive therapeutic stance toward Eleanor she would have to communicate her personal limits. Not making her limits clear to Eleanor would constitute therapy-interfering behavior. The therapist decided to put this on the agenda in the next session.

THERAPIST (after reviewing the diary card and identifying a quality-of-life goal to target): Eleanor, in addition to talking about your phone call with your mother, I have a difficult issue to raise having to do with therapy-interfering behavior on my part. I have a feeling that this will be upsetting for you but I am bringing it up because I want to make sure nothing gets in the way of our therapy. It has to do with the hugs at the end of session – I have been becoming more uncomfortable with them. It has nothing to do with you – it has to do with my own personal limits. I have not been clear with you about them and that is my fault.

ELEANOR (VISIBLY UPSET): What's wrong with needing a hug? Why is it uncomfortable for you? You have been asking me to rely on you by calling for coaching, and I have been feeling closer to you, and have been starting to trust you, and now you are saying that I am too needy! This is exactly what I was afraid of!

THERAPIST: You have every right to be angry and upset with me. You have been working really hard and doing so well in therapy. I know that you have been taking risks. I want to encourage you and to be a support for you. And there is nothing wrong with wanting and needing hugs – I am not thinking that you are too needy. I really want you to understand that I think you deserve to get what you need, including hugs.

My feelings about the hugs have nothing to do with you. They are a personal limit of mine that I would like to explain to you if you are willing to hear me out.

ELEANOR: Go ahead.

THERAPIST: Thanks, I really appreciate your willingness to listen. Eleanor, when you first asked for a hug, I felt that I wanted to support you, especially since you had taken the risk of calling for coaching. At the time I didn't pay attention to some feelings of discomfort that I had. But as time has gone on, and the hug became kind of automatic at the end of each session, my discomfort with it became more apparent to me. I have thought about it a lot to try to understand what exactly is uncomfortable for me about it. First of all, I am not an overly physically demonstrative person. In my personal life, I am not quick to hug people. That is a particular personal characteristic of mine. Second, the fact that it became something automatic at the end of each session made it feel forced to me, and it took away the opportunity for me to feel like giving you a hug. I was wondering if it felt real to you – it didn't feel real to me.

ELEANOR: But I need the hug! It is the only hug I get all week! It does feel good!

THERAPIST: I totally agree that you need the hug. You need the hug, and I need to observe my personal limits, which are to be able to have the opportunity to hug you when I also feel like it. My limits prevent me from hugging you as often as you need. That doesn't mean that you shouldn't need or want it.

ELEANOR: I don't know – I am really angry at you. I do hear what you are saying though. I will have to think about it.

THERAPIST: Okay, you definitely should think about it and please tell me what you are thinking. I am hoping that we can continue to talk about it and work it out together.

Over the course of the next few sessions, Eleanor was able to express her anger with her therapist and was also able to radically accept her therapist's limits because she felt validated for wanting and needing the hugs and for being angry about not being able to have them. After a few months, Eleanor came into session and shared a personal achievement with the therapist. The therapist felt that she wanted to give Eleanor a hug, told her so, and asked her if it would be okay. Eleanor was very pleased and said yes.

By observing natural limits with BPD patients, the therapeutic relationship with DBT clinicians is providing a model for the negotiations and interactions that must be learned for effective interpersonal functioning across all life situations. In any given interpersonal interaction, it is necessary to learn to respect the natural limits of the individual with whom you are engaged. These limits vary depending on a number of variables, including temperament, the nature and definition of the relationship, and life circumstances. The same is true for the clinician – individual temperament and life circumstances have an impact on the extent to which the clinician is available, willing to self-disclose, etc.

A real learning opportunity presents itself when the clinician's natural limits conflict with a natural need of the patient. There is a dialectic tension between the need of clinicians to observe their personal limits and the real need of patients to have, for instance, greater availability on the part of the clinician. Again DBT assumptions can be of use here in nonjudgmentally framing the situation as a dialectic that needs synthesis, rather than as an aggressive, selfish attempt on the part of the patient to transgress boundaries. Observing arbitrary limits does not prepare an individual for the differences in limits that they experience with different people and in different situations in their lives. This may be one of the aspects of conventional therapy that cause patients to feel that the therapeutic relationship is not a "real" relationship.

> **Case example**
>
> Cary requested a late evening therapy appointment time due to her work schedule. Although it was not very convenient for the therapist, he decided to accommodate her request. After a few months, Cary requested another change in her therapy appointment time from the evening to late afternoon so that she could start a yoga class that only met on that evening. Cary knew that a patient in the skills group met with the therapist before group and she wanted the therapist to ask that patient to switch appointment times with her. She became enraged with the therapist for not agreeing to do so. She thought the therapist could do more to support her in starting her yoga practice, which was part of her plan to become more skillful, and she did not understand why he was not willing to do this for her. She accused the therapist of never doing anything helpful for her. This made him extremely angry since he had gone out of his way originally to see her later in the evening. His anger made him very reluctant to go out of his way to switch his schedule around again, even though he knew it was possible and he would be willing to do if for a patient who was more appreciative, less angry, less demanding, and would not make him feel coerced. He had to think carefully about his natural limits. If he offered to change his schedule for her again, would his resentment interfere with his ability to maintain a therapeutic stance? Or if he did not offer her this time, would he be unnecessarily withholding and behaving in a therapy-interfering manner?

The dilemma of this DBT clinician may not be an issue in therapeutic approaches where clinicians are not encouraged to explore their natural limits. In such a situation, arbitrary limits of non-DBT therapy would clearly prevent the clinician from accommodating the patient's request for another change in schedule. In conventional therapy, the assumption is that it is in the patient's best interest to refrain from "gratification" [9, 10] of such requests, which might short-circuit a full exploration of the feelings and expectations that are being expressed. Alternatively, some approaches would suggest changing the schedule without any examination of personal limits and reactions.

From the DBT perspective, it is more helpful to the patient for the clinician to either grant or refrain from requests after an honest assessment of the patient's needs and the ability of the clinician to accommodate them.

Guidelines for observing natural limits regarding between-session availability

While clinician availability for between-session in vivo skills coaching is a requirement of DBT practice, the specifics regarding what the patients can expect regarding when and how the clinician is available is subject to the clinician's natural limits.

Hours of availability

Most DBT clinicians we have worked with are available for skills coaching every day, including weekends, except for vacation days or other times in which their work or weekend schedule interferes with their ability to answer calls. During the week, some clinicians limit their availability in the evening. Others request a "blackout period" in the evening hours and then resume their availability later. Often these determinations are based on differences in sleep patterns, evening work/recreational schedules, and family obligations. DBT clinicians arrange paging coverage when they are on vacation or unavailable for an extended period of time. In standard DBT, clinicians are expected to be available 24/7. We have made modifications to this in our private practice. We observe our natural limits regarding availability for coaching and explain to our patients that if they call late or in the middle of the night, we may be asleep, or we will be too tired to be able to provide effective coaching. We encourage them to call as soon as they are aware that they might be heading for trouble, preferably during the evening hours.

Immediacy of response to a call, message, or page

Clinicians should make every effort to respond in as timely a manner as possible when contacted for skills coaching. This does not mean that the clinician must drop everything in order to answer a call immediately. During the orientation to treatment, clinicians should inform the patients as to what they should expect regarding response time. We tell our patients that we will answer a call or message as soon as we can. However, this could mean that they may have to wait an hour, in some cases even between two and three hours. For example, DBT clinicians do not interrupt a session with one patient to return a call of another. Patients are expected to use skills while they are waiting to hear back from the clinician. Clinicians and patients can devise a list of skillful behaviors for the patients to try during the waiting period. Whenever possible, we return a call immediately, even if it is just to tell the patient that we cannot talk at this moment and to set up a time to speak later on at our mutual convenience. We also encourage our patients to contact us again if they have not heard from us, since phone calls or voice mail messages sometimes do not go through.

In some cases, depending on the patient and the situation, we have found that it may be helpful to take a little time to respond to a call in order to provide the patient with an opportunity to use skills on his or her own. This is when the patient calls only when he or she is in a state of emotional dysregulation, and the clinician knows the patient well enough to have confidence that the patient will wait to hear back before engaging in suicidal behavior. When the clinician calls back immediately, the patient is unable to calm down and unable to utilize the coaching. However, by waiting 20–30 minutes, the clinician will reach the patient in a calmer state because he or she has left the message, "shared his or her distress," and has had the opportunity to use skills on his or her own. At that point, the coaching is much more effective. Thus, over time and experience with particular patients, clinicians can gauge the most effective timing.

Paging versus phone messages, emergency versus nonemergency calls

DBT clinicians vary in terms of how they would like to be contacted and for what reason. When we were first trained in DBT we used pagers. Since that time, we have found it more convenient to use our cell phones. Some clinicians are not comfortable giving out their personal cell phone numbers. In such cases, there are other modalities for contact. Using a number (e.g., Google phone numbers) that can forward calls to a cell phone or landline is a good option. Some clinicians welcome and encourage nonemergency pages for coaching in order to intervene to prevent a crisis. Others prefer to be paged only in an emergency, and otherwise they check their phone messages frequently to pick up nonemergency requests for skills coaching. With the advent of e-mail and texting, it is important for the clinician to be very clear regarding whether or not these forms of communication or contact are acceptable. In general, we advise that clinicians who are comfortable communicating with their patients through e-mail or texting do so for scheduling purposes only, and not for actual skills coaching. Although we realize that sometimes text messaging is the most effective way to reach our patients, and we use it if necessary in an emergency, we strive to set the expectation for and observe the limit of conducting coaching person to person through direct phone calls.

Missed calls. Invariably, a clinician unintentionally misses a call, either because they do not hear it, it does not go through, or the phone is accidently shut off or on vibrate mode. Such an occurrence provides an opportunity for problem solving, skills coaching, and dialectic synthesis in the individual therapy session. The clinician can validate the patient's anger, the difficulty of reaching out for help and then receiving no response, and the feelings of abandonment and disappointment. What are the patient's interpretations of why the clinician did not return the page? The clinician and patient can explore whether the view is in line with the actual reason or not. Perhaps the interpretation is distorted in terms of the current situation but valid in terms of the patient's past history with disappointment and abandonment.

How can patients use skills to handle the anger and disappointment? They can use emotion regulation skills to observe and describe their interpretations and to generate alternative interpretations. They can recognize that they do not know why the clinician did not call back and can use distress tolerance skills to tolerate not knowing instead of assuming that their interpretation is correct before checking it out.

Often patients invalidate their own anger, and try to talk themselves out of it because they know that the clinician did not intend to disappoint and, therefore, there is "no (legitimate) reason" to be angry. This results in confusion and self-doubt, which creates distress and suffering in addition to the original feelings of anger. Clinicians can point out the dialectic synthesis of such a situation: "Your anger about not getting a call back is valid, and so is the reason that I did not call you back. Both things are true and valid. Even though I didn't intend to disappoint you, the result was that you reached out for help and did not receive it." Such a synthesis can help patients self-validate so that they do not experience the intense suffering of self-invalidation, self-hate, and self-doubt. This synthesis also helps clinicians maintain a validating stance that prevents burnout from unnecessary feelings of burden, guilt, or anger. Just because the patient is angry with the therapist does not mean that the therapist did something wrong. Similarly, the fact that the therapist did not do anything wrong does not invalidate the patient's anger.

Balancing dependency and autonomy

As stated earlier, a major criticism of encouraging between-session contact is that it induces a "pathological" level of dependency of the patient on the clinician. Indeed, if patients are sufficiently engaged in treatment, they will certainly become extremely dependent on their DBT clinicians. It is difficult to imagine a productive therapy in which a borderline patient is not dependent upon the clinician.

As in every area, DBT adopts a dialectic stance toward dependency and autonomy. The tension between encouraging dependency and insisting upon patients' responsibility for their behavior presents an opportunity for dialectic synthesis throughout the treatment.

Learning to ask for help skillfully

Contrary to popular notion that BPD patients are demanding of clinicians, it is often the case that BPD patients act overly independent. Or, more accurately, they vacillate between being overly independent and extremely needy and helpless (exhibiting the dialectic that Linehan [11] has termed "apparent competence versus active passivity"; see Chapter 16). They often do not ask for help, and rely on self-destructive behaviors to self-soothe and take care of themselves. This is a coping response to avoid the shame of feeling that they are too needy, or the unbearable disappointment or rage they feel when their needs are invalidated or not adequately met. Or, they engage in unskillful help-seeking behaviors that, over time, alienate and burn out the people on whom they depend.

Therefore, in the beginning of treatment, the main focus is on building a treatment alliance in which patients are encouraged to call for skills coaching and rely on the clinician to develop new and more skillful ways of asking for help and/or taking care of themselves. Dependence is encouraged in order to ultimately develop greater autonomy by being able to function more skillfully. The dialectic synthesis is to achieve the ability to be interdependent – to be able to learn when you need help and skillfully ask for it, while also knowing your capability to help yourself (and not be overly helpless).

Conversely, there are some patients who will reach out for between-session contact frequently and indiscriminately, to communicate distress but not necessarily to request help with skills, and will become very angry if not responded to in the way they want. These individuals need to be taught how to ask for help appropriately, and it is likely that the lack of skill in asking for help is causing interpersonal difficulties outside of the therapy as well. It is very helpful to point this out to patients and to draw the link immediately between therapy and the rest of their lives. The availability of the clinician for between-session skills coaching presents the opportunity to make this a target goal of treatment (second in the hierarchy of goals since it is therapy-interfering behavior). Clinicians can shape the behavior by gently reminding patients of the parameters of between-session availability (for skills coaching or relationship repair). In addition, clinicians can gently but firmly observe limits during a phone call by informing patients that unless they are interested in engaging in skills coaching, the phone call will end for the moment. Clinicians will invite patients to call again when they are ready for skills coaching. Such a response on the clinician's part may be experienced as an aversive consequence and is designed to shape behavior. If these approaches are not effective in getting the behavior under control, then the misuse of between-session contact can be placed on the agenda as a therapy-interfering behavior during the individual therapy session, and subjected to a behavioral analysis, as described previously. However, as we have mentioned, this case is more the exception than the rule. Practitioners new to DBT have to take a leap of faith when instituting intersession contact and trust that if they adhere to the parameters of this type of contact they will not be spending inordinate amounts of time on the phone.

Weaning from between-session coaching

In most cases, we have found that calls for skills coaching naturally decrease over the course of a successful DBT treatment except that they can increase during periods of stress. Intersession contact becomes less frequent and the contacts that are made are briefer. Patients often report that although they think about calling, they already know what their clinician is going to say and they are able to figure out what to do by themselves. Sometimes they report having an imaginary conversation with the therapist or they even picture the therapist sitting on their shoulder whispering in their ear. This is a desired outcome – through repeated instances of being coached to use a skill in the moment, patients internalize the experience and become more independently skillful. Furthermore, the quality of phone coaching changes over time from the clinician making most of the suggestions about what skills to use to the therapist becoming less active and encouraging the patient to generate ideas about the skills to employ. The need for skills coaching calls typically reduces as a natural consequence of this process.

Sometimes the process of reducing reliance on between-session skills coaching needs to be more explicitly addressed. When clinicians determine that their patients are calling when they do not really need to anymore, and that the patients are ready to learn how to rely on their own skills base, the clinician will recommend a taper from between-session contact. The clinician uses commitment strategies (see Chapter 8) to collaborate with the patients in setting this treatment goal, and balances this recommendation for change with validation of any feelings of anxiety, abandonment, or anger on the patients' part.

Often this is not a difficult process. Clinicians and patients work together to design a taper schedule – which might consist of having patients try two skills by themselves before they pick up the phone to call for coaching. Over time, the number of skills, or the amount of time between coaching calls, might increase. The goal of this taper is an increased sense of mastery on the part of the patients.

Sometimes patients, even if they agree to a taper, begin to feel abandoned and have trouble tolerating the decrease in support and attention. Patients might then regress and exhibit older, unskillful behaviors in order to reinstate the more frequent contact with the clinician. This can be addressed as therapy-interfering behavior, balanced with heavy validation of the fact that becoming more skillful does indeed usually result in having less help from those around you. Patients can be invited to look at the pros and cons of being skillful and getting less help versus being unskillful and more reliant on others for assistance. Clinicians can also work with patients to learn how to experience a sense of mastery around being more skillful and independent. In these cases, the tapering off from between-session contact is a very gradual, back-and-forth process.

Summary

Clinician availability for between-session contact is a powerful change intervention unique to DBT. Between-session skills coaching enhances patient motivation and capability by providing support for learning and generalizing more skillful behaviors within the context of real-life situations. Parameters for between-session clinician availability enhances clinician motivation and capability – clinicians are able to directly intervene to decrease life-threatening behaviors, and witness increased skills acquisition in their patients. Rather than "setting boundaries," the DBT concept of "observing natural limits" informs the clinicians' ability to make themselves available in this manner while preventing a sense of resentment or burnout toward their patients.

There are clear parameters for between-session contact that are fully explained to the patients at the outset of treatment. Clinicians often need to initiate and shape this help-seeking behavior in their BPD patients. Inability or failure to follow the parameters is addressed in session as therapy-interfering behavior, and is subjected to nonjudgmental problem solving.

Calling for between-session coaching and for the purpose of therapeutic relationship repair provides an opportunity to learn effective interpersonal help-seeking behaviors, as well as to synthesize the dialectic between dependency and autonomy.

Questions to consider about between-session availability

As a clinician, in thinking about whether you might consider making yourself available to your patients in this way, here are some questions to consider:

1 What are your feelings/fears about being available to patients for telephone consultation between sessions?
2 What are some (arbitrary) limits that you currently set as part of the way you were trained to conduct psychotherapy?
3 What are some of the ways that you have found yourself "deviating" from your usual limits? Are there certain patients that you make "exceptions" for? How do you feel about making these exceptions?

Suggested activity for examining arbitrary versus natural limits

Think about how you would handle a request for rescheduling a therapy session in the following two circumstances with two different patients.

The first patient always attends sessions on time, pays on time, is working hard and making progress in therapy. One week, she asks for an uncharacteristic change in her appointment time for the following week due to having to take her child to a medical appointment with a specialist who only has the one time available.

Assuming that you had some other possible appointment times available, would you grant a change in appointment time? What factors would you consider in whether or not to grant the request for a change in appointment time?

The second patient struggles to attend therapy regularly. She periodically misses sessions, sometimes calls in advance to cancel, and at other times she misses without calling. She is often late to sessions. She pays on time, and pays for missed sessions as well. One day, she calls one hour prior to her scheduled session time to cancel because she is too depressed to get out of bed. She really needs to come in and asks if you have time to reschedule the session for later in the week.

Assuming that you had some other possible appointment times available, would you grant a change in appointment time? What factors would you consider in whether or not to grant the request for a change in appointment time?

Suggested activity for responding to a between-session coaching call

> **Case example**
>
> A patient calls at 7:30 p.m. on a Tuesday evening. She just had an argument with her mother, is feeling extremely upset, and is having urges to take five sleeping pills in order to make sure she can calm herself down. Although she called for coaching, she is currently very emotional and having trouble taking in any suggestions for coaching.

Think about how you might respond to this patient. What interventions might you use to calm her down? Once you were able to do this, what skills would you suggest? What steps would you take to assess her safety and to feel a sense of calm yourself once the phone call is ended?

References

1. Foa, E.B., Yadin, E., Lichner, T.K. (2012) *Exposure and Response (Ritual) Prevention for Obsessive–Compulsive Disorder: Therapists Guide*, Oxford University Press, Oxford.
2. Limbrunner, H., Ben-Porath, H., Wisniewski, L. (2011) DBT telephone skills coaching: Preliminary findings in individuals with eating disorders. *Cognitive and Behavioral Practice*, 18, 186–195.

3. Linehan, M.M. (1993) *Cognitive Behavioral Treatment of Borderline Personality Disorder*, Guilford Press, New York, pp. 498–500.
4. Linehan, M.M. (1993) *Cognitive Behavioral Treatment of Borderline Personality Disorder*, Guilford Press, New York, pp. 319–338.
5. Cabaniss, D.L., Cherry, S., Douglas, C.J., et al. (2011) *Psychodynamic Psychotherapy: A Clinical Manual*, Wiley-Blackwell, Oxford.
6. Gabbard, G.O. (ed.) (2009) Professional boundaries in psychotherapy, in *Textbook of Psychotherapeutic Techniques*, American Psychiatric Publishing, Inc., Washington, DC.
7. Bender, D.S., Dolan, R.T., Skodol, A.E., et al. (2001) Treatment utilization by patients with personality disorders. *American Journal of Psychiatry*, 158 (2), 295–302.
8. Cabaniss, D.L., Cherry, S., Douglas, C.J., et al. (2011) *Psychodynamic Psychotherapy: A Clinical Manual*, Wiley-Blackwell, Oxford, p. 91.
9. Cabaniss, D.L., Cherry, S., Douglas, C.J., et al. (2011) *Psychodynamic Psychotherapy: A Clinical Manual*, Wiley-Blackwell, Oxford, p. 93.
10. Schlesinger, H.J. (2003) *The Texture of Treatment: On the Matter of Psychoanalytic Technique*, Analytic Press, Hillsdale, pp. 195–197.
11. Linehan, M.M. (1993) *Cognitive Behavioral Treatment of Borderline Personality Disorder*, Guilford Press, New York, pp. 84–85.

Chapter 13

Management of suicidal behavior

Top 10 questions to be addressed in this chapter:

How do clinicians help patients manage their chronic suicidal ideation, threats, and gestures in outpatient settings without becoming dysregulated themselves? How can clinicians refrain from becoming either overly anxious and overreactive or disinterested and immune to suicide ideation and behaviors?

When should an individual with BPD be hospitalized and how can clinicians avoid unhelpful, repeated hospitalizations?

The orientation in DBT is to maintain and support patients' functioning in outpatient settings as much as possible and to avoid hospitalization if at all possible. This is done with the purpose of avoiding interruptions in the process of building and maintaining a normal life (in DBT parlance, "a life worth living") and because there is little support that hospitalization "works" especially for patients with BPD. In this chapter, we review DBT-informed interventions for providing support to patients and clinicians in managing suicidal behaviors on an outpatient basis.

Key points

- Filling the gap in the standard level of care
- Detailed history of past suicidal and self-harm behavior
- Safety planning
- Obtaining commitment to making suicidal behavior a top priority treatment target
- Behavioral analyses
- Availability for between-session contact
- Contingency management
- Suicide crisis protocol

The Dialectical Behavior Therapy Primer: How DBT Can Inform Clinical Practice, First Edition. Beth S. Brodsky and Barbara Stanley.
© 2013 John Wiley & Sons, Ltd. Published 2013 by John Wiley & Sons, Ltd.

Filling the gap

> **Case example**
>
> A therapist is currently conducting weekly psychotherapy sessions with a 25-year-old single female graduate student who is struggling to maintain her grades. She has extreme fluctuations in functioning related to problems she is having in her romantic relationship. As long as the relationship is stable, her mood, behaviors, and ability to perform her schoolwork are stable. However, she gets into frequent arguments with her boyfriend, which sometimes results in threats (on both sides) to end the relationship. At these times, the patient becomes suicidal. In the past, she has taken low-lethality overdoses with intent to die. Today the patient comes in for her psychotherapy session in a dysregulated emotional state, reporting that she had a serious fight with her boyfriend and he broke up with her. Given her past history, it seems likely that her suicide risk is elevated.

How does one go about making a clinical assessment of suicide risk in such a case? The standard procedure consists of the following steps:

1. Assess the presence of *suicidal ideation*.
2. Find out if the patient has a suicide *plan and whether there has been any recent suicidal behavior*.
3. Inquire into the patient's *intent to act* on the plan.
4. Evaluate whether or not the patient has *access to means*.
5. *Develop a plan* with the patient to reduce suicide risk.
6. When a patient is *unable to maintain safety*, hospitalize.

Unfortunately, as we have previously mentioned, there is no evidence for the effectiveness of safety contracts [1]. And, although hospitalization may be a short-term life-saving step, it is not a long-term strategy for individuals with chronic suicidal ideation and impulsive behavioral patterns. The standard protocol focuses on suicidal ideation and not NSSI, because we are concerned about behavior that could result in death, and generally NSSI is not immediately life threatening. Thus, the standard protocol does not aid the clinician in determining suicide risk when NSSI is present, and individuals with BPD who engage in NSSI are often hospitalized unnecessarily due to misconceptions regarding suicide risk. Over time, revolving-door hospitalizations lead to increased demoralization and hopelessness, and therefore suicide risk [2].

As we described in Chapter 5, the phenomenology of suicidal and nonsuicidal self-harm behaviors characteristic of BPD requires an alternative perspective regarding how to predict and effectively intervene in reducing and preventing self-harm behaviors. DBT was one of the first, if not the first, psychotherapies to fill the gap by developing outpatient interventions designed to maintain safety and avoid hospitalization. Both clinicians and patients need tools and support to be able to instill a sense of control over acting on suicidal urges. We present both DBT and DBT-informed interventions for maintaining safety in chronically suicidal and impulsive BPD patients on an outpatient basis.

Comprehensive history taking

It is well known that a past suicide attempt is the most reliable predictor of future suicide attempts [3] and that NSSI is a risk factor for suicidal behavior. Therefore, at the outset of treatment with an individual at risk for suicidal and self-harm behavior, a comprehensive history taking, along the lines we suggested in Chapter 5, will provide a solid foundation for effective monitoring of suicide risk and treatment planning. Such history taking can also help the clinician distinguish between suicidal and non-suicidal self-injury. For each past suicide attempt, clinicians should obtain information regarding the following:

1. *Method* used and how the patient obtained access
2. Level of *medical lethality*
3. *Precipitant*
4. *Vulnerability* to the precipitant
5. *Intent to die*
6. *Other intentions*
7. *Consequences* of the behavior
8. *Cognitions*
9. *Presence of drug or alcohol use at the time of the attempt*

Several research measures have been developed for use in taking a comprehensive suicide history. The Columbia Suicide Severity Rating Scale [4] is one such measure that has been modified for clinical use, and provides a guide to obtaining detailed information on suicide ideation, planning, attempts, method used, medical lethality, and preparatory acts. The Beck Lethality Rating Scale [5] offers a detailed description of the levels of medical lethality associated with various methods.

Method

The most frequently used method for attempting suicide in individuals with BPD is overdose on either prescription or over-the-counter medications [6]. Obtain information regarding the number of pills, what type, and what dosage. Find out whether they took the pills all at once, or whether they started out taking a few and then continued to take more pills over a period of time. If the method used is cutting or stabbing, find out what type of instrument they used to cut and where on the body the cuts were inflicted. Less frequently reported methods are firearms, ingestion of poison, jumping from bridges, high places, from cars or in front of cars or trains, asphyxiation through hanging or carbon monoxide. For each of these methods, obtain as much information as possible regarding access and availability. However, these methods are much higher in lethality and, if used, it is likely that the event ended in death. For patients who have a history of multiple suicide attempts, notice patterns in whether the method choice remains the same or whether the individual chooses different means each time.

Medical lethality

Gather as much information as possible regarding the extent of physical damage for each past suicide attempt. The medical lethality of a given attempt can be measured by both the actual damage to the body and the level of medical care required (the Beck lethality scale offers helpful guidelines). Obviously, for different methods, the type of physical damage will vary. For sedatives, obtain details regarding level of consciousness (drowsy, fell asleep, slept for a long time, was easily awakened or not). For cuts or stab wounds, the depth of the wound and the amount of bleeding are indications of the physical damage. In terms of the level of medical care required, distinguish between whether the patient required medical hospitalization or if emergency care without hospitalization was sufficient (such as gastric lavage or suturing). For more highly lethal attempts, the patient may have sustained organ damage, or perhaps entered into a comatose state. At the highest levels of medical lethality short of death, the patient's vital signs are affected, requiring ventilator and/or intensive care treatment.

Precipitant

If possible, have the patient identify an event that preceded and may have triggered the attempt (e.g., an interpersonal conflict, some type of disappointment or feeling of failure, a personal or financial loss, bad medical news, or a reminder of a past traumatic experience). Although identifying a trigger is particularly difficult for patients, especially in retrospect, it is worth asking for, since this type of information is extremely helpful in learning how to predict and manage future suicide risk.

Vulnerability to suicidal behavior

Several diagnoses, in addition to BPD, increase risk for suicidal behavior: major depression, bipolar disorder, substance use disorders, and schizophrenia. A history of childhood trauma also increases risk. In addition, situational factors that increase risk include an ongoing stressful situation, such as family discord, physical illness, work or school expectations, and interpersonal problems.

Intent to die

Intent to die can be assessed both by subjective patient report and by certain objective factors. Objective factors include the timing of the attempt and any other precautions against being discovered, whether or not a suicide note was written, or any preparatory behaviors such as giving away personal items and making arrangements [5].

Other intentions

As previously mentioned, individuals with BPD make suicide attempts and perform other acts of deliberate self-harm for the purpose of affect regulation and wanting to escape from unbearable emotional pain. So, although it seems paradoxical, individuals with BPD will describe both NSSI episodes and suicide attempts as efforts to make themselves feel better.

Consequences

For each suicide attempt, obtain information regarding whether the patient felt regret or relief, whether they received caretaking attention, whether or not they were hospitalized, whether or not they lost a job or status in school, and whether or not these were experienced as reinforcing (relief from pressure, more caretaking) or aversive (large hospital bills, unpleasant hospital experience, feeling of failure) consequences.

Cognitions

Examine the core beliefs and automatic thoughts that might have contributed to the decision to make an attempt ("I can't take the pain anymore," "I am a failure," "I will always feel this way").

Substance use related to the attempt

Substance use can be related to suicidal behavior in two ways. Drug and alcohol use results in disinhibition, which impairs judgment and increases likelihood of acting on suicidal urges. Alternatively, these substances may be used as the method, or to enhance the method, of self-harm. Typically, alcohol is used in conjunction with pills to either enhance medical lethality and/or to increase disinhibition and help the individual to act on the urges.

Safety planning

Based on this history, the next step at the beginning of treatment is to develop a safety plan with the patient. The SPI is not a formal part of DBT but utilizes strategies and techniques that are employed in DBT as well as other forms of CBT. It will be described in detail in the following chapter.

Obtaining commitment

Clinicians working with suicidal individuals have a heightened sense of responsibility to guard patient safety. This can result in a high sense of burden unless the patient also accepts responsibility for working with the clinician to stay safe. In DBT, shared responsibility is made explicit, through the use of commitment strategies and by the constant revisiting of the commitment when it seems to be flagging. As described in Chapter 8, patient and clinician make an agreement to work together to reduce life-threatening behaviors. The clinician offers skills and support for the patient to be able to maintain the commitment.

Prioritizing suicide as a treatment target

Making a commitment to target suicidal behaviors means that direct inquiry is made at each and every psychotherapy session regarding the presence of suicidal ideation, any intent to act, or urges to self-injure. In DBT, patients monitor their suicidal ideation and self-harm urges and behaviors on the diary card, and whenever significant ideation or behavior is present, it is addressed directly during the therapy session. This may seem straightforward. However, in the absence of an explicit commitment to focus on suicidal behavior, or interventions such as active monitoring with a diary card, clinicians may not think to ask and patients will not think to report.

Chain analysis

In accordance with the explicit emphasis on targeting suicidal behavior, all significant life-threatening behaviors are subjected to a chain analysis. Each analysis provides detailed information regarding the types of triggers, vulnerabilities, automatic thoughts, feelings, and behaviors that lead to an episode of suicidal or nonsuicidal self-harm. The chain analysis aids in identifying patterns and developing skill-based problem solving specific to the individual patient. The chain analysis can provide information that can be used to create and modify a patient-specific safety plan.

Between-session contact

Although between-session contacts in DBT are not limited to crisis management, patients are encouraged to call their therapists before they engage in self-harm behaviors if they are unable to utilize skills to effectively cope with their urges. Clinician availability for between-session coaching serves to manage suicidality in a number of ways:

1. Skills coaching gives the clinician a chance to intervene before distress escalates into suicidal urges.
2. Clinician anxiety can be reduced by the knowledge that patients will call for coaching before engaging in destructive behaviors.
3. Through repeated exposure to their patients during times of distress, clinicians can gain more information regarding patients' emotional responses, automatic thoughts, and which skills will be most effective in riding them safely through the crisis.
4. Clinicians can incorporate between-session contact into a safety plan as well as a plan for crisis management (see suicide protocol later).

Contingency management

Each of the aforementioned interventions is conducted with particular attention to contingency management. Clinicians strive to provide aversive (but not punitive) consequences to unskillful behaviors, as well as to seek opportunities to reinforce skillful behaviors whenever possible. Thus, DBT clinicians are not only trained to ask, they are encouraged to inquire in excruciating detail about a self-harm episode. The chain analysis, although intended to promote skillful behavior, can be a tedious, laborious, and painful process, thereby serving as an aversive consequence, which will hopefully reduce the likelihood of the behavior in the future. In order to prevent reinforcing suicidal crisis behavior, between-session skills coaching is made available anytime the patient wants to use skills to avert a crisis.

Managing contingencies in the environment

Whenever possible, the clinician can use consultation to the environment strategies (see the next Chapter 14) to manage the contingencies surrounding suicidal behavior outside of the therapy. Thus, if a family member or partner is inadvertently reinforcing suicidal behavior by responding with increasing caretaking or by backing off on interpersonal demands or expectations, the clinician might invite these significant others into the therapy sessions to increase awareness of this dynamic and offer guidance as to how to refrain from such reinforcement.

Sometimes an opportunity may arise for the clinician to intervene with other mental health service providers to create aversive consequences for suicidal behaviors. Consider the case of Nicole:

> **Case example**
>
> Nicole called her DBT therapist on a Sunday morning to say that she had taken seven pills of prescribed Klonopin in response to feeling stressed about a family situation in which she was being asked to attend her aunt's funeral later in the week. She indicated to her therapist that she was feeling suicidal and wanted to go to the hospital. The therapist suspected that Nicole was having trouble telling her family that she was afraid to attend the funeral and felt that being hospitalized was the best way to avoid the funeral without having to express her fears. The therapist encouraged Nicole to go to her nearest ER to make sure she was physically stable after the overdose on Klonopin. The therapist indicated to Nicole that she had a choice in how she presented herself to the doctors in the ER – she could either tell them that she has active suicidal ideation and does not feel safe or she could decide to tell them that she has an appointment with her therapist the following day and will be able to stay safe until then. Nicole should also ask the ER doctors to call the therapist to consult.
>
> The therapist told the ER staff to fully evaluate Nicole and make an independent decision about her safety. The therapist also expressed her desire to try to avoid a hospitalization, and indicated that she was available to see Nicole the next morning and work with her to stay safe on an outpatient basis. The therapist and ER staff collaborated to encourage Nicole to not insist on hospitalization. After a full day in the ER, Nicole called her therapist to complain that the ER staff was "having trouble processing her insurance" and this resulted in a long, uncomfortable wait in the ER. She was feeling better and just wanted to go home, and was able to tell the ER that she was safe and was released to see her therapist the following day.

In this case, the clinician consulted with the ER staff to avoid what the clinician felt would have been an unnecessary hospitalization. This intervention blocked what may have been a reinforcing consequence for Nicole, who wanted to avoid stress by becoming suicidal and getting hospitalized.

Immediate crisis management

Immediate crisis management is needed when a patient is expressing a high intent to commit suicide and is not responding to the aforementioned interventions. In such a case, the clinician should stay in contact with the patient until a plan for safety is secured. This might necessitate either extending a psychotherapy session or a phone call until a plan is in place. The safety plan that was originally developed should be used as a guide.

Individuals identified as emergency contacts, as well as third-party friends or family members, should be involved whenever possible in providing support and/or implementing the safety plan.

Summary

In this chapter, we review DBT-informed, hands-on techniques that reduce anxiety and enhance effectiveness, thereby increasing the capacity of the clinician and patient to successfully stay safe and manage suicidal behaviors on an outpatient basis. These include interventions to identify a particular individual's triggers and vulnerabilities for suicidal behavior, as well as comprehensive assessment of suicidal intent and medical lethality based on past behaviors.

The capacity for impulsive suicidal episodes is one of the most anxiety-provoking aspects of working with BPD patients. Despite the many interventions we review to learn how to identify warning signs, vulnerabilities, and suicidal risk, prediction of an acute suicidal crisis is not always possible. Therefore, these interventions also encourage a collaborative therapeutic relationship and include the availability of between-session skills coaching, which are crucial to maintaining a sense of calm and safety in working with these patients.

In Chapter 14, we review safety planning, an intervention that provides the patient with concrete steps for identifying and managing their suicidal feelings, as well as for skillfully reaching out for help when necessary. Safety planning includes anticipating and addressing the obstacles for taking these steps in order to enhance compliance with the plan.

References

1. Garvey, K.A., Penn, J.V., Campbell, A.L., et al. (2009) Contracting for safety with patients: Clinical practice and forensic implications. *American Academy of Psychiatry Law*, 37 (3), 363–370.
2. Soloff, P.H., Fabio, A. (2008) Prospective predictors of suicide attempts in borderline personality disorder at one, two, and two-to-five year follow-up. *Journal of Personality Disorders*, 22 (2), 123–134.
3. Oquendo, M.A., Currier, D., Mann, J.J. (2006) Prospective studies of suicidal behavior in major depressive and bipolar disorders: What is the evidence for predictive risk factors? *Acta Psychiatrica Scandanavica*, 114 (3), 151–158.
4. Posner, K., Oquendo, M., Gould, M., et al. (2007) Columbia Classification Algorithm of Suicide Assessment (C-CASA): Classification of suicidal events in the FDA's pediatric suicidal risk analysis of antidepressants. *American Journal of Psychiatry*, 164 (7), 1035–1043.
5. Beck, A.T., Beck, R., Kovacs, M. (1975) Classification of suicidal behaviors: 1. Quantifying intent and medical lethality. *American Journal of Psychiatry*, 132 (3), 285–287.
6. Stanley, B., Gameroff, M.J., Michalsen, V., et al. (2001) Are suicide attempters who self-mutilate a unique population? *American Journal of Psychiatry*, 158, 427–432.

Chapter 14

The Safety Planning Intervention

In this chapter, we describe the Safety Planning Intervention (SPI), based on principles and strategies of DBT and CBT but not part of DBT as developed by Linehan.

> **Key points**
>
> - Individuals with BPD are frequently suicidal and have difficulty managing suicidal feelings.
> - Safety planning provides a structured way for individuals with BPD to handle their suicidal crises.
> - The SPI has six steps arranged in a hierarchical order, developed collaboratively between the clinician and suicidal individual.

As we have reviewed throughout the previous chapters, individuals with BPD frequently struggle with suicidal urges. It seems shocking that they can become suicidal from what appear to be relatively minor provocations (e.g., an argument with a boyfriend or unreturned phone calls or texts). Unfortunately, because suicidal feelings are so frequent in BPD, clinicians, family members, and friends can become inattentive to them. This is a dangerous result because completed suicide occurs at a high rate in this population.

At the same time, reacting to each suicidal expression may inadvertently reinforce suicidal ideation and behaviors as "effective" means of communication. And, in fact, it can result in sought-after attentiveness in the short term but, ultimately, the opposite effect often occurs. Consequently, clinicians, friends, and family members, as well as the suicidal individuals themselves, can feel at a loss to cope with the frightening nature, and the frequency and strength of these urges. In this chapter, we describe an intervention, Safety Planning Intervention (SPI), developed by one of this book's authors (Barbara Stanley)

Adapted with permission from Stanley, B., Brown, G.K. (2012) Safety planning intervention: A brief intervention to mitigate suicide risk. *Cognitive and Behavioral Practice*, 19, 256–264.

The Dialectical Behavior Therapy Primer: How DBT Can Inform Clinical Practice, First Edition.
Beth S. Brodsky and Barbara Stanley.
© 2013 John Wiley & Sons, Ltd. Published 2013 by John Wiley & Sons, Ltd.

and Dr. Gregory K. Brown [1] designed to help suicidal individuals manage their self-destructive feelings and urges on their own and to reach out to others appropriately.

The Safety Planning Intervention

SPI is a written, prioritized list of coping strategies and sources of support that individuals can use to alleviate a suicidal crisis. It was developed for suicidal individuals irrespective of diagnosis and has been used with suicidal patients who have BPD. SPI has been identified as a "best practice" by the Suicide Prevention Resource Center/American Foundation for Suicide Prevention Best Practices Registry for Suicide Prevention (www.sprc.org).

Given that suicidal crises may be relatively short-lived and have an ebb and flow pattern, an intervention that helps people cope with these crises is useful, even if the intervention is only used for a brief period of time. People do not remain at a constant level of acute suicidality for long periods of time even if they are chronically suicidal. The chronically suicidal person typically has periods of lower levels of suicide ideation punctuated by exacerbations when the ideation can get dangerously elevated. It is for this reason that restriction of access to means (e.g., removal of guns from the home; limiting the amount of psychotropic medications available) is effective in preventing suicidal behavior. In other words, the usefulness of means restriction is largely based on the fact that suicidal thoughts tend to subside over time. Similarly, if suicidal individuals are given tools, like SPI, that enable them to resist or decrease suicidal urges for brief periods of time, then the risk for suicide is likely to decrease.

The SPI is unique in that it is a systematic and comprehensive approach to maintaining safety in suicidal patients. Prior efforts have primarily focused on a single aspect of safety (e.g., means restriction or emergency contacts). Furthermore, the explicit focus on utilizing internal coping and distracting strategies as a step in an emergency plan to deal with suicidal urges is not typically an aspect of most safety plan efforts even though it is an aspect of therapies targeting suicidal feelings (e.g., CT and DBT).

The SPI, a very brief intervention which takes approximately 20–45 minutes to complete, provides patients with a prioritized and specific set of coping strategies and sources of support that can be used should suicidal thoughts reemerge. The intent of the safety plan is to help individuals lower their imminent risk for suicidal behavior by having a predetermined set of potential coping strategies and a list of individuals or agencies they can contact. While we recommend that the interventions be followed in a stepwise manner, it is important to note that, if a patient feels at imminent risk and unable to stay safe even for a brief time, then the patient should immediately go to an emergency setting. Furthermore, some individuals may feel that they cannot or do not wish to use one of the steps in the safety plan. In this instance, they should not feel that they must do so since the intent of the safety plan is to be helpful and not a source of additional stress or burden. For example, one of the steps on the safety plan is to contact family or friends who can offer support and assistance. However, for some individuals with BPD, they may be hard-pressed to identify people who they can turn to because they have had so many crises in the past and have lost sources of support. Furthermore, despite the sense that individuals with BPD are demanding, our experience is that many have difficulty asking appropriately for help owing to a sense of being undeserving and a fear of rejection.

The SPI is best developed with the patient following a comprehensive suicide risk assessment [2]. During the risk assessment, the clinician should obtain an accurate account of the events that transpired before, during, and after the recent suicidal crisis, as is done in a chain analysis described in Chapter 9. Individuals typically are asked to describe the suicidal crisis including the precipitating events and their reactions to these events. This review of the crisis facilitates the identification of warning signs to be included in the safety plan.

The basic components of the safety plan include: (a) recognizing warning signs of an impending suicidal crisis; (b) employing internal coping strategies; (c) utilizing social contacts as a means of distraction from suicidal thoughts; (d) contacting family members or friends who may help to resolve the crisis; (e) contacting mental health professionals or agencies; and (f) reducing the potential use of lethal means. The first five components are employed when suicidal thoughts and other warning signs emerge. The sixth element, reducing access to means, is discussed after the rest of the safety plan has been completed often with the aid of a family member or friend, for an agreed-upon period of time. Each of these steps is reviewed in greater detail.

The steps of safety planning

Step 1 – Recognition of warning signs

The first step in developing the safety plan involves the recognition of the signs that immediately precede a suicidal crisis. These warning signs include personal situations, thoughts, images, thinking styles, moods, or behaviors. One of the most effective ways of averting a suicidal crisis is to address the problem before it fully emerges. Examples of warning signs include feeling irritable, depressed, hopeless, or having thoughts such as "I cannot take it anymore." Similarly, individuals can identify problematic behaviors that are typically associated with suicidality, such as spending increased time alone, avoiding interactions, or drinking more than usual. Generally, more specifically described warning signs will cue the individual to use the safety plan than warning signs that are more vaguely described. For individuals with BPD, their warning signs often involve feeling emotionally dysregulated and out of control or feeling all alone or unloved. In addition, because depression is a frequent comorbidity with BPD, feeling hopeless is also a common warning sign in BPD.

Step 2 – Internal coping strategies

As a therapeutic strategy, it is useful to have individuals attempt to cope on their own with their suicidal thoughts, even if it is just for a brief time. Ultimately, the goal in all therapeutic interventions, including the SPI, is to have individuals learn how to cope on their own. In this step, individuals are asked to identify what they can do, without the assistance of another person, should they become suicidal again. Prioritizing internal strategies as a first-level technique is important because they enhance individuals' self-efficacy and can help to create a sense that suicidal urges can be mastered. This, in turn, may help them feel less vulnerable and less at the mercy of their suicidal thoughts. Such activities function as a way for individuals to distract themselves from the crisis and prevent suicide ideation from escalating. This technique is similar to those described in DBT, in which we teach individuals to employ distraction techniques when they are experiencing intense urges to make a suicide attempt. Examples of these coping strategies include going for a walk, listening to inspirational music, going online, taking a shower, playing with a pet, exercising, engaging in a hobby, reading, or doing chores. Activities that serve as "strong" distractions vary from person to person and, therefore, the individual should be an active participant in identifying these activities. Engaging in such activities may also help individuals experience some pleasure, sense of mastery, or facilitate a sense of meaning in their lives. However, the primary aim of identifying and doing such activities is to serve as a distraction from the crisis.

After the internal coping strategies have been generated, the clinician may use a collaborative, problem-solving approach to ensure that potential roadblocks to using these strategies are addressed and/or that alternative coping strategies are identified. If individuals still remain unconvinced that they can apply the particular strategy during a crisis, other strategies should be developed. Clinicians should help individuals to identify a few of these strategies that they would use in order of priority; the strategies that are easiest to do or most likely to be effective may be listed at the top of the list.

Step 3 – Socialization strategies for distraction and support

If the internal coping strategies are ineffective and do not reduce suicidal ideation, individuals can utilize socialization strategies of two types: socializing with other people in their natural social environment who may help to distract themselves from their suicidal thoughts and urges or visiting healthy social settings. In this step, individuals may identify individuals, such as friends or family members, or settings where socializing occurs naturally. Examples of the latter include coffee shops, places of worship, and Alcoholics Anonymous (AA) meetings. These settings depend, to a certain extent, on local customs, but individuals should be encouraged to exclude environments in which alcohol or other substances may be present. In this step, individuals should be advised to identify social settings or individuals who are good "distracters" from their own thoughts and worries. Socializing with friends or family members, without explicitly revealing their suicidal state, may assist in distracting individuals from their problems and their suicidal thoughts; this strategy is not intended as a means of seeking specific help with the suicidal crisis. A suicidal crisis may also be alleviated if individuals feel more connected with other people or feel a sense of belongingness.

Step 4 – Social contacts for assistance in resolving suicidal crises

If the internal coping strategies or social contacts used for purposes of distraction offer little benefit to alleviating the crisis, individuals may choose to inform family members or friends that they are experiencing a suicidal crisis. This step is distinguished from the previous one in that individuals explicitly reveal to others that they are in crisis and need support and assistance in coping with the crisis.

Given the complexity of deciding if individuals should or should not disclose to others that they are thinking about suicide, the clinician and individual should work collaboratively to formulate an optimal plan. This may include weighing the pros and cons of disclosing their suicidal thoughts or behavior to a person who may offer support. Thus, for this step, someone who may help to distract individuals from their suicidal urges may not be the best person for assisting individuals with a suicidal crisis when suicidal thoughts are disclosed. Individuals should be asked about the likelihood that they would contact these individuals and whether these individuals would be helpful or could possibly exacerbate the crisis. If possible, someone close to the individual with whom the safety plan can be shared should be identified and should be named on the plan. It should be noted that sometimes individuals are unable to identify someone because they may not feel comfortable sharing the plan with family or friends.

Step 5 – Professional and agency contact to help resolve suicidal crises

This component of the plan consists of identifying and seeking help from professionals or other clinicians who could assist individuals during a crisis. The clinicians' names and the corresponding telephone numbers and/or locations are listed on the plan and may be prioritized. Individuals are instructed to contact a professional or agency if the previous strategies (i.e., coping strategies, contacting friends or family members) are not effective for resolving the crisis. If individuals are actively engaged in mental health treatment, the safety plan may include contact information for this provider. However, the safety plan should also include other professionals who may be reached, especially during nonbusiness hours. Additionally, contact information for a local 24-hour emergency treatment facility should be listed as well as other local or national support services that handle emergency calls, such as the national Suicide Prevention Lifeline: 800-273-8255 (TALK). Consistent with DBT, individuals should resort to this step *prior* to engaging in self-harm behavior and not afterward.

The safety plan emphasizes the accessibility of appropriate professional help during a crisis and, when necessary, indicates how these services may be obtained. The clinician should discuss the individuals' expectations when they contact professionals and agencies for assistance and discuss any roadblocks or challenges in doing so. Individuals with BPD may be reluctant, at times, to contact professionals and disclose their suicidality for fear of being hospitalized. As with the other components of the plan, the clinician should discuss any concerns or other obstacles that may hinder individuals from contacting a professional or agency. Only those professionals whom individuals are willing to contact during a time of crisis should be included on the safety plan.

Step 6 – Means restriction

The risk for suicide is amplified when individuals report a specific plan to kill themselves that involves a readily available lethal method [3]. Even if no specific plan is identified by individuals, a key component of the safety plan intervention involves eliminating or limiting access to any potential lethal means in the environment. This may include safely storing and dispensing of medication, implementing firearm safety procedures, or restricting access to knives or other lethal means. In developing a safety plan, means restriction is addressed after individuals have identified ways of coping with suicidal feelings because, if they see that there are other options to acting on their suicidal urges than committing suicide, they may be more likely to engage in a discussion about removing or restricting access to means. Depending on the lethality of the method, the manner in which the method is removed or restricted will vary. Generally, clinicians should ask individuals which means they would consider using during a suicidal crisis and *collaboratively identify ways to secure or limit access to these means*. Clinicians should routinely ask whether individuals have access to firearms, regardless of whether it is considered a "method of choice," and make arrangements for securing them. For methods with lower lethality (such as drugs or medication with a low level of toxicity), clinicians may ask individuals to remove or restrict their access to these methods themselves when they are not experiencing a crisis. For example, if individuals are considering overdosing, having them ask a trusted family member to store the medication in a secure place might be a useful strategy.

The urgency and importance of restricting access to a lethal method is greater for highly lethal methods. For methods of high lethality, such as a firearm, asking individuals to temporarily limit their access to such means themselves by giving it to a family member or other responsible person may be problematic, as individuals' risk for suicide may increase further as a result of direct contact with the highly lethal method. Instead, an optimal plan would be to restrict individuals' access to a highly lethal method by having it safely stored by a designated, responsible person – usually a family member or close friend, or even the police [4]. Individuals who are unwilling to remove their access to a firearm may be willing to limit their access to the firearm by having a critical part of the firearm removed or by using a gunlock and having the gunlock key removed. Clinicians should also be aware that restricting access to one lethal method does not guarantee individuals' safety because they may decide to use another one. The specific behaviors necessary to make the individuals' environment safer should be noted on the safety plan and the length of time (e.g., one month, two weeks) that this restriction should be in place can be noted.

Implementation of the safety plan

It is important to note that the SPI should be administered in a collaborative manner with individuals. The coping strategies, external supports, and triggers to suicidal urges are generated together by the clinician and individual, and the individual's own words are used in the written document. The collaborative nature of this intervention is essential to developing an effective safety plan. A clinician-generated list of coping strategies is unlikely to be helpful to an individual in the absence of knowing what strategies are most engaging. Similarly, "typical" triggers to suicidal feelings are not useful if they do not have personal relevance. On the other hand, the individual is not left alone to struggle with identifying his or her triggers and best means for coping. Instead, clinicians can offer suggestions and inquire in a supportive manner to help the individual complete the intervention.

After the SPI is complete, clinicians should assess the individual's reactions to it and the likelihood he or she will use the safety plan. One strategy for increasing individual motivation to use the safety plan during a crisis is to ask the individual to identify the most helpful aspects of the plan. If the individual reports or the clinician determines that there is reluctance or ambivalence to use the plan, then the clinician should collaborate with the individual to *identify* and *problem solve* potential obstacles and difficulties to using the safety plan. Role-playing the use of the SPI may be helpful if clinicians have sufficient time available and the individual is willing to engage in this exercise. Once individuals indicate their willingness to use the safety plan during a crisis, then the original document is given to the individual to take with them and a copy is retained by the clinician. The clinician also discusses where the individual will keep the safety plan and how it will be retrieved during a crisis. This may include making multiple copies of the plan to keep in various locations or changing the size or format of the plan so that it could be stored in a wallet or electronic device that is easily accessible. In order to increase the likelihood that the safety plan would be used, the clinician may consider conducting a role-play during which the individual would describe a suicidal crisis and then would provide a detailed description of locating the safety plan and following each of the steps listed on it.

Safety Plan Intervention: An illustrative case example

Case example

A 24-year-old, single mother with BPD presented at the local hospital emergency department following a suicide attempt having taken an overdose of anxiolytic medication prescribed by her general practitioner. She reported that she simply felt overwhelmed when her one-year-old baby began crying and was inconsolable. She said that this came on the heels of the man she had been dating telling her that he did not want to go out with her any longer because her life was just too "complicated" and he found her "just too needy." She became quickly demoralized and one thought kept running through her mind: "No one is ever going to want to be with me. I am always going to be alone." She took one pill thinking it would calm her down and when it did not, she took another. When the second pill didn't help, she took several more thinking she wanted to end it all. But she got scared that no one would be there to take care of her baby and called her neighbor, who took her to the local ER. During the evaluation, she said that she often feels that her emotions get out of control and when they do, it feels unbearable and she becomes suicidal. She reported that she had taken "several" overdoses in the past with suicidal intent but none of them involved taking as many pills as she had that day. She denied hallucinations, delusions, and homicidal ideation. Her tentative diagnosis was BPD with a possible depressive disorder. The patient told the ER physician that she was no longer suicidal and that she needed to go home to take care of her baby. Her risk for suicide was determined to be moderately high but not at imminent risk. She also revealed that she had recently begun seeing a therapist who she felt was helpful. The ER contacted this clinician, who confirmed that the patient was seeing her and that she had an appointment later in the week. The patient was then discharged from the ER and not hospitalized. Prior to discharge, a safety plan was developed with her to help her better manage her suicidal feelings.

In the safety plan, this patient's primary warning sign was identified as feeling emotionally dysregulated and out of control. She also felt that she could not think straight. Her internal coping strategies included listening to her iPod, watching talk shows on television, and exercising to DVDs. Social distracters, where suicidal feelings are not revealed, included going to the playground to be with other young mothers, going to the local coffee shop, and talking with her sister. She then identified her mother as the only person she could think of to talk with and reveal she was feeling suicidal. The therapist's name and number, the local ER name and number were listed, as well as the suicide prevention hotline number. A copy was placed in the individual's chart and the individual was given a copy on discharge. The individual stated that she would make another copy so that she could keep one copy in her apartment on the refrigerator and another in her purse. Table 14.1 shows an example of a safety plan that was developed with this patient.

Table 14.1 Sample safety plan

Safety Plan Form [1]
Warning signs that crisis is developing 1. Feeling out of control 2. Inability to think straight
Internal coping strategies 1. Listen to iPod (upbeat songs) 2. Watch talk shows on TV 3. Exercise to DVDs
External strategies People/places to go to help distract from crisis 1. Sister.. 2. Playground to be with other mothers 3. Go to local coffee shop
People to ask for help 1. Mother.. 2. Best friend
Professionals to ask for help Primary Mental Health Professional: Dr. Mary Smith Phone: 212 777-1234   Emergency #: 646 777-1234 Hospital ER: North General Medical Center Address: 1487 Franklin St, Hillside, N.Y.
Steps to make the environment safe Limit access to prescribed medication. Ask mother to holds meds and dispense weekly

Summary

In this chapter, we reviewed the SPI that provides the clinician and patient with a concrete tool for anticipating and managing suicidal crises. The SPI provides guidance to follow six steps to collaboratively create an individualized plan for the prevention of suicidal behavior and also to reduce the likelihood of hospitalization if at all possible. The SPI includes anticipation and addressing of obstacles that might get in the way of plan implementation, to increase the likelihood that the individual will be able to use the plan when necessary.

References

1. Stanley, B., Brown, G.K. (2011) Safety planning intervention: A brief intervention to mitigate suicide risk. *Cognitive and Behavioral Practice*, 19, 256–264.
2. American Psychiatric Association. (2003) *Practice Guideline for the Assessment and Treatment of Patients with Suicidal Behaviors*, American Psychiatric Association, Washington, DC.
3. Joiner, T.E., Steer, R.A., Brown, G., et al. (2003) Worst-point suicidal plans: A dimension of suicidality predictive of past suicide attempts and eventual death by suicide. *Behavior Research in Therapy*, 41, 1469–1480.
4. Simon, R.I. (2007) Gun safety management with patients at risk for suicide. *Suicide and Life Threatening Behavior*, 37, 518–526.

Chapter 15

The three C's of consultation

Top 10 question to be addressed in this chapter:

What are the ways of effectively managing behaviors that are referred to as "splitting" in treatments where there are multiple clinicians?

An assumption of DBT is that clinicians treating individuals with BPD need support. DBT provides structure and guidelines for consultation and collaboration with colleagues. DBT practitioners consult with colleagues on their DBT consultation team, consult to their patients, and consult with other clinicians.

> **Key points**
> - BPD patients often have multiple treatment providers.
> - This chapter reviews DBT concepts and guidelines for effective collaboration and support.
> - Support for clinicians treating individuals with BPD – the DBT consultation team.
> - Parameters for consultation to the patient.
> - Parameters for consultation to third-party treaters.
> - How does DBT conceptualize and manage splitting behaviors?

The three C's – consult with DBT colleagues, consult to patient, consult with other clinicians

Due to the complex nature of the BPD disorder and its presenting symptomatology, there is often a need for multiple treatment modalities, resulting in the involvement of numerous mental health clinicians providing care for one patient. Thus, clinicians treating individuals with BPD rarely function in isolation. This chapter reviews concepts and guidelines for peer consultation and support, for coaching patients to advocate for themselves with multiple care providers, and collaboration with other members of an outpatient "treatment team." This chapter also addresses the phenomenon of "splitting" and how it is understood and approached from a DBT perspective. As in other DBT interventions, these concepts are informed by a dialectic approach.

The Dialectical Behavior Therapy Primer: How DBT Can Inform Clinical Practice, First Edition.
Beth S. Brodsky and Barbara Stanley.
© 2013 John Wiley & Sons, Ltd. Published 2013 by John Wiley & Sons, Ltd.

Consulting with colleagues: The DBT consultation team

DBT has a built-in support system for the clinician in the form of the DBT team/peer supervision group, called the DBT consultation team. Besides providing support in times of crisis, the consultation team meets on a weekly basis and is composed of individual clinicians and group skills leaders. The consultation team meeting provides an opportunity for each clinician to present their ongoing individual cases and to receive consultation.

The team performs a number of functions in promoting the individual therapy. A primary goal is to encourage and support the clinician to remain in the therapeutic relationship. A unique function of the DBT consultation team is to assist the clinician in maintaining an optimum balance between validation and change in relation to the patient, helping the therapist stay on track and keeping the treatment focused on and moving toward addressing treatment goals. This includes helping the therapist explore and observe his or her own personal limits with a particular patient. The team provides the context within which the treatment is conducted.

The following example illustrates how the DBT consultation team assists the therapist in balancing change with validation, getting the therapy back on track and observing limits:

Case example

CLINICIAN (presenting her patient Alice in the consultation team): My patient Alice is having a really hard time right now. She hates her job and is threatening to quit. I am trying to help her manage the stress and to hold off on leaving the job until she has another job lined up. If she quits her job, she will be in financial trouble, may have trouble paying her rent, and her problems will become even worse. Her stress at work is making her extremely irritable and needy. I really want to be a support to her, and I have been coaching her to use distress tolerance skills while she is at work. Sometimes she calls me two to three times a day and it doesn't seem to be enough to help her manage her distress. She is alienating her boyfriend, which also compounds her level of distress and leads to increased binge eating, and last week she cut herself after an argument with him. I'm not sure what else I can do.

TEAM MEMBER: Wow, you are really doing so much for Alice. I can understand how worried you are about her and I can see how much you want to help her. I am concerned, though, that you are taking on too much responsibility and doing too much of the work yourself. I think we may have to help you figure out how to get Alice to take a little more of the responsibility for her situation, to use your coaching and support more effectively. I'm afraid that you may not be observing your limits with her and you will get frustrated and resentful. Ultimately, that won't be helpful to Alice.

CLINICIAN: I *am* starting to feel burdened by her phone calls and the fact that my coaching doesn't seem to help her become more skillful in dealing with her job or her boyfriend. But I am really concerned about her losing her job and I don't want her to lose it.

TEAM MEMBER: It is stressful to consider the possibility of her losing her job. But she doesn't seem to be on board with the idea of keeping the job until she has another one lined up. Right now that is *your* goal for her, not hers. Maybe you can step back a bit, and tolerate the distress of the possibility of Alice losing her job, and see if you can work with her to commit to figuring out how to tolerate this job until she finds another one. Or, you may need to radically accept that she won't keep this job. After all, she has been out of

> CLINICIAN: a job in the past and has survived. Also, we should look at what is happening during these coaching calls. Is she receptive to using the skills? She is not exactly open to using the skills. She often calls me to tell me that she can't handle the job anymore and I ask her to try to hang in there and use interpersonal effectiveness and distress tolerance skills. But you are helping me to see that I am trying too hard to get her to change. Maybe I need to be more validating of her distress. If I validate how hard the job is for her right now, and how hard it is for her to use the skills that I am suggesting, maybe she will be able to see for herself why it is important to try, and she might feel more supported. Or maybe she won't, and I will have to accept that she is not ready to stick with this job.
>
> TEAM MEMBER: Yes, I think that balancing the emphasis on change with more validation might be the way to go. Alice might feel more supported, and you won't have to do all of the work to get her to change – which won't work anyway. Then the two of you can collaborate on how to proceed with her situation.

In this next example, the team helps the therapist overcome an impasse with a suicidal patient.

> ### Case example
>
> CLINICIAN: (presenting her patient, Kim in the DBT consultation team): My new patient, Kim, comes into my office, sits down in the seat across from me, looks down at the floor, and refuses to speak. I don't know how to get her to say something and to engage with me. And I am really worried about her suicidality – she has a lot of pills at home and she has made serious overdoses in the past. I am trying to get her to make the commitment to stop life-threatening behaviors and want to do some safety planning with her. I know I shouldn't be getting angry, but I feel that she is angry with me, and last session I kind of lost it with her and started insisting that she tell me that she is angry with me. That didn't help.
>
> TEAM MEMBER: It must be so frustrating to sit in the room with her when she is not making eye contact and not answering any of your questions. I wonder if it is because she finds it very difficult to come to her session, and she is really nervous when she is in the office with you. It might be the best she can do to just show up.
>
> CLINICIAN: You know, that makes a lot of sense. It didn't occur to me at all, I wonder why? When I am sitting with her for some reason I feel anger in the room – maybe it is mine. But I will definitely approach her differently next session and see if that helps.
>
> TEAM MEMBER: It's difficult sometimes when you are in the room with the patient to step back and see the larger picture. Good luck!
>
> (A week later in team)
>
> CLINICIAN: I had a much better session with Kim last week – I shared what the team suggested about how perhaps she is really afraid to come to session and she is doing her best just to show up. She lifted her head, looked me straight in the eye, and nodded her head. I then apologized for my therapy-interfering behavior, for not realizing this before, and for getting angry with her. After that, we were able to proceed with safety planning. She actually agreed to bring her extra pills in to me so that she wouldn't have access to taking them in overdose.

In this illustration, the clinician felt comfortable to share her frustration and have her feelings validated by the team. The team offered support and a helpful suggestion without judgment. This enabled the clinician to feel supported and to regain a validating stance toward a difficult patient.

The DBT consultation team also serves as a support for the clinician in times of crisis intervention and suicide management. There are instances in which a between-session skills coaching call can become a suicide crisis call and the clinician coaches her patient to use skills to stay safe. After such a call, the clinician may need to consult with a team member to manage anxiety and to maintain a therapeutic stance.

Case example

A few weeks later, Kim contacted her clinician to let her know she was feeling suicidal and was not sure she could control her urge to go to the office building of her new job and jump from the window of her office on the 12th floor.

CLINICIAN: It's great that you called, Kim. I hope you are willing to work with me to stay safe.
KIM: I'm not sure I can, but I guess if I called you I want to try.
CLINICIAN: What is going on that you are having such strong urges, Kim?
KIM: I am feeling really lonely and my boyfriend is with his friends and said he can't come over until later. I hate being so dependent on him. He has a right to see his friends but I can't tolerate it.
CLINICIAN: It is hard to feel so lonely and also so dependent on one person. I am confident that we can work together in therapy to help you learn to tolerate feeling alone and not needing him quite as much. In the meantime, can you try to use some self-soothing skills? Why don't you try taking a bath, maybe taking a nap until you can contact your boyfriend and find out when he can come over? Or, is there another friend you can call to feel less lonely?
KIM: My boyfriend is supposed to call me within a few hours. I guess I can try to use distress tolerance skills until he calls.
CLINICIAN: That sounds great, Kim. Will you promise to contact me again if you feel you can't follow through on this plan?
KIM: Okay. I will.

After the call, the clinician felt uneasy and decided to call a team member for consultation. The clinician did not know Kim very well and was feeling unsure about whether she could rely on her to follow through. The team member reminded the clinician that Kim had given her pills to the clinician as part of her safety plan, and also called her for coaching, so that she is demonstrating a certain amount of connection and willingness to work with the clinician to stay safe. The team member suggested that the clinician try to use distress tolerance skills herself to distract herself from her anxiety about Kim. The team member also suggested that if, after an hour or two, the clinician wanted to she could call Kim to feel out whether Kim was feeling connected enough to the clinician and to the plan to stay safe. The clinician decided to use skills to handle her own anxiety about Kim, and Kim ended up calling her two hours later to let her know she was feeling better. The clinician was relieved.

This example illustrates the way in which the team can support the clinician in both tolerating the distress surrounding suicide management and in providing a safety net for the patient. In this example, the clinician wanted to give Kim a chance to use skills to stay safe, and therefore used the support of the team to be able to tolerate her own distress about Kim's suicidality. In addition to giving the clinician sound advice regarding how to intervene with Kim, the team member was able to give feedback based on his own knowledge of Kim's course of treatment thus far (from the team meetings).

Guidelines for a DBT consultation team meeting

Within a standard DBT treatment, consultation teams meet regularly (usually weekly) and are composed of a team of DBT clinicians. Ideally, each patient has an individual DBT clinician and a skills trainer who attend the same consultation team meetings. One clinician is the "team leader" responsible for helping the team set the agenda for the meeting.

The same principles and basic structure for DBT sessions with patients are applied to team meetings. Each DBT team meeting begins with a mindfulness exercise (see Chapter 11), followed by a few minutes of sharing experiences of the mindfulness exercise. This is the way in which group skills training sessions begin. This opening promotes regular mindfulness practice among team members, as well as helps team members to cultivate a one-mindful, nonjudgmental presence during the meeting. The designated team leader, which can be a rotating function, then directs the team in creating an agenda for the team meeting. The agenda is established using the hierarchy of goals (see Chapter 8). Clinicians whose patients are engaging in life-threatening (Target 1) behaviors present their patients first. Patients who are engaging in therapy-interfering (Target 2) behaviors are presented next. Patients presented next are those engaging in quality-of-life-interfering (Target 3) behaviors.

As clinicians present their patients, the team members consult by validating the clinician as well as highlighting the areas that require change on the part of the clinician's approach. Team members listen carefully to hear if the clinician is being validating enough of the patient, and if the clinician is also pushing enough for change. Skills trainers add their observations of the patient. When the team expresses differences in the view of the patient, the team leader encourages a dialectic synthesis of the various points of view. Sometimes the team decides to engage in didactics regarding DBT interventions and concepts by choosing a reading assignment and discussing it. At times the team might view a videotape of an individual DBT session or a DBT skills group to be able to learn and offer consultation.

The concept of a consultation team is extremely valuable for clinicians who are incorporating DBT interventions and concepts in their treatment of BPD patients. We believe that the team is a crucial component of DBT that should and can be adapted to private practice. A team of colleagues who are treating patients with impulse control and behavioral difficulties (BPD, eating disorders, suicidal behaviors, substance use disorders) can decide to create a team that meets regularly to consult on cases. Meeting weekly to practice mindfulness, set an agenda, and provide and receive consultation guided by dialectic synthesis of validation and change can be a great support for clinicians working with difficult patients.

Having a team in place is also extremely useful for between-session crises and coverage during therapist absences. In our experience, team members who are familiar with our patients and with the DBT approach are best able (and willing) to cover our private practices when we are away. The team support allows for more optimal patient care as well as peace of mind for a clinician during an absence. Members of our consultation team are available for between-session coaching, and are also trained to handle suicidal crises in a way that gives the patient a chance to stay safe without being hospitalized.

Non-DBT collaboration and coordination of treatment

Coordinating the outpatient mental health care of an individual patient across disciplines and areas of specialization presents a challenge. There is no coherent approach, nor clear guidelines in place, for communicating with other health-care providers in the current mental health-care system. Of course, certain procedures for confidentiality and consent for release of information exist [1]. These procedures are a crucial component of ethical and sound clinical care, and they allow for the respectful and appropriate flow of clinical information between providers.

However, the parameters regarding the timing of and mechanism for sharing the information are less clear. Clinicians are trained to respect confidentiality to the point where they may choose not to reach out to a co-provider even when it may be appropriate and/or helpful to do so. Conversely, and more commonly, clinicians often consult with other professionals involved in their patient's care, with permission, in a way that excludes the patient from the flow of information, or discourages patient responsibility and involvement. These represent two extremes of clinical approaches to third-party contact that require a dialectic synthesis in order to find the most appropriate intervention for a given patient in a given situation.

Splitting

In the case of individuals with BPD, the matter is even more complex due to the issue of "splitting." The concept of "splitting" stems from psychoanalytic theory and the conceptualization of "borderline personality organization" [2]. The phenomenon of splitting as a defense mechanism and its vicissitudes in psychotherapy is the subject of a rich literature, and a full detailed discussion of splitting is beyond the scope of this book. Very briefly, from a psychoanalytic perspective, early disruptions in emotional development leave individuals with BPD unable to experience an integrated view of themselves, of other people, and of the world. Their internalized self-other representations are split into "good" and "bad" object representations, which causes them to view experiences and people from a good/bad, all or nothing perspective. They also have difficulty integrating emotional experiences so that when they are in one emotional state, it is almost impossible for them to imagine or remember experiencing any other type of emotion. This leads to extreme mood dependency and compartmentalization, which is extremely disruptive of identity development as well as interpersonal and vocational functioning. In addition, the inability to integrate cognitive, emotional, and interpersonal experiences has particular clinical implications.

Clinical lore is filled with examples in which a borderline patient evokes strong reactions on inpatient staff [3], outpatient clinicians, family members, and friends by rigidly categorizing the people involved with them as either good or bad in regard to them and their treatment. What this means in terms of treatment is that the clinician who is seen as "all good" becomes idealized and can feel that they are the only person who understands and who can help the patient. Such idealization can be quite seductive and can lead to a loss of therapeutic perspective and an overly positive stance toward the patient, which might then translate into a lack of recognition of the patient's difficulties. The clinician who is devalued, on the other hand, often experiences intense hostility and anger from their BPD patients and can feel that everything they do is inadequate, wrong, and hurtful. Under these circumstances, it is easy to lose therapeutic perspective and develop a strong negative stance, which might lead to a lack of compassion for the patient. In both instances, the patient's care is compromised in that the clinicians do not maintain an optimal therapeutic stance. The idealized clinician might be more inclined to make less demands on the BPD patient, might be more enabling of the patient's pathology, and miss opportunities to encourage change. The devalued clinician might be overly focused on change (which might drive the patient away), or have little patience to maintain the treatment relationship (might emotionally give up on a patient or refer the patient elsewhere).

The drastic differences in perspective regarding one patient can have a negative impact on the collaboration between the idealized and devalued clinicians. The devalued clinician might start to blame the idealized clinician for being too indulgent and enabling. The idealized clinician might blame the devalued clinician for their unwillingness to put up with the patient, and for not recognizing the patient's limitations.

An atheoretical description of splitting, adopted as a diagnostic criterion for BPD in the current version [4] of the *DSM* (APA), is defined as: "a pattern of unstable and intense interpersonal relationship characterized by alternating between extremes of idealization and devaluation." Thus, individuals with BPD also demonstrate splitting in relation to the same person, in which their regard for the other person fluctuates between an idealizing and devaluing stance. In the experience of mental health providers as well, individuals with BPD are observed to "split" within one therapeutic relationship (the clinician may be idealized until they disappoint in some way, and then they are devalued). However, as mentioned earlier, BPD patients are also known to split between providers, so that one provider is idealized while the other is devalued, in such a manner as to possibly interfere with the coordination of a treatment. This can be experienced or interpreted by the clinician as an attempt on the patient's part to manipulate, such as when a child hears "no" from one parent and then approaches the other parent to try to get what they want.

Many clinicians are concerned about the possibility of splitting when approached to be an adjunct in the treatment of a BPD patient. For example, psychopharmacologists are often unwilling to take on the medication management of these patients, despite the fact that they would not be the primary clinicians in the treatment team. In addition to being put off by the threat of suicidal behavior, they often cite the interpersonal difficulties they anticipate with a patient diagnosed with BPD, including inappropriate anger, oppositionality, noncompliance, and splitting behavior.

DBT and splitting

The dialectic worldview of synthesizing opposites and viewing all behavior within the larger context of the whole is quite effective in addressing (eliminating) what is commonly referred to as "splitting" behavior on the part of the patient. From a DBT perspective, splitting is not conceptualized as something that the BPD individual does. Rather, splitting is something that occurs within the course of treatment with BPD patients [5]. Splitting is seen as taking place when the different individuals involved disagree regarding how to best treat the patient. Splitting is considered to be a failure of dialectical synthesis, and the treatment providers are expected to take responsibility for using interpersonal skills and dialectical synthesis to resolve disagreements. Splitting among staff regarding a patient usually falls along the lines of seeing the patient as either "fragile" or needing of "a tough stance." This "either/or" dichotomy is clearly anti-dialectical, and surely both perceptions have some truth to them. The application of DBT principles such as taking a nonjudgmental and respectful stance toward both clinicians and patients can mitigate the phenomenon of splitting as well. Staff are encouraged to adopt a stance of acceptance and validation of both the patient and clinician as "doing the best they can" and balancing that with an understanding that they both need to do better.

Thus, from a DBT perspective, the phenomenon of "splitting" in treatment is an iatrogenic result of the standard approach to the coordination of care, and can be resolved through dialectic synthesis on the part of the treatment team. In addition, as we will describe, the DBT intervention of "consultation to the patient" can circumvent these types of "splits" in treatment.

Coordination of care – DBT model

Consultation to the patient

In a standard DBT treatment, one patient will have at least two clinicians – an individual clinician and a skills training group leader. As mentioned earlier, these clinicians comprise the DBT consultation team, which meets regularly to coordinate treatment. More often than not, there is also a psychopharmacologist to provide medication consultation and management. And, when there is a hospitalization, a visit to the emergency department, a day treatment program, or a family therapy component, there is a need for coordination of care external to the team.

When there is a need for communication between multiple treatment providers, the bias in DBT is that the DBT clinician refrains from stepping in whenever possible, in order to provide an opportunity to enhance the patient's ability to engage in self-care. The orientation in DBT is to teach, coach, and encourage the patient to take charge of managing their environment through effective interaction with their network of care providers. In other words, as much as possible, the DBT clinician serves the role of coach to the patient in relation to other providers in much the same way as the therapist coaches the patient in any other relationship. Thus, the DBT therapist avoids getting in the middle of a disagreement between the patient and another provider. The main innovation of DBT in this regard is the explicit role of the clinician as a consultant to the patient regarding how they can interact effectively with their clinicians. The primary objectives of this approach are to discourage passivity and avoidance and to increase respect for the patient. Thus, the patient is coached to provide the information necessary for their care to their other mental health providers. This may seem startling and annoying to other clinicians involved in the patient's care who do not practice DBT. The specific strategies for consulting to the patient, in order to facilitate and develop their ability to effectively interact with their treatment providers, are illustrated later.

In our experience, both patients and other mental health providers need to be educated regarding the consultation to the patient philosophy. As one new patient put it, "I don't want to act as a 'go-between' between my psychiatrist and you." The clinician might validate that the patient would feel more taken care of if the clinician would make the direct call to the psychiatrist, but still encourage the patient to advocate for herself.

In another example, a patient was not being adherent to her medication regimen. Upon exploring the reasons for this in session, the patient told her DBT clinician that she wanted to take a different medication but did not feel her psychiatrist would listen to her. She requested that the clinician call the psychiatrist to make the suggestion. Instead, the DBT clinician offered to coach her patient to use the DEAR MAN interpersonal skill (see Chapter 11) to effectively ask her psychiatrist for a change in medication. The patient agreed and made the request at her next visit with her psychiatrist. The psychiatrist then called the DBT clinician to complain that this patient was getting very angry with him and resisting and devaluing his efforts to help her. The clinician explained that the patient was working in therapy to learn interpersonal effectiveness skills to assert herself with him. After speaking with the clinician, the psychiatrist was then able to take a more validating approach and be more receptive to the patient, who was finally learning to assert herself (perhaps clumsily at first) in her treatment. Thus, consultation to the patient sometimes necessitates consultation to the provider to be more receptive to collaboration with the patient.

As this example illustrates, the consultation to the patient approach may result in less accuracy or efficiency in the relaying of information, can leave more room for misinterpretation, and requires more effort on the part of the clinician (and patient). It is similar to how parents encourage a young child to dress himself or do certain tasks to build his sense of mastery and independence, at the cost of having the task done less efficiently. Overprotective parenting can interfere with skills acquisition. Thus, unless there is a crisis or an immediate need for more direct, comprehensive information, this is a worthwhile price to pay to teach self-advocacy.

Besides having positive long-term effects of building competence, such an approach also sets an example for and cultivates a stance of radical acceptance (see Chapter 11) of the system the way it is and having to cope with it. The clinician does not collude with an unrealistic expectation that the world will change, or that someone will magically swoop down to fix a problem or situation.

Consultation to the patient and splitting

By consulting to the patient rather than stepping in to intervene, the clinician avoids taking sides in any of the disagreements between treatment providers, and thus avoids involvement in, or contribution to, the type of therapeutic split that might otherwise occur. The clinician maintains the stance of coaching patients to advocate for themselves. In the face of disagreements between clinicians and other providers, a dialectical stance would consist of integrating the various points of view rather than dichotomizing them. Thus, a clinician could validate a patient's dissatisfaction with a particular treatment provider, but also firmly communicate that it is ultimately the patient's responsibility to manage the relationship, albeit with help, support, and skills coaching from the DBT clinician.

Clinicians do not have to take the side of other clinicians. As consultants to the patient, they can validate the patient's experience of the "offending" treatment provider and then direct the patient to skillfully negotiate her needs with this person. The clinician does not feel compelled to be on the same page with another clinician in order to "present a united front." Nor does the clinician need to take the patient's side. Rather, the therapist encourages the patient to use skills to interact with the "treatment-interfering" clinician. The patient may have been trying to convince one clinician to intervene on her behalf with the other clinician and, if done, may inadvertently contribute to the patient's avoidance and passivity. The clinician can validate without taking sides, and without feeling compelled to rush in and "fix" the problem.

Case example

ALICE: (initiating a coaching phone call to her clinician and sounding very upset): I just came from skills group – I asked Terry (the skills group leader) if I could ask a question and she said "No." Can you believe that? She was being really mean.

CLINICIAN: Wow, that does sound kind of off-putting, I can understand why you are upset.

ALICE: I am really upset. I want her to know that she really hurt my feelings! Can you call her and tell her that she shouldn't do that to me again? Otherwise I'm not going back to group.

CLINICIAN: I totally get it that you are upset and I think you have every right to feel that way. I would really hate it, though, if you made any big decisions about group right now when you are so upset. And I am really glad that you called me so we could do some skills coaching. How about reviewing some emotion regulation skills to get into a less emotional state of mind first? If I can help you find "wise mind," then maybe we could problem-solve about how to use your interpersonal effectiveness skills to speak with Terry yourself and let her know how she made you feel. What do you think?

ALICE: (still very agitated): How could she speak to me that way? She is an awful therapist –she doesn't know the first thing about how to run a group!

CLINICIAN: It must have felt terrible to have her say no like that, especially in front of everyone else in the group.

ALICE: Exactly! How could she do this to me? I feel so humiliated.

CLINICIAN: Yes, being told no in front of the others must have felt humiliating. I really get that. What do you think we can do about it?

ALICE: I don't know but I have to say something – she really hurt my feelings.

CLINICIAN: Yes, I think you should definitely say something. How about this? Why don't you write down all of your thoughts and feelings about what happened? Then you can identify exactly what you would like to say to Terry, using the DEAR MAN (interpersonal) skills so that you can let her know what you want and how you feel in a skillful manner.

ALICE: I guess I can try that.

In this example, the clinician accepted Alice's report of the events at face value. The clinician did not assume that the patient was distorting the interaction with the skills leader (although she may have been). The clinician also did not advocate for the skills leader or try to correct any possible distortions in Alice's interpretation of the incident (by saying things like – what do you think she meant by it or why do you think she said that, perhaps you heard wrong, maybe she was upset about something else at the time, etc.). And the clinician makes a point of not assuming that Alice did something to provoke such a response from the skills leader (although she may have). Each of these approaches would have added to Alice's experience of invalidation at that moment. The clinician will take note of some of these other issues to address at a future point in time, when Alice may be more receptive to examining the ways in which she may have contributed to or misunderstood what happened. But for the time being, during the phone call, the focus was on letting Alice feel that the clinician was on her side, by both validating and encouraging her to use her skills.

The clinician was able to make Alice feel supported and validated without engaging in negative judgment of the skills leader. The clinician's neutral stance regarding the skills leader's behavior (as reported by Alice), modeled using the skill of radical acceptance (see Chapter 11), in this case led to accepting the fact that skills leaders are human and make mistakes. Or it could result in radical acceptance of the fact that life is not always fair and people still have to use their skills to make the best of it. The clinician also modeled the skill of "effectiveness," as taught in skills training, also referred to as "doing what works," indicating that it is more effective to focus on how to use skills rather than to belabor the unfairness or injustice of the situation. Therefore, the clinician shifted the focus away from blame finding, and toward the skills Alice could use to calm herself down and skillfully assert herself with the skills leader. The fact that the clinician validated Alice probably helped to cultivate a willingness on Alice's part to use skills.

Thus, a dialectic stance toward third-party clinicians helps to avoid the pitfalls of getting in the middle. By validating and encouraging effective skillful behavior rather than dwelling on the patient's interpretations of being victimized, the patient can be encouraged to avoid passive avoidance and to let go of needing to blame, or to split in order to feel validated.

Consultation to third-party clinicians

Given the "consultation to the patient" orientation, DBT offers a specific perspective regarding the conditions under which, and the manner in which, a clinician consults with third-party treaters or involved family members or friends. This perspective allows for mindful consideration of the therapeutic goals involved in making such an intervention, or in deciding not to. There are parameters for third-party consultation, both within the treatment team (interaction between clinician and/or group clinician) and without (family, friends, institutional representatives, psychopharmacologists, nutritionists, etc.).

Direct intervention is indicated when the patient is unable to act and the outcome is very important (e.g., when the patient is incapacitated by a drug overdose). Direct consultation by the clinician with a third party is also indicated when the environment demands the intervention of a "professional," such as when dealing with insurance companies, interacting with entrenched bureaucracies such as hospitals, ERs, and day programs with application and other procedures.

Clinicians are, of course, mandated to intervene when the patient's life is at stake. Furthermore, DBT clinicians are encouraged to consider whether intervening on behalf of the patient is the humane thing to do if no harm will result. When considering such an intervention for a patient, therapists are trained to ask themselves whether they would intervene in such a way for a friend and not do less for their patients than they would do for other important people in their lives with respect to this type of intervention. An example of this might be if a patient is having trouble contacting their psychiatrist in an emergency. The DBT therapist would consider using his or her personal connection and access to the physician to facilitate communication.

Summary

There is a dialectic regarding the treatment of individuals with BPD or other impulse control disorders (such as eating disorders) in that these individuals usually require a team of multiple providers, while at the same time the phenomenon of splitting often complicates the coordination of care. In this chapter, we reviewed DBT concepts that help guide the clinician in obtaining support while avoiding the pitfalls of splitting that often adversely affect the effectiveness of treatment. First, DBT reconceptualizes splitting as a failure of dialectic synthesis on the part of treatment providers, and therefore places responsibility for splitting with the clinician rather than the patient. DBT guidelines for consultation to the patient and to third-party providers help the clinician make thoughtful decisions regarding the coordination of treatment that both empower and provide a safety net for the patient. The DBT consultation team provides support for the clinician in maintaining a dialectic therapeutic stance toward patients.

References

1. American Psychological Association. (2002) *American Psychological Association Ethical Principles of Psychologists and Code of Conduct*, Standard 4. http://www.apa.org/ethics/code2002.html. Accessed on 8 February 2013.
2. Kernberg, O.F. (1967) Borderline personality organization. *Journal of the American Psychoanalytic Association*, 15 (3), 641–685.
3. Book, H.E., Sadavoy, J., Silver, D. (1978) Staff countertransference to borderline patients on an inpatient unit. *American Journal of Psychotherapy*, 32 (4), 521–532.
4. American Psychiatric Association. (2000) *Diagnostic and Statistical Manual of Mental Disorders* (4th ed., text rev.), American Psychiatric Association, Washington, DC.
5. Linehan, M.M. (1993) *Cognitive Behavioral Treatment of Borderline Personality Disorder*, Guilford Press, New York, pp. 431–433.

Chapter 16

DBT case formulation

Now that we have described DBT theory and interventions, we present guidelines for a detailed case formulation, developed at the beginning of treatment. It provides the basis for the DBT treatment plan and serves as the road map for treatment. Some aspects of the DBT case formulation can be found in most treatment approaches case formulations (e.g., case history) while others are unique to DBT (e.g., patient's dialectical dilemmas).

Key points

- A DBT case formulation includes several components
- Brief case history based on the biosocial theory of BPD
- Outline of the hierarchy of primary treatment goals as well as secondary goals that are addressed to achieve the primary goals
- Summary of skills deficits and behavioral excesses
- Conceptualization of the patient's "dialectical dilemmas"
- Detailed formulation of the contingencies in self and in the environment that reinforce unskillful behaviors
- Detailed treatment plan regarding how the behavioral goals, skills deficits, and contingency management will be targeted

Our goal is to provide a clear and comprehensive overview of DBT psychotherapy for the treatment of BPD and other impulse control disorders. We describe the theoretical basis of DBT and how it informs a unique conceptualization of and therapeutic approach to the diagnosis and presenting problems in individuals with BPD, distinguishing it from other treatment approaches. We describe the history and theory of the BPD diagnosis, etiology, and phenomenology, as well as the dialectic theory that provides the foundation for the DBT therapeutic stance and interventions. We also present how the dialectic approach of the DBT model represents a synthesis of a Zen/mindfulness orientation with acceptance/validation strategies and learning theory. We illustrate how these theoretical underpinnings translate into specific treatment interventions that effectively target the problematic

---

The Dialectical Behavior Therapy Primer: How DBT Can Inform Clinical Practice, First Edition.
Beth S. Brodsky and Barbara Stanley.
© 2013 John Wiley & Sons, Ltd. Published 2013 by John Wiley & Sons, Ltd.

behaviors presented by BPD individuals. These include self-harm and other destructive behaviors, as well as emotional and interpersonal dysregulation that often lead to suicidal (and other destructive) behaviors as well as therapist burnout and treatment dropout. We present the rationale for skills training and review the DBT skills modules and training format.

In this chapter, we present the case of Kim to illustrate the DBT approach to case conceptualization. Kim has many Stage 1 (life-threatening and "quality of life"- interfering) behaviors, and, therefore, the case conceptualization, although mentioning Stage 2, focuses mostly on Stage 1. The case of Kim illustrates the integration of DBT concepts and interventions into a DBT case formulation [1]. We will present a brief outline of how to think about and formulate a case from a DBT perspective. The case formulation is mainly for the purposes of treatment planning.

DBT versus psychodynamic formulation

DBT case formulation is driven by social learning and CBT principles, and, therefore, is largely focused on observable behavior. Thus, as opposed to psychodynamic case conceptualization, there is no reference to unconscious mechanisms or processes. A purely behavioral approach to understanding psychopathology discourages speculation regarding what might be happening in the mind [2], and makes inferences based on behaviors and the visible antecedents and consequences of these behaviors (refer to Chapter 6 for a description of learning theory and basic behavioral principles). When the purely behavioral approach is modified to include a focus on cognition, as in CBT and DBT, the formulation includes some inference into what type of interpretation the patient is making (which is not explicitly "observable"). However, this inference is highly reliant on patient report and not on speculation regarding some "unconscious motivation" or process that is outside the patient's awareness.

DBT case formulation

Brief history

In DBT, only a *brief history* of the patient, one that is informed by the biosocial theory of the etiology of BPD (Chapter 4), is included. This brief history highlights factors related to the biological predisposition to emotional dysregulation and characteristics of the invalidating environment that are believed to be directly relevant to the patient's presenting symptomatology. A brief psychiatric history of the patient's symptoms and past treatment is also included.

The presenting problem

Second, *the presenting problem* is described very clearly in specific detail regarding primary goals to be targeted in treatment, according to the hierarchy of goals. Target 1 behaviors are listed first. These include suicide attempts, NSSI, active suicidal ideation, suicidal threats, homicidal ideation, or behaviors that might harm others. Other life-threatening behaviors considered to be Target 1 might include reckless driving or unsafe sexual practices. In the treatment of someone with a primary eating disorder, any binge/purge/restricting behaviors might be prioritized as Target 1, particularly in the absence of suicidal behavior and NSSI and if the eating disorder behavior is potentially life threatening. If a patient has a primary substance use disorder, Target 1 behaviors might be expanded to include substance abuse. Any therapy-interfering behaviors (Target 2) are considered next. Examples include: lateness to therapy, poor attendance, not attending skills sessions regularly, not doing assigned homework, not following the parameters of between-session contact (see Chapter 12), and not calling for coaching when necessary. Finally, any other quality-of-life behaviors that are to be targeted in the absence of Targets 1 and 2 behaviors should be prioritized and listed. These might include shoplifting or stealing, interpersonal verbal abuse, anger outbursts, avoidance behaviors, eating disorder or substance use behavior that is not prioritized as Target 1, relationship problems, and work/school problems.

Case example

Kim's brief history

Kim is a 28-year-old single white woman living with two roommates. She came to outpatient DBT from a day program she had attended for three months following hospitalization for a suicide attempt. The suicide attempt consisted of a serious overdose of her roommate's sleeping pills, which she took impulsively after an argument with her boyfriend. She lost consciousness, was found by her roommate, and taken to the ED where her stomach was pumped. She regained consciousness after a few hours. She was referred to DBT because she was diagnosed with BPD and was intermittently suicidal. She experienced suicidal ideation, and, in addition to three prior suicide attempts, she occasionally engaged in NSSI, which consisted of making cuts on her inner arm without intent to die, her mood fluctuated from depression to anger to feelings of emptiness, she had interpersonal difficulties, and was guarded and suspicious when she experienced stress.

Kim is an only child. Her parents divorced when she was four years old. Her father moved to another state and had only sporadic contact with her for two years. He then remarried and had more children, became very involved with his new family and had little to no contact with Kim. Kim's mother had a number of boyfriends and then remarried when Kim was seven years old. Kim reported a severe history of repeated sexual abuse at the hands of her stepfather between the ages of 8 and 12. When drunk, he would come into her room at night, would frighten her into having intercourse, and to remain quiet about it. This abuse ended when her mother and stepfather divorced. Kim suspected that her mother knew about it but was not sure. Kim became unable to trust her own perceptions, not sure what were real feelings and actions and what were not. She has a very conflicted relationship with her mother, whom she perceives as unprotective of her, and weak, and in need of protection herself.

Kim first sought treatment at age 24, consisting of outpatient psychotherapy and psychopharmacology. She has a history of the one psychiatric hospitalizations and is chronically self-injurious and has made two low-lethality suicide attempts in the past, three including the most recent overdose. In her first suicide attempt at age 22, she turned on the gas stove with reported intent to die but was interrupted by a roommate. In her second suicide attempt at age 26, she swallowed an unknown number of pills,

(Continued)

> (*Continued*)
> most likely a mixture of the three medications she was taking at the time, and then called someone to help her. She had her stomach pumped in the ED and was released, with no other medical consequences. She has had the following medication trials in the past: selective serotonin reuptake inhibitor (SSRI), monoamine oxidase inhibitor (MAOI), low-dose atypical antipsychotic medications, and is currently on 150 mg Effexor qd, which she feels is helpful in preventing her from feeling very hopeless and suicidal when she is depressed. She has a history of substance abuse of cocaine and marijuana; currently her substance use consists of smoking small amounts of marijuana on a daily basis, by her report, in order to relieve tension and prevent self-harm behaviors.
>
> Kim is currently taking college writing courses and looking for an office job. After graduating from college she had worked as an administrative assistant at a financial firm for about two years until she became depressed and angry and either did not show up to work or got into altercations with coworkers. As she described it, "I stopped going to work because I felt as if my boss was deliberately trying to give me a hard time."

Statement of Kim's presenting problem – Stage 1

Target 1. Kim engages in NSSI behavior consisting of making small, superficial cuts on her arms and sometimes her stomach with an Exacto knife. At the beginning of DBT treatment, she was engaging in this behavior approximately once a month. Kim has also made three suicide attempts in her life and has intermittent suicidal ideation, which is mostly passive and consisting of thoughts of wishing that she were dead. Sometimes her thoughts become more actively suicidal and she starts thinking about ways she could kill herself. She has a number of methods that she considers, including overdosing on pills, jumping from a high window, or asphyxiation by placing her head into an oven. These behaviors are almost always precipitated by negative interpersonal interaction, mostly with her boyfriend but also with employers, friends, and family members.

Target 2. Kim periodically misses her individual psychotherapy session, particularly after a session in which she felt invalidated. At these times, she does not call to say she will not be attending the session. She also has difficulty calling for coaching when she should in order to use skills to fight urges to hurt herself.

Target 3. Kim often has temper outbursts, usually precipitated by feelings that she is being criticized, which lead to escalating fights with her boyfriend and result in his staying away for a few days and not speaking to her. She would like to gain control over her temper outbursts and fights with her boyfriend. She also is not working right now and is interested in returning to work as an administrative assistant. A longer-term goal is to pursue a creative interest in writing but this is thwarted by her difficulty in completing writing assignments.

Primary targets

The primary targets for treatment are outlined according to the hierarchy of goals for the purpose of treatment planning. If the treatment is targeting life-threatening (Target 1) behaviors, the patient is considered to be in Stage 1 of DBT treatment. If the patient is not engaging in any life-threatening behaviors, has addressed the most significant quality of life issues, and is in need of exposure therapy for trauma, Stage 2 is entered (see Chapter 17).

Kim's Primary Targets: Stage 1.

1 Refrain from engaging in suicidal behavior, decrease suicide ideation, and eliminate NSSI.
2 Increase adaptive coping skills, particularly emotion regulation and interpersonal effectiveness.
3 Decrease therapy-interfering behaviors of treatment avoidance (i.e., missing sessions and not calling for coaching when needed).
4 Decrease temper outbursts and severe arguments, increase job-seeking behaviors, maintain employment, and remove obstacles to achieving long-term goals.

Secondary treatment targets

Secondary targets are conceptualized in terms of the four areas of dysregulation, which also must be addressed in order to target the primary treatment goals. The dialectical dilemmas [3] are also considered in formulating secondary treatment targets. Secondary targets, and how they contribute to the primary treatment goals, should be identified and described in clear terms, specific to the particular patient and their behaviors. For example, in general, secondary targets that are related to the reducing suicidal and self-harm behaviors might be emotional dysregulation (increasing the capacity to regulate emotions, decreasing the experience of negative emotions, and decreasing emotional reactivity), behavioral dysregulation (impulsivity, poor judgment, and difficulty controlling urges to act unskillfully), cognitive dysregulation (distorted interpretations, dysfunctional thoughts, and core beliefs), or interpersonal dysregulation (overdependency on significant others for self-definition and self-soothing). Secondary targets that are related to reducing therapy-interfering behaviors might be behavioral dysregulation (avoidance behaviors) or interpersonal dysregulation (feeling overly dependent or not wanting or knowing how to ask for help).

Kim's Secondary Targets

The following areas of dysregulation contribute to Kim's suicidal behaviors, ideation, and cutting behaviors:

1 *Emotion dysregulation.* Kim exhibits extreme mood lability – she can be feeling euthymic and then suddenly can very quickly swing to feeling either hopeless and depressed, or angry and irritable, or start experiencing feelings of intense shame. She also has upswings in which she feels overly energized. She also experiences these feelings, particularly anger, very intensely. When she is in these emotional states, she often exhibits poor judgment. She considers suicide when she is hopeless, and she cuts herself to escape feelings of anger and shame.
2 *Behavioral dysregulation.* When Kim is in an emotionally dysregulated state, she often feels the urge to act impulsively. When depressed and hopeless, her suicidal ideation is triggered and often accompanied by urges to act on it in some way – by

either planning ways to kill herself or communicating to someone that she is thinking about suicide. When she is feeling anger and shame, she also experiences a sense of self-hatred, which becomes too difficult to tolerate and she starts having urges to cut herself. When she is in a more elevated, "hypomanic" mood, she makes unrealistic plans, which she is unable to fulfill.

3 *Cognitive dysregulation.* Kim often misinterprets the feelings and motives of her boyfriend, friends, and employers. Whenever her boyfriend wants to hang out with his friends or has some type of interaction with another woman, she becomes suspicious that he will cheat on her. She often thinks that her friends are leaving her out and do not want to be with her. When employers give her instructions, she quickly assumes that they are not interested in her ideas and feels disrespected by them. These interpretations trigger the emotional states that lead to her self-harm behaviors.

4 *Interpersonal dysregulation.* Kim is highly dependent on her boyfriend for reassurance and for modulating her sense of self and self-esteem. When she receives what she needs from him, it feels satisfying. However, much of the time she feels very vulnerable and afraid of losing him. This, in turn, contributes to her emotional dysregulation. She also starts to hate herself for needing him so much. This vulnerability makes her more susceptible to the emotional triggers that lead to self-harm behaviors.

Dialectical dilemmas in a DBT formulation

In addition to understanding primary target behaviors (self-harm, therapy-interfering, and "quality of life"-threatening behaviors) from a behavioral and social learning theoretical perspective, Linehan has identified three "dialectical dilemmas"[4] which are destructive patterns of behavior common to BPD patients that have developed in response to the transaction between emotional dysregulation and an invalidating environment. These behavioral patterns are dialectical in that they are characterized by extreme swings from one end of a continuum to the other, and that each end of the continuum also contains its antithesis (or the other side of the continuum).

The first dialectical dilemma, *emotional vulnerability versus self-invalidation*, describes how individuals with BPD swing from becoming very emotionally dysregulated in the face of invalidation (escalating in order to "prove" that their feelings are valid and to get a validating response – "I have a right to be upset") to becoming extremely self-invalidating ("What is wrong with me – there is no reason for me to be feeling this way") due to having lost control over their emotional experience. This leads them to try to take too much control over their emotions by not seeking validation, which results in starting to feel invalidated and then escalating again in order to seek validation.

The second dialectical dilemma is termed *active passivity versus apparent competence*. Active passivity is a learned behavioral pattern in which the individual learns to "cope" with overwhelming situations by becoming passive in terms of trying to problem-solve, and by actively expressing distress in ways that will prompt others to rush in to help.

Apparent competence describes the ways in which individuals with BPD have learned to hide their negative feelings and act as if everything is fine. Or, they are in a mood state in which they forget that they have negative feelings and in which they believe that everything *is*, and will be, fine. In this mode, patients have unrealistic expectations regarding what they can do on their own, they disregard their emotional limitations (the mood dependency that interferes with a consistent level of functioning), and are unwilling to reveal "weakness" by asking directly for help. Active passivity and apparent competence represent two ends of a continuum that play into each other. The appearance of competence leads to feeling overwhelmed and alone by having taken on too much and being unwilling to ask for help directly. The individual becomes actively passive by either avoiding or refusing to do what is needed in a given situation, which is experienced by the others involved as a cry for help.

Linehan identified a third dialectical dilemma, which she calls *unrelenting crisis versus inhibited grieving*. Unrelenting crisis refers to the ways in which an individual both creates and is controlled by a never-ending series of aversive events. Individuals with BPD, due to their emotional and behavioral dysregulation, react impulsively when distressed, and often create crises for themselves. They have temper outbursts, which lead to the loss of jobs and relationships, impulsive behaviors that lead to financial loss, health problems, and hospitalizations. These crisis-generating behaviors are often due to attempts to avoid feeling distress, or inhibited grieving. These individuals have learned to survive extremely difficult life circumstances and trauma by not allowing themselves to feel pain and negative emotions. Impulsive reactive behaviors represent their best attempts to avoid feeling distress, and inadvertently create more distress in the process. In addition, reacting to crisis, as painful as it might be, might also serve to distract from the experience of deep loss. Thus, the example of Laura from Chapter 6 who was stalking her boyfriend when he broke up with her illustrates this dialectical dilemma. He might decide to call the police when she is outside banging on his door, intoxicated and refusing to leave. Her unwillingness/inability to accept the loss of her boyfriend (inhibited grieving) is leading to crisis-generating behavior. Having to deal with the consequences of her behavior also is a distraction from having to accept the loss.

In our work with BPD patients, we have identified two other dialectical dilemmas in addition to Linehan's original three. We see a pattern which we have described as being *overly trusting versus overly guarded* that contributes to interpersonal dysregulation and subsequent self-harm and therapy-interfering behaviors. Individuals with BPD often cannot tolerate the in-between period of getting to know and build trust with another person. Their deep need for connection and help leads them to become overly trusting with someone they do not know very well. This quickly sets them up to become overly mistrustful as soon as they feel misunderstood, invalidated, or if the person behaves in a way that is unexpected and disappointing. They then feel too distant and disconnected, and push away their mistrust to become overly trusting again. This failure of dialectical synthesis is disruptive to a more realistic trust-building process and the development of intimacy in interpersonal relationships.

Finally, there is the dialectical dilemma of feeling *entitled versus undeserving*. We find that the experience of individuals with BPD is that they feel very self-hating and undeserving most of the time. We are then caught by surprise when we experience them as feeling very entitled, such as insisting on having things their way, or spending a lot of money on themselves. We have come to understand that when BPD individuals feel invalidated, especially because they have a pervasive sense of feeling undeserving, they need to overcompensate to validate themselves by flipping into a more entitled position. After they have behaved in an entitled manner, they feel guilty and revert to the position of feeling undeserving. This dialectic is similar to the first, emotional dysregulation versus self-invalidation, but it has a specific contribution to emotional and interpersonal dysregulation.

These dialectical dilemmas are unique aspects of DBT case conceptualization. Secondary targets related to the dialectical dilemmas include increasing self-validation, decreasing self-invalidation, decreasing inhibited grieving (increasing emotional experiencing), increasing active problem solving, and decreasing mood dependency of behavior.

Kim's Dialectical Dilemmas

1. *Emotion vulnerability versus self-invalidation.* Kim often becomes very emotionally dysregulated when she is trying to get her boyfriend to understand how she feels. This can lead to feeling that she is crazy and there is something wrong with her for losing control over something that was really not such a big deal.
2. *Active passivity versus apparent competence.* When Kim is not suicidal, she denies that she will ever feel suicidal again and she is reluctant to plan ahead and problem-solve around preventing suicidal urges or having a safety plan in place, since she believes she will not need one. Also when she is feeling energized, she puts a lot of pressure on herself to be productive and not needy and de-emphasizes her need for help. When she is upset, she will not show up for session and will not let the therapist know what is happening, leading the therapist to worry and try to reach her for skills coaching.
3. *Unrelenting crises versus inhibited grieving.* Kim tries to avoid situations that remind her of her sexual abuse but cannot completely avoid triggers. When she is triggered, she quickly reacts with urges to self-harm in order to rid herself of feelings of shame and anger.
4. *Overly trusting versus overly guarded.* Kim has difficulty trusting anyone in her life and she does not exhibit this particular dialectical dilemma.
5. *Entitled versus undeserving.* Kim can become very entitled in terms of trying to get her boyfriend to do and say things that she wants/needs him to do. She has trouble when he needs her, and sees his neediness as detracting from her need for attention. This leads to guilt, which then makes her feel undeserving of being taken care of. When she feels that she is not getting enough attention from her boyfriend, she starts to feel entitled to his attention again. She feels that his lack of attention is his way of saying that she is undeserving, and she cannot tolerate that.

Thus, for Kim, secondary targets related to the dialectical dilemmas include increasing self-validation, decreasing self-invalidation, decreasing inhibited grieving (increasing emotional experiencing), increasing active problem solving, and decreasing mood dependency of behavior.

Stage 2 – treatment goals

Once life-threatening behaviors are under control, and the patient has made significant progress in the reduction of therapy-interfering behaviors and is exhibiting more stable functioning in terms of quality-of-life behaviors, they are ready to enter Stage 2 DBT. In this stage of treatment, exposure to trauma is the main treatment target. Trauma work typically does not commence in DBT until the patient learns skills to effectively cope with life and "quality of life"-interfering behaviors, unless the trauma is recent and then it is addressed immediately. The rationale for this approach is that exposure to trauma will undoubtedly trigger extremely painful emotions, which increases the risk for the patient to regress back to less skillful forms of coping. For many patients, it is difficult for them to delay trauma work but an analogy to running a marathon is helpful in explaining the rationale to patients. We do not decide to go out and run a marathon one day and just do it. In order to run this race, runners must train and be prepared and, in doing so, they protect themselves from injury. Similarly, in order to address past traumatic experiences, patients must "train" and have the necessary skills in place so that under the stress of the "marathon," they do not injure themselves (e.g., engage in NSSI or suicidal behavior). In Stage 2, in addition to trauma exposure work, life-interfering, therapy-interfering, and "quality of life"-interfering goals are monitored and become the focus of treatment if and when they reemerge.

Although we are focusing on the formulation for a Stage 1 DBT, we add this description of Kim's goals for Stage 2 since she (as is common for many BPD patients) agreed to the Stage 1 goals in order to prepare for trauma work, her main therapeutic objective.

Kim's Stage 2 Treatment Targets

1. Exposure to sexual abuse experienced as a child
2. Monitoring suicidal ideation, urges to engage in self-cutting
3. Addressing therapy-interfering behaviors if they are present (on both patient's and therapist's part)
4. Addressing any unskillful behaviors that arise in her relationships and vocational functioning

Current stage of treatment

As can be seen from the detailed nature of this case formulation, it takes some time to develop it. Thus, while it is developed early in treatment in order to guide the course of therapy, it is completed after the patient and therapist have had a chance to get to know and work with each other and develop an idea of how to understand and best approach the patient's treatment goals. The treatment plan is developed around this understanding as well as around how the treatment has progressed (or not) thus far.

Kim's Current Stage of Treatment. Kim is currently in Stage 1 and is stable within treatment. She comes to individual and skills training sessions more often than not and fills out her diary card. She periodically misses sessions without calling to cancel, although she never misses more than one session at a time and invariably shows up for the next appointment after missing one. She has started to call for coaching when she is feeling suicidal but also misses opportunities to call. A tentative treatment alliance has been established and continues to be developed. Kim expresses some mistrust regarding the therapist's intentions and sometimes feels that the therapist is "hiding" what she is really thinking about Kim. This frightens Kim because she is afraid that her therapist will one day reveal these "true" feelings and show her rage and hatred of the patient. The primary treatment goal is to refrain from suicidal behavior, and decrease NSSI and suicidal ideation. Sessions are largely spent on behavioral chain analyses of episodes in which Kim has engaged in self-cutting or has had spikes either in urges to cut or in suicidal ideation. Kim and her therapist review weekly progress using the diary card, and problem solve using DBT skills to intervene at different points along the chain. The therapeutic dyad addresses therapy-interfering behaviors such as when she does not call for help in fighting an urge to self-harm, which leads to addressing the treatment alliance issues – she feels diminished by her position as a "patient," by feeling at the therapist's mercy when waiting for a returned phone call. Kim responds well to the direct nonjudgmental approach to addressing therapy-interfering behaviors, which includes addressing her sense that the therapist is concealing her true feelings (what she sees as the therapist's therapy-interfering behaviors). She also finds reassurance in using the diary card and the chain analysis. All of these approaches are experienced as transparent to her and, therefore, increase her sense of safety and free her from worrying that something unexpected will occur in the therapy.

The treatment plan

The treatment plan is then organized by the behavioral treatment targets and by an analysis of behavioral excesses and skills deficits, and the patient's dialectical dilemmas. Hypotheses are made as to the environmental precipitants, the contextual events, and vulnerability factors as well as the secondary, intervening variables that trigger and contribute to the target behavior. The DBT modes, strategies, and interventions that are to be applied to address the target goals based on this analysis are clearly delineated.

Kim's treatment plan

Environmental precipitants. Kim's suicidal ideation is often triggered by interactions with her boyfriend. When he wants to spend time with his friends, Kim feels abandoned, then becomes suspicious of his interactions with other women and imagines that he is cheating on her. Kim's boyfriend then distances himself by not seeing her for a few days after he has been wrongfully accused of cheating. Kim's urges to cut herself are usually triggered by feeling criticized or invalidated by her friends, therapist, and employers. Feeling criticized, disrespected, or invalidated also contributes to avoidance behaviors (not showing up) in therapy and at work.

Contextual events/Vulnerability factors. Kim's vulnerabilities are principally within the domain of emotion dysregulation, consisting of experiencing rage as a physical reaction (skin starts to "tingle," feels pressure on her temples), the inability to tolerate intense negative affects such as shame and anger, and depression and hopelessness, accompanied by suicidal ideation. She also experiences intense feelings of emptiness. This makes her vulnerable in the interpersonal domain, since she is overly reliant on significant others for a sense of feeling whole and emotionally stable. As a result of her interpersonal vulnerability, she is hypervigilant to feeling abandoned and criticized, which contributes to cognitive vulnerability in the form of distorted perceptions of the behaviors and motives of others. Contextual events are also prominent. She sometimes feels triggered to cut herself at the sight of her scars from having cut in the past.

Excesses. Kim often experiences anger, accompanied by a high level of physiological arousal. She has crisis-generating patterns as a consequence of her hypervigilance to perceived criticism and abandonment, and mistrust and misperception of the intentions of others. She is overly dependent on others, and when she is not upset she becomes too self-reliant and overly trusting of others.

Kim's excessive, inappropriate anger usually leads to either a temper outburst or shame-induced self-attacking ruminations referring to herself in negative terms (e.g., "I'm a piece of garbage."), feeling toxic, feeling her skin tingling, and experiencing escalating internal physical pressure that finds release in self-cutting.

In her more energetic spurts, usually after an outburst or an episode of cutting, she "sets herself up" by trying to take on everything at once (starts job hunting, decides to be completely trusting of her boyfriend). She tries to avoid experiencing negative emotional states of anger and depression (inhibited grieving) by forgetting that she ever felt mistrustful or criticized by others and idealizes the people in her life.

Deficits. Kim has great difficulty controlling her experience of her anger, a deficit in ability to process emotional experience through cognitive mechanisms and verbal outlets. Anger becomes solely a physical sensation, experienced as pressure on her head that she can only alleviate by having temper outbursts or by cutting herself. She lacks self-soothing skills, has difficulty getting support from others in her environment, and has a tendency to ruminate about the ways in which she feels abandoned, criticized, and betrayed by others.

She also has trouble with realistic decision-making and judgment – when she is in an elevated mood, her mind becomes flooded with ideas about all of the things she can and should do: find a job right away, be much more open and trusting, enroll in more writing classes. She eventually and inevitably fails to follow through with these plans. This, in turn, results in greater disappointment, demoralization, and recriminations.

Kim demonstrates deficits in the following skills:

Mindfulness. When Kim is ruminating, she loses all ability to be nonjudgmental.

Interpersonal. Kim focuses on self-respect to exclusion of relationship effectiveness and has an immediate need to express herself without considering the long-term consequences. Kim also has difficulty finding a balance between self-reliance and appropriately seeking help.

Emotion regulation. Kim has difficulty identifying current emotional state, synthesizing emotional and rational states of mind (i.e., wise mind), validating her own emotions, and distinguishing between thoughts, feelings, physiological states, and actions urges. She does not maintain a regular schedule of sleep, eating, and taking care of her other physical needs.

Distress tolerance. When feeling physical sensation of agitation, pressure, or toxicity, Kim can no longer tolerate these feelings and often resorts to NSSI. She is able to tolerate distress temporarily by giving herself permission to self-injure later. She also attempts to completely eliminate distressing experiences or feelings through avoidance or compartmentalization.

Secondary targets related to Kim's excesses and deficits:

1. Increase self-soothing skills
2. Increase skills for reducing physiological arousal
3. Decrease rumination
4. Increase ability to recognize and challenge distorted interpersonal interpretations
5. Increase interpersonal effectiveness in communicating with boyfriend
6. Develop self-validation of her emotions
7. Learn to label affect, find verbal expression for emotional experience
8. Learn to distinguish between feelings of anger from feelings of physical pressure
9. Decrease vulnerability to negative emotions

Consequences of Target and Skillful Behaviors

Reinforcers of Target 1 behaviors. Kim has immediate internal reinforcers for her cutting behavior. She experiences an immediate reduction in physiological and emotional tension, which serves as a negative reinforcer. She also feels euphoric and energized. With respect to her anger outbursts, her immediate response is that they feel appropriate because she has a sense of standing up for herself, not allowing herself to be taken advantage of and feeling vulnerable to betrayal. An immediate external reinforcer for NSSI is that sometimes her boyfriend will be more attentive and will agree to remain with her instead of going out with his friends.

Reinforcers of Target 2 behaviors. An immediate internal reinforcer for missing sessions and avoiding work is that Kim avoids the negative emotions that arise in those situations.

Reinforcers of skillful behavior. Kim sometimes feels a sense of mastery when she is able to ride through an urge to self-injure, but it is not as immediate nor as powerful a reinforcer for her. An external reinforcer is that she will not have to do a behavioral analysis in the therapy session and she can discuss something other than Target 1 behavior. Although Kim experiences behavioral analyses as helpful, she would prefer not to revisit yet another episode of self-harm behavior in session.

Negative consequences of effective behavior. For Kim, the challenge is that there are many punishing and less reinforcing consequences for skillful behaviors. Most consequences are in relation to her internal state. When Kim uses skills, she has to tolerate more stress and feelings of anger and self-hate. She becomes aware of feelings of fear that arise when she does not immediately act on urges to either self-harm or start a fight with her boyfriend. Also, when she is skillful, she feels increased pressure and expectations from herself and others to have to continue to use skills. She is overwhelmed by the prospect that she will always have to tolerate distress and fears that it will never get easier for her. In addition, there is increased disappointment when she relapses, and a relapse eradicates all feeling of progress. Furthermore, when she is skillful, she feels that despite the hard work, whatever she does is not enough. She feels diminished when she has to call for coaching help.

Negative consequences of target behavior. The punitive consequences of Kim's unskillful behaviors – her suicide ideation, her cutting, her temper outbursts, and her avoidance of work and of therapy – are not immediate and, therefore, these behaviors do not seem to be so negative to Kim.

But she, nevertheless, does experience the negative consequences after some time passes. Kim feels accountable to her therapist and her boyfriend and wants to please them. There are negative effects of her self-injury within herself as well. She hides her scars and her cutting behavior from her boyfriend and this causes stress for Kim. Furthermore, sometimes the scars bother her and make her feel ugly and damaged.

With regard to relationships, there are many negative consequences. The fact that her boyfriend distances himself from her after she engages in anger outbursts and unsubstantiated accusations toward him is a punitive effect of her anger outbursts. Kim also desires to get married and have a family one day and feels that missing therapy or work, having repeated arguments with her boyfriend, and dealing with upset by cutting reduce her chances of getting what she wants in life.

DBT Modes and Strategies

DBT treatment modes. Kim has been attending weekly individual therapy sessions and weekly group skills training. To date, Kim's boyfriend has attended two couples sessions at his request and with Kim's agreement, to address her boyfriend's feelings of being left out of "the loop" of Kim's treatment, to encourage increased communication, and to acknowledge difficulties in communication. During these couples sessions, the therapist took a stance of both consulting to the patient and consulting to the third party – the boyfriend. The therapist encouraged Kim to describe the treatment as well as to express some of her concerns and to discuss with her boyfriend in a skillful manner how he could help her. The therapist also did some psychoeducation regarding the BPD diagnosis and described the treatment approach and conceptualization of Kim's problems. The boyfriend was also encouraged to express his concerns and ask questions. He expressed an interest in knowing what he could do to help Kim, and the therapist also explained how skillful behaviors might be reinforced by him.

Adjunctive psychopharmacological interventions. Kim is taking antidepressant medication that seems to help relieve depressive mood symptoms and ward off suicidal ideation and extreme hopelessness.

Dialectical strategies. In individual sessions, the therapist strives to achieve an effective balance acceptance and change. Usually, the therapist needs to constantly shift between emphasis on radical acceptance and emphasis on change. Kim often focuses on the need for change and engages in self-invalidation, only to quickly feel criticized when the therapist tries to engage her in problem solving. At these times, the therapist needs to quickly switch to validation and expresses how difficult it is to be told that she might be able to do things differently, and how that feels like a criticism or as if she is being blamed for having her problem. Other times, Kim will overly focus on the need to change to the exclusion of self-acceptance. She gets upset when the therapist encourages radical acceptance, as if this is permission to self-injure. The therapist and patient are in a constant balancing act around these two poles. When Kim becomes discouraged after a "relapse," and she feels all of her progress has been eradicated, the therapist uses metaphors, for example, about exercise, how if you take a break from it after getting in shape, it takes less time to get in shape when you start exercising again. The therapist plays devil's advocate when recommitment to goals is necessary, questioning whether it really is a good time to be working on these goals and that maybe Kim is trying to do too much. Due to Kim's interpersonal sensitivity, the therapist does not feel comfortable being irreverent with Kim at this point in treatment. As it is, just validating Kim when she is in "self-invalidation" mode seems irreverent to her and usually gets her attention.

Problem solving. Kim and the therapist work together to generate ways to fight urges to self-harm by distracting, self-soothing, and keeping her goals in mind. Sometimes she is able to distract herself by painting and writing poetry. At times, both of these activities are about her self-injury. She takes walks in the park, reads her skills book, and watches children playing to remind herself of her desire to start a family.

Chain analyses are conducted to identify stressors, triggers, and sensations that signal the beginnings of an urge. Patterns that have emerged from these analyses are that Kim first begins to feel angry or upset (about feeling abandoned or neglected by her boyfriend). She experiences anger as a physical tingling sensation on her skin or pressure on her temples. She also has self-attacking ruminations (due to thoughts that she is overly needy of her boyfriend) that lead to physical sensations on her skin that are experienced as tension, and this tension, in her mind, requires physical release.

The first 3 months of treatment focused on problem solving around how to fight urges as well as therapy-interfering behavior of not attending treatment regularly. The treatment then moved into targeting how to short-circuit urges to self-injure by observing and labeling emotions. Insight strategies include alerting Kim to behavior patterns that lead to urges, such as setting unrealistic goals and then crashing with disappointment when she is unable to maintain "model" behavior.

Chain analyses of missing sessions have led to an understanding that the therapist is sometimes inadvertently invalidating Kim by focusing too much on trying to help her fight urges instead of validating the reasons she has these urges (which according to Kim have to do with her history of sexual abuse). When Kim feels invalidated in this way, she leaves the session feeling upset and makes up her mind not to come to session next week. She ruminates the whole week about how the therapist does not understand her, does not care about her, and does not want to hear about her trauma. After she misses a session, she starts to fear that the therapist will lose interest in her and that she is missing a chance to work on her goals. The therapist welcomed the opportunity to try to be more aware of the ways in which she may be invalidating Kim. They also agreed that Kim would try to call the therapist for relationship repair if this happened again.

Validation. Problem solving is balanced with emotional validation for how difficult it is to constantly fight urges to self-injure. Cheerleading all problem-solving efforts serves as a form of validation. When Kim becomes hopeless that her efforts will not really make a difference, the therapist continues to express hope. The therapist focuses on Kim's strengths, tries to point out faulty assumptions in her strongly held beliefs that she is always to blame. Emotional experiencing of anger and frustration is encouraged, although often Kim becomes suspicious that the therapist is trying to induce anger and then it is dropped.

Communication strategies. The strategy of playing devil's advocate is useful with Kim to increase her commitment to change. One such example is, "Maybe now is not a good time to work on getting a job."

Summary

In this chapter, we presented how to develop a DBT case conceptualization. We described the case of Kim to illustrate how DBT theory and interventions inform a comprehensive case conceptualization and detailed treatment plan. In contrast to some therapeutic approaches, the DBT case formulation and treatment plan is clearly focused on behavioral principles and a social learning understanding of the development of human behavior. Treatment goals are operationalized and defined in behavioral terms. Behavioral problems are understood as the product of inborn and environmental behavioral excesses and deficits, and internal and environmental consequences of behavior. DBT treatment strives to define the behaviors that need to change; takes a nonjudgmental approach toward change; identifies and validates the historical, biological, and environmental forces that maintain unskillful behaviors; applies contingency management to modify these forces and to encourage the reinforcement of more skillful behavior; and addresses skills deficits through the teaching of behavioral skills.

References

1. Koerner, K. (2012) *Doing Dialectical Behavior Therapy. A Practical Guide*, Guilford Press, New York, pp. 32–69.
2. Skinner, B.F. (1974) *About Behaviorism*, Knopf, New York.
3. Koerner, K. (2012) *Doing Dialectical Behavior Therapy. A Practical Guide*, Guilford Press, New York, pp. 10–12.
4. Linehan, M.M. (1993) *Cognitive Behavioral Treatment of Borderline Personality Disorder*, Guilford Press, New York, pp. 74–78.

Chapter 17

Beyond Target 1 – Therapy and "quality of life" interfering behaviors

Top 10 question to be addressed in this chapter:

How do practitioners assess capability in BPD patients and help patients set realistic goals and achieve a good quality of life?

While DBT has become known as a treatment of choice for suicidal and nonsuicidal self-injury (Target 1) in BPD and these behaviors are, in fact, a major focus, there are two additional primary treatment targets in this initial phase of therapy: therapy-interfering behaviors (Target 2) and "quality of life"-interfering behaviors (Target 3). In this chapter, we discuss how DBT addresses these behaviors and we describe in detail the DBT approach to addressing Target 2 (therapy-interfering behavior), as well as Target 3 (quality of life interfering behaviors). We will present some of the ways we have come to understand the application of the dialectic philosophy to treatment decisions regarding quality of life goals and medication treatment.

> **Key points**
> - Addressing therapy-interfering behaviors
> - Quality of life goal setting
> - Addressing quality of life goals
> - Applying dialectical thinking to medication decisions and adherence

Therapy-interfering behaviors

Clearly, the main emphasis of Stage 1 DBT is on the elimination of suicidal, self-harm, and other life-threatening behaviors. The dialectic strategy of balancing validation and change is aimed at reducing these behaviors while keeping the patient and clinician engaged in the treatment process. Any behaviors that interfere with the conduct of therapy on the part of the patient or clinician must also be addressed in order to facilitate treatment

---

The Dialectical Behavior Therapy Primer: How DBT Can Inform Clinical Practice, First Edition.
Beth S. Brodsky and Barbara Stanley.
© 2013 John Wiley & Sons, Ltd. Published 2013 by John Wiley & Sons, Ltd.

engagement, reduce premature termination of treatment (either by the patient or therapist), and maintain progress toward treatment goals. Some psychotherapeutic approaches, particularly those that are psychodynamically oriented, attend to therapy-interfering behaviors on the part of the patient – lateness, missing sessions, not making progress – through interpreting "treatment resistance" on the patient's part. As stated previously, treatment "resistance" is a concept from psychodynamic psychotherapy that has become ubiquitous in therapeutic parlance to describe what the patient is doing to "oppose" the process of therapy. Resistance is considered to be both conscious and unconscious, stemming from an individual's reluctance toward and defense against thinking about or facing certain feelings or experiences [1, 2].

DBT explicitly attends to therapy-interfering behaviors on both the patient's and clinician's part. The emphasis on *behavior* removes inferences about motivations. DBT takes the same matter of fact, nonjudgmental, dialectic stance of balancing validation with problem solving toward the identification and targeting of any behaviors that interfere with therapy. There is no assumption of treatment "resistance" per se. That is not to say that the thoughts and feelings associated with the behavior are not considered. Lateness, missing sessions, non-adherence to certain aspects of the treatment – all of these can definitely be indications of avoidance, fear, shame, and ambivalence about the painful process of engaging in therapy. But the matter-of-fact problem solving approach facilitates open, nondefensive discussion. The DBT therapist adopts the stance, "We have a problem, you seem to get to your appointments when with only 20 minutes left. Let's try to figure out why so that we can have the entire session to get our work done." This discussion usually takes place in the context of a chain analysis with the lateness as the "problem behavior."

Thus, in DBT we do not assume that the motivation behind the therapy-interfering behaviors is necessarily related to ambivalence about the therapy itself. We investigate and posit hypotheses that we test out, based more on social learning theory. We understand behaviors in terms of the reinforcing contingencies that increase the likelihood of these behaviors. We also examine how skills deficits contribute to problematic behaviors, with the understanding that treatment-interfering behaviors can be a result of a lack of skill. And then there are times when a patient's treatment-interfering behaviors might be a reaction to treatment-interfering behavior on the part of the clinician. For example, if a therapist begins sessions a few minutes late, the patient may react by coming even later.

At the beginning of an individual session, the clinician reviews the diary card with the patient. In addition to any Target 1 behaviors, the clinician is always thinking about whether to add any therapy-interfering behaviors to the agenda. At this time, the clinician and patient both identify behaviors that they have observed that are interfering with the therapy process. Lateness to session, failure to complete the diary card or do any other assigned homework, missing individual or skills group sessions, not observing clinician's limits, not calling for skills coaching when necessary, communicating angry feelings in a non-skillful manner – these are all examples of behaviors that might be considered therapy-interfering on the part of the patient. If any of them are present, they are placed on the agenda to be addressed during the session. The best way to address these behaviors is by subjecting them to a behavioral chain analysis, which aids in identifying the thoughts, feelings, and unskillful behaviors related to the therapy-interfering behavior.

Identification of therapy-interfering behavior on the part of the clinician is often less straightforward. Although you might expect that borderline patients are very quick to point out ways in which the clinician is being critical or unhelpful, it is very often the case that patients are reluctant to complain or to take initiative to raise the topic. Patients are more inclined to blame themselves and are often not aware that the clinician may be doing something that is interfering with the therapy. For example, if patients have trouble following through on homework assignments, they might automatically blame themselves for being lazy. This should alert clinicians to inquire as to whether the assignment was too difficult, and possibly take responsibility for pushing too hard for change and setting unrealistic goals for their patients. Furthermore, therapists, even though it can be uncomfortable, can model and facilitate discussion of therapy-interfering behaviors by identifying their own behaviors that can interfere with the process. For example, in Sarah's case, someone knocked on the therapist's clinic office door during the prior session and the therapist stepped out of the office to respond to the question, Sarah reacted to it by feeling "less important" than the person in the hall and did not then complete the assigned homework for the next session because she felt that the therapist would not think that would be "important" either. The chain analysis, in this instance, revealed a great amount of rich clinical detail that helped the patient understand her behavior in this instance as well as others outside the treatment.

Thus, it is important that the clinician be alert to any possibility that therapy-interfering behavior on the part of the patient might be related to something the clinician did. Another example would be the clinician inadvertently invalidating the patient, which results in the patient missing the next session, or coming in very angry. Although missing session and dysregulated expressions of hostility are unskillful responses to feeling invalidated, and, therefore, constitute therapy-interfering behavior on the part of the patient, there is also an opportunity in these instances for the clinician to take responsibility for interfering with the therapy as well, and not place sole focus on the patient's behavior. Such an approach often mitigates much of the hostility and therapy-interfering behavior on the part of the patient. The patient will feel less criticized or blamed, and will be encouraged to self-validate and not blame themselves as much for their unskillfulness.

Clinicians are also encouraged to check in with the patient directly with regard to whether there is any behavior that the patient is experiencing as invalidating or that is in any way making it more difficult for the patient to engage in therapy.

A chain analysis allows for a matter of fact, nonjudgmental investigation and hypothesis testing of therapy-interfering behavior. The chain analysis helps both clinician and patient understand and highlight the contingencies of the behavior. Often what emerges from a chain analysis is the understanding that a short-term immediate reinforcing consequence can, in the moment, override all of the negative consequences of the therapy-interfering behavior that are less immediate and more long range. In addition, the positive consequences of more skillful behaviors often consist of the absence of negative consequences rather than the presence of something positive, which makes these consequences less reinforcing. This illustrates, in a nonjudgmental way, the challenges of replacing unskillful with more skillful behaviors.

In this vignette, Neil and his DBT clinician conduct a chain analysis of his lateness to therapy.

Case example

TARGET BEHAVIOR:	30 minutes late to therapy session
TRIGGER:	Phone rang just as Neil was about to leave the house
VULNERABILITY:	Neil is afraid to leave the house
CHAIN ANALYSIS:	Neil and his clinician decide to start the chain analysis from when he woke up in the morning.
NEIL (ACTION):	I woke up early, which gave me a lot of time to get things done before I needed to leave my home for our appointment
ACTION:	I took a shower, got dressed, fed the cats, ate breakfast. I was ready to leave 30 minutes early
COGNITION:	I thought about leaving early but then decided to read the newspaper.
CLINICIAN:	Is there anything about coming to therapy that feels uncomfortable and makes you want to avoid it?
NEIL (GETTING UPSET):	No – I really want to get to therapy and it really bothers me that I made so much effort to get here and I only have 30 minutes after travelling all that way!
CLINICIAN:	Any other thoughts about why you decided to read the paper instead of leave your apartment? Did you think about taking the paper with you to read on the bus?
NEIL (FEELING):	I feel comfortable in my apartment and feel some anxiety about leaving. I also don't like reading on the bus. I felt relief in the moment when I decided to stay and read the paper.
CLINICIAN:	Can you say more about that feeling of anxiety about leaving the house?
NEIL (FEELING):	I'm not sure – I just kind of dread walking out the door and facing the world. I feel much safer and more in control when I'm home. I get very angry when I am out on the streets – I look at people and judge them or think they are looking at me in a mean way and I get upset.
BODY SENSATIONS:	I feel butterflies in my stomach and shortness of breath when I think about leaving my apartment. Also, I hate getting to your office early – I feel uncomfortable waiting in the waiting area.
CLINICIAN:	What feels uncomfortable about being in the waiting area?
NEIL (FEELING):	I feel exposed, feel like other people are looking at me, I just can't stand waiting for anything. I get very impatient, it feels like a waste of my time (Cognition).
CLINICIAN:	So do you think you didn't allow enough time for travelling to get here on time because you don't like leaving the house and don't like getting places early and having to wait?
NEIL:	Yes, although at the time I think that I am leaving enough time – it should only take 45 minutes to get from my home to your office.
CLINICIAN:	Is that leaving enough time for any possible delays since you take public transportation?
NEIL (COGNITION):	I guess not. I think that it should only take 45 minutes and I am not willing to build in time for delays.
CLINICIAN:	Does that happen when you are late to meet a friend or to getting to work?
NEIL:	I guess so. I never really thought about that.
CLINICIAN:	Would you be willing to work on leaving the house on time or even a bit earlier?
NEIL:	I guess I should.

CLINICIAN:	Let's continue with the analysis and then we will do some problem solving.
NEIL (ACTION):	So I was reading the paper, and started to get lost in reading the paper.
EVENT:	The phone rang. I looked at the clock and it was exactly the time I would need to leave to make it here on time. I really wanted to pick up the phone. I was waiting for a call from my friend to make plans. I knew I shouldn't but the feeling to pick it up was too strong, I didn't feel I could leave the house not knowing who was calling. So I picked up the phone and it was my friend and we got into a conversation and made the plans. By the time I got off the phone I was 20 minutes late and then I rushed out of the apartment and ran to the bus.
CLINICIAN:	Did you still feel anxious once you left the house?
NEIL (FEELING):	I felt a little less anxious – I was in a hurry so I didn't focus on the other people in the street as much.
EVENT:	The bus was 10 minutes delayed and so I arrived 30 minutes late.
FEELING:	I really hate it that I can't seem to make it here, or anywhere, on time. My boss keeps warning me that if I continue to be late I may lose my job.
	Identifying the consequences of leaving the house late:
IN SELF:	Temporary immediate relief from anxiety – feel as if I am being productive and feel more in control by taking the phone call
LONG TERM:	Feel like a failure, am angry at myself, because I got to therapy late
IN ENVIRONMENT:	Short term: missed half of the therapy session, had to do this behavioral chain analysis
LONG TERM:	If I keep doing this I will lose friends, jobs, miss out on things I want/need to do

Solution Analysis:

Distress tolerance skills to use: Radical acceptance that I need to allot a full hour for travelling to therapy. I can validate that I feel that I shouldn't have to, but then I have to turn my mind to accept that even though I think it should only take 45 minutes, I need to accept the reality of the situation. Also I can write out a pros and cons analysis of waiting to leave versus leaving the house. I can try to remember how I will feel when I get here late.

Emotion Regulation – Opposite action to emotion – avoid avoiding. I need to figure out how to push myself to leave the house. Maybe there is a way I can feel that I am taking control by leaving on time. I can observe and describe my feelings of anxiety about leaving the house. Be mindful of the emotion and my interpretations, that I will feel more vulnerable and exposed outside of my house.

Mindfulness – I can work on being less judgmental and controlling negative thoughts when I am outside, in the train, and in the waiting room. I can be in the present moment and not think too far ahead about how I will feel in a given situation in the future. Also to be effective by leaving enough time to get somewhere, rather than focus on what "should" be. Practice not "cutting off my nose to spite my face."

CORRECTION/OVERCORRECTION:	Make a commitment to come early next time and read skills book in the waiting area.
HOW TO AVOID TRIGGER IN FUTURE:	Turn the phone ringer off when I am getting ready to leave the house.

(Continued)

> (Continued)
>
> HOW TO WORK ON THE VULNERABILITY: Observe, describe, and challenge the distorted interpretations that lead to anxiety about leaving the house. Also behavioral rehearsal of leaving the house even when I don't have anywhere I need to be, just to buy a cup of coffee or run an errand. Practice being nonjudgmental when I am around other people.

In this chain analysis, the clinician asked Neil whether his lateness had to do with feeling ambivalent about coming to his therapy session. This line of questioning upset him, since in his experience his lateness had nothing do to with therapy, and because he made so much effort to get to the session and felt invalidated by the insinuation that he did not want to come. He is late in many situations and the common factor is that he is indeed avoiding uncomfortable feelings of anxiety and anger that come up for him when he is exposed to other people in general. Neil and his clinician were able to generate some ideas to use mindfulness and emotion regulation skills to address his fear of being outside and around others.

By getting as much detail as possible about the thoughts, feelings, body sensations, and sequence of events, Neil and his clinician were able to identify a number of other areas for problem solving. He became aware of his "willfulness" in terms of allotting enough time to travel to his clinician's office. Many BPD patients focus on what they feel they "should" be expected to do rather than what will work best for them. As a solution, Neil will practice "radical acceptance" and effectiveness – "doing what works."

Neil became more aware of the contingencies of his behavior. He experienced an immediate sense of relief when he decided to delay leaving the house and this feeling took precedence over any future negative feelings he might have when he was late to his session. Part of the solution for this is to write down the pros and cons of the immediate versus long-term consequences of his delaying behaviors.

Medication nonadherence

Medication nonadherence can be a form of therapy-interfering behavior. Medication is not a formal part of standard DBT treatment, and DBT practice encourages patients to work toward ending their reliance on psychopharmacological interventions, if possible, in favor of using skills. In part this is due to a lack of strong empirical evidence for the efficacy of any particular class of psychotropic drugs in the treatment of BPD [3–5]. However, the co-morbidity of BPD with Axis I disorders [6, 7] that are known to be responsive to medication such as major depressive disorder, bipolar disorder, schizoaffective disorders, anxiety disorders and eating disorders results in the inclusion of psychopharmacological intervention in the treatment plan of many BPD patients.

As in the case of other therapy-interfering behaviors, both patient and clinician can contribute to the problem of medication noncompliance. By medication noncompliance we are referring to the patient's non-adherence to a prescribed regimen to which both the patient and prescribing physician agreed. This involves behaviors such as abruptly discontinuing a medication that the patient has taken over a long period of time or missing doses that result in initial withdrawal reactions. A dialectical approach to medication adherence, decision making, and monitoring is useful in improving medication compliance and diminished power struggles between patient and clinician regarding medications.

The dialectics of prescribing medication

> **Case example**
>
> Brandy is a 39-year-old Hispanic single woman with a long history of amphetamine dependence currently in full remission. She had been diagnosed with ADD by her previous psychiatrist and was prescribed Adderall. When she came to Dr. Green, a psychiatry resident, for DBT psychotherapy and medication management, she was taking a high dose of Adderall and asked Dr. Green to continue prescribing the same dose. Brandy was working at a nursing home during the day and attending nursing school at night, and she was adamant that she needed the Adderall to get everything done. Given her history, he initially agreed that it would be helpful for her to continue and he prescribed the Adderall. However, Brandy started exhibiting signs of paranoid thinking in relationship to her boss at work. Dr. Green was troubled by this and was especially concerned that Adderall might be contributing to what he thought might be some mild psychotic symptoms. He consulted with his psychopharmacology supervisor who agreed that they should try to taper Brandy off Adderall. Dr. Green made a very strong recommendation to Brandy that they work together to get her off the Adderall. She became extremely upset, panicked about not being able to have the medication she felt she needed, and became hostile and threatened to get the Adderall off the street if she had to, or to even start using crystal meth again. Dr. Green backed down and continued to work with his DBT team and his psychopharmacology supervisor to figure out how to balance her insistence on getting the Adderall with his discomfort with prescribing it to her. He felt as if he was doing her a disservice.
>
> The team viewed this situation as one that required a dialectical synthesis. Dr. Green would need Brandy to collaborate with the medication regimen in order to increase her compliance. Her threats to go against his medical advice were therapy interfering on her part. Dr. Green's suggestion to stop the medication without addressing Brandy's fears was also interfering with the treatment and getting in the way of a collaborative approach. Dr. Green started to validate Brandy's concerns about going off the Adderall and her feelings of reliance on the medication to maintain the life she felt was meaningful for her. He was then able to express his concerns that the Adderall might be contributing with the disturbing experiences she was having with her boss at work. Dr. Green used commitment strategies of trying to get Brandy's foot in the door to consider other medication options and the possibility of learning to live without stimulant medication. He communicated that he would work with her and not just make a unilateral decision about the medication. They were then able to agree on a plan in which she would lower the dose rather than completely stopping the medication, and have a say in when and how the taper would take place.

In this case, Dr. Green was engaging in therapy-interfering behavior by missing opportunities to validate Brandy's fear of losing the Adderall, as well as her belief that she needed Adderall to be able to function. It is often the case that clinicians err by inadvertently invalidating their patients, especially in the context of anxiety over life-threatening behaviors, or in this case when Brandy's unwillingness to comply with medication recommendations made Dr. Green anxious about an increase in dangerous symptoms. Once Dr. Green, with the help of his DBT team, became aware of his need to validate, he was able to acknowledge that he was placing an over-emphasis on change, which encouraged a more collaborative approach with Brandy regarding the way to take both of their concerns into consideration. A dialectical synthesis was reached regarding the way to proceed with the medication regimen.

Quality of life goal setting – Target 3

Although quality of life goals are technically the third priority in a Stage 1 DBT treatment, they are of primary importance in terms of "creating a life worth living" [8]. In addition, "quality of life"-interfering behaviors often are secondary targets that lead to, and therefore need to be addressed in order to prevent, life-threatening behaviors.

However, realistic assessment of a patient's vocational and social (Target 3) goals is not quite as straightforward as is Target 1 and Target 2 goal setting. Individuals with BPD suffer from unrealistic expectations of maintained high functioning. They are constantly engaging in self-invalidation and attributing their inability to function in a particular task or area of their lives to laziness and "not being good enough."

The extent to which individuals with BPD can appear extremely high functioning, and often *are* under certain, highly structured, non-interpersonally stressful circumstances, leads everyone in their lives (themselves, their families, and their clinicians) to raise the bar of expectation. As much as high expectations can be a sign of caring and a vote of confidence, they can also create a setup for failure and demoralization.

DBT identifies this dilemma as a dialectic of "apparent competence" versus "active passivity" [8] to illustrate the fluctuations in functioning that result from the extreme dependency in BPD patients (see Chapter 16 for detailed discussion of apparent competence-active passivity and other dialectical dilemmas). Although we believe the term "apparent" competence is, in part, a misnomer because the competence is quite real in certain situations, the concept is helpful in understanding the fluctuations in functioning because the ability to cope and respond with skillful behaviors is not consistent across situations. Or, it is "apparent" because patients' own expectations of what they can accomplish is sometimes unrealistic and does not take their emotional vulnerability into account. Under circumstances of high stress, lack (or perceived lack) of support, the individual not only does not act skillfully, but actively relinquishes responsibility to engage in skillful behavior and expresses an urgent need for someone else to take over (and, thus, becomes actively passive). Often, when patients are in an actively passive frame of mind, they tend to feel "uncared for" when asked to use skills.

A crucial and delicate task in the treatment of BPD is determining the appropriate balance between expectations of high functioning and acceptance of limitations, either in level of achievement or the pace at which the individual can be expected to progress, or both. The challenge to the clinician and, ultimately, the patient, is to maintain a synthesized view of the patient that includes and accepts both strengths and limitations in functioning.

A related concept is the tendency for individuals with BPD to engage in mood-dependent functioning. Mood-dependent functioning is when individuals feel that they have to behave in accord with the mood that they are experiencing. So, if individuals with BPD are feeling depressed, the notion of going to work or school, exercising, and socializing may seem alien. They feel that their behavior should be dictated by their mood. So, staying at home or in bed can seem like the appropriate course of action. Psychoeducation can be particularly helpful here so that the process of helping patients engage in their important daily functions irrespective of mood, can begin.

BPD patients can also compartmentalize their higher functioning selves from a recognition and acceptance of certain limitations. They convince themselves, as well as those around them, that their self-destructive episodes are momentary lapses in behavior in which they cannot even recognize their "normal" selves. They then resume their high stress pursuits (school, work, social interactions) without acknowledging their vulnerability to the next "episode." After repeated setbacks in which all of the progress they have made is lost during a lapse in functioning, patients become increasingly demoralized and hopeless about ever being able to achieve their goals and have a life worth living. They (and those around them) also attribute their setbacks to deliberate, intentional behavior on their part, such as laziness or a poor work ethic, or self-sabotage, rather than recognizing their vulnerability to the stress of maintained high functioning.

Individuals with BPD are often highly intelligent and talented. This can be another reason their vulnerabilities and limitations are easy to overlook. Even clinicians often over-estimate the abilities of the Ivy-league college student who returns home in the middle of the school semester due to a low-lethality suicide attempt. Both patient and family ask the clinician whether the patient can return to school the following semester, and the clinician feels pressured to and also wants to believe in the patient's capability. The process of synthesizing the strengths and vulnerabilities and arriving at the appropriate level of expectation involves a dialectic process of careful trial and error, a lot of balancing of change with validation, and often challenging the patient's own emphasis on the need to change with more self-acceptance. Acknowledgment of limitations requires "radical acceptance" of the reality of the situation.

We have observed certain areas of limitations in individuals with BPD that disrupt consistent functioning. One involves their extreme sensitivity to criticism or real or perceived failure. Thus, these individuals have less resilience in maintaining functioning in highly competitive vocational settings in which failure or negative feedback is routine and expected (e.g., medical school or performing arts auditions). Increasing demands in the face of success also presents a negative consequence to high functioning and can result in a regression in these individuals, since they have difficulty in self-reinforcing and recognizing a sense of mastery in the absence of positive feedback. PTSD reactions also present limitations, when work or school situations trigger past traumatic experiences. Sensitivity to interpersonal rejection, and cognitive factors such as automatic beliefs that they cannot function when they are depressed or upset also contribute to disruptions in functioning. However, BPD patients who are talented and have experienced themselves as capable, will have a very hard time accepting their limitations. How does a clinician proceed to address this? Let's consider the case of Tara.

Setting realistic quality of life goals

Case example

Tara is a 25-year-old single white woman, a graduate student who is struggling to complete her Master's degree at a prestigious university. The program is quite competitive and required a design portfolio for admission. Tara is clearly talented and has demonstrated ability in this area. She was referred for DBT by her college counseling center for NSSI. She periodically cuts herself with an exacto knife on her forearms, which she states are designed to relieve feelings of self-hate. This behavior has increased in frequency, exacerbated by the stress of her academic commitments Tara feels capable of understanding the work that is required. However, she finds that she is constantly comparing herself with her fellow students and always determines that her work is not as good as theirs. She begins to become convinced that the teachers and other students are also thinking the same thing, which leads her to avoid attending class. She stays home in bed, certain that she is worthless and feeling even worse because she is not going to class and not doing her work. This, in turn, leads to feelings of self-hatred that build up and become a physical sensation of tension. She takes a knife and starts cutting her arms and legs until these feelings are released. Feeling better, she is able to go to the art studio and to make up the work that she has missed. In a spurt of energy, she completes the work and starts to feel like her "old self." This cycle repeats itself twice during the course of the semester. In the middle of executing her final project, a creative idea that had initially excited her, she begins to doubt herself again, convinces herself that she does not care, and gives up on the project mid-stream. She drops out of sight for three weeks, not attending school or her therapy sessions. She is unable to graduate. She insists that she has a poor work ethic, is lazy, and that is why she did not follow through on her final project. Her mother also sees it this way. When the clinician shares her view that she avoids her work in order to escape painful feelings, and that she might consider that the competitive atmosphere is difficult to handle, she becomes angry and insists that she needs to punish herself in order to motivate herself to do the right thing. When she requests a letter from the clinician stating that she is ready to return to school to complete the semester, the clinician uses this as an opportunity to explore whether or not she feels ready to withstand the stress of competition.

TARA (ANGRY): I can't believe you are saying that I can't handle going back to school. If I don't go back and finish my degree, I won't be able to get the type of job that I really want and I'll be stuck in this job that I hate.

CLINICIAN: I am not saying for sure that you cannot handle it. I know that you are capable of doing the course work itself. Look Tara, I want you to succeed. This is a big decision. I know that it might be difficult to think about the challenges of going back to school but I would like to help you think it through carefully.

TARA (BEGRUDGINGLY): So what do I need to think about?

CLINICIAN: Well, how about thinking back to some of the difficulties that you encountered last time you were in school, the difficulties that you still have sometimes in work situations, in which you start comparing yourself negatively to your peers. You become depressed, stay in bed, and miss work to avoid feeling inferior to your colleagues. This leads to a downward spiral in which you fall behind in your work. When you are feeling confident, you are very capable of putting a lot of effort and achieve an excellent level of work. But when the

	negative comparisons are triggered by a comment by a supervisor or peer, it is difficult for you to maintain that level of achievement. We have been working on practicing mindfulness to refrain from judging yourself and others, and challenging some of the distorted interpretations you make when you start making comparisons, and you have made some progress with this.
TARA:	Yes, I have been better at getting to work more consistently and not spiraling down as much but I still feel that I am not good enough to compete with the other students. This program is so competitive. I will really have to work on controlling my negative thinking. Maybe I'm not ready yet. Maybe I'll never be ready.
CLINICIAN:	Well, how about this? Perhaps you can try taking one course without matriculating and see if we can help you learn those skills with one course instead of taking on a full course load all at once.
TARA:	But it will take me forever to finish school if I do that.
CLINICIAN:	Yes, you may have to radically accept that going slowly and building your skills to handle the stress will in the long run increase your chances of completing the program. It is very hard to accept that you may not be ready to go back to school full time right now. You might have to remind yourself every day that you are working toward your goals, even if it is at a slower pace. Remember the fable of the tortoise and the hare – slow and steady wins the race.

Although Tara is very angry at first with the clinician for suggesting that she might not be able to handle the stress of returning to school at this point in time, Tara is able to consider that perhaps she needs to have more skills in place to help her avoid comparing herself so much, and to challenge her interpretations that she and everyone else judges her work as inferior. The clinician "plunges in where angels fear to tread" by confronting Tara with her limitations (her vulnerability to interpersonal comparisons), but also validates and cheerleads by highlighting how Tara's mood fluctuations, rather than her lack of ability, interferes with her ability to achieve. The clinician offers a solution that is a dialectical synthesis between applying for full time school versus not going to school at all – which is to take one class so that Tara can have an opportunity to improve her skills in a lower stress situation.

Finding the balance between capability and limitations: A trial and error process

Determining an individual's actual capabilities in the face of fluctuating sense of self and apparent competence requires a delicate trial and error process. There is no sure way to know in advance what the patient is capable of and at what pace they would best be able to achieve their social and vocational goals. We have found that maintaining a dialectic stance is the clinician's best aid in avoiding the pitfalls of either overestimating or underestimating the patient's capability, both of which would lead to demoralization. Informed by dialectics and DBT, we have identified the following guidelines for clinicians to consider in approaching the task of realistic quality of life goal setting:

1 *History taking*. The clinician obtains a comprehensive history of the patient's level of functioning and the circumstances under which they were able to achieve their highest level of functioning, as well as the situations that triggered a regression in their ability to function. The history can inform the parameters of the goal setting process.
2 *Transparency*. The clinician shares with the patient that they are collaborating in a trial and error process in which the clinician does not know for sure what the realistic goal should be, and cannot be sure regarding the pace at which the patient can best achieve this goal. The clinician will serve as a guide, partner, and support to the patient in the trial and error process.
3 *Breaking a goal down into steps*. One of the ways to determine if a goal is realistic is to break it down into smaller steps and then take one step at a time. As in Tara's case, in order to see if Tara is ready to return to school full-time, she might take one course first preceded by doing some of the tasks that are required for successful completion of a course on her own.
4 *Preparing for failure and reassessment*. As part of the trial and error process, the clinician needs to prepare the patient for the "error" that might occur if the step that has been agreed upon is not achievable. One way to accomplish this is for the clinician to take responsibility for therapy-interfering behavior in encouraging the patient to take a step that is too large. Another is to emphasize that this is a trial and error process and to use distress tolerance skills and radical acceptance that "error" is a necessary part of the process. The clinician can reframe the patient's inability to take the step as a success in that it provided more information regarding how to reassess and make the steps more doable.
5 *The use of dialectic strategies*. First and foremost, the clinician must rely heavily on validation to balance the change of working toward quality of life goals. This includes Level 4 validation (how could it be otherwise given your history and your emotional vulnerability), and Level 5 validation (normalization of the fits and starts of trying to work toward a goal). When a patient is focused on wanting to change, the clinician must "plunge in where angels fear to tread" in highlighting the obstacles that might get in the patient's way. When the patient has trouble taking the agreed upon steps and then becomes mired in demoralization and self-invalidation, the clinician can use self-involving self-disclosure to normalize how everyone is in the position of taking on more than they can handle at times. The use of metaphors can also be extremely effective, as we will illustrate in the following text.

The case of Lucy

> **Case example**
>
> Lucy is a 36-year-old woman who is living with her long-term girlfriend. She is currently unemployed. She enrolled in medical school but was asked to take a leave the year before because of failure to attend classes regularly. She often called in sick when on clinical rotations. Lucy had difficulty being an older student around the younger 20-year-old

> medical students, and also had difficulty with the hierarchy in the medical profession and being in a "lowly" position as a medical student. Lucy is thinking about not returning to medical school but instead enrolling in a doctoral program in biology. She realizes that she might not be ready to go to school, but she wants to build up to it. Lucy has difficulty getting out of bed on certain days. Her girlfriend works and supports her financially, but Lucy is expected to do the housework. Sometimes she is able to function at home and feels a sense of mastery when she does. However, on most days she feels that doing household chores is beneath her and that it is a waste of her intelligence and her abilities.
>
> Lucy's "quality of life" goal is to be able to either get a job or go back to school. She realizes that she needs to first be consistent with attendance and following through on her commitments. With the help of her therapist she decided to get a part-time volunteer job in order to practice following through on her responsibilities even on days when she has trouble getting herself out of bed. Both she and the therapist thought it might help her to have more structure, and to be accountable to a job where people are relying on her to show up and contribute. Both Lucy and her therapist agree that this will be a process of trial and error. Lucy wants to commit to 20 hours per week, but the therapist encouraged her to consider starting with fewer hours at first. Lucy uses her diary card to keep track of the days that she feels able to attend work, and which days she has the urge to call and cancel. She and the therapist devised a plan for the days that she does not feel like going to work. On these "down" days she is supposed to call her therapist for coaching to make sure she avoids avoiding. She developed a pros and cons list to remind her of the reasons she would be better off pushing herself to go. Lucy and her therapist also came up with a "bare bones" plan for the days that Lucy feels like cancelling, such as pushing herself to go but not taking on any extra tasks at home that day, or giving herself the option to leave work early if she is really feeling badly once she is there.
>
> After a few weeks of working, she still called in sick sometimes, but also used the skills to push herself to go. The fact that Lucy could push herself sometimes but not others was confusing to her. She had trouble understanding the difference between her capabilities and her limitations. The therapist agreed that it was not clear and that they needed to figure this out together. They conduct behavioral analyses of the days that Lucy called in sick. They also examine what made the difference for her on the days that she successfully pushed herself to go.

In Lucy's case, the jury is still out as to whether she will be able to develop the ability to tolerate the negative sense of self that she experiences in work and academic settings, and overcome her avoidance behaviors. Lucy and her therapist will continue to work through trial and error, conducting behavioral chain analyses of the thoughts and feelings that lead to Lucy's avoidance behaviors, and breaking down the steps as much as possible to decrease the stress and increase her ability to cope in these situations.

Making slow and steady progress toward quality of life goals

Fluctuations in mood and mood dependency wreak havoc on the ability of BPD patients to maintain steady progress toward their goals. In low stress, highly structured situations, these individuals tend to feel very capable, energized, and focused and are able to work skillfully and effectively toward their goals. They make quite a bit of progress and see the results of their efforts. However, as we saw in the case of Tara, one small trigger (seeing the work of a classmate that she feels is better than hers, for example) can lead to an inability to maintain skillful functioning. Depending on the severity of the reaction, most or all of the progress made during the high functioning period can be lost. The patient, once feeling better, is left to start over from scratch to rebuild. After repeated episodes of functioning/dropping out, regaining and losing progress, the patient becomes increasingly hopeless and demoralized. We have often used the metaphor based on the myth of Sisyphus to describe this plight. Working toward a goal is much like pushing a huge boulder up the side of a mountain. You can see the progress of your hard effort. However, when you get tired and start to feel you will never make it to the top of the mountain, you give up and let the boulder roll backward down to the base of the mountain. Then you are left to start from the beginning again.

Thus, another aspect of working toward quality of life goals is to help patients learn how to ride out the periods of emotional dysregulation without losing all of the gains they have made during a period of being in "wise mind." Here are some guidelines for addressing this task.

1 *Learn to expect disruptions in routine and schedule.* This involves helping patients to understand, and to radically accept, that they cannot rely on ideal circumstances for optimum functioning. Triggers happen, and structures and routines that are relied upon invariably break down or get interrupted. For example, we often see that our patients who are college students may be doing quite well during a semester but then struggle to get back on track after the spring break. They have difficulty transitioning from their class schedule to a week off in which they usually have to study for exams or work on projects independently. This can result in not completing their final exams and projects, and the loss of all of the work they accomplished in the first half of the semester.

2 *Learn how to contain the damage.* There will be times when patients are feeling strong and capable and able to move forward. The idea is to learn how to take advantage of those periods to make as much progress as is possible. However, rather than counting on and hoping that conditions will always be favorable, the patient needs to radically accept that there will be times when they feel like giving up, or that they cannot face interactions with others or face their work or school obligations. During these "down" times, the patient will have to learn how to "contain the damage" by maintaining their position rather than reversing all of their progress. The clinician can work with them to identify what it would take to function at a "bare minimum" on bad days, rather than give up, so that they will not lose their gains. This involves finding a dialectic synthesis between giving up and moving forward. To use the Sisyphus metaphor, they can learn how to put in the effort required to hold the boulder in place rather than let it go completely and let it roll all the way down the mountain. Another useful metaphor is to think of working toward the goal as if you were swimming across a large lake. Sometimes you are feeling strong and you can swim and make progress in the water. At other points you are exhausted and feel like giving up. Instead of completely letting go (and letting yourself drown), you use a small amount of energy to tread water, which will keep you in place until you are feeling ready to move forward again.

Accepting limitations

Even when patients are willing to entertain the possibility of their own limitations, they often have to face the denial of family members who understandably want to believe that their loved one is capable of high levels of achievement within "normal" time frames. This creates a negative consequence for the efforts of patients to find and accept the appropriate level of expectation for progress. The challenge for the clinician in framing this for the patient is illustrated in the case of George.

Setting realistic quality of life goals – George

Case example

George is a 28-year-old white male who lives with his girlfriend. He was referred to DBT for the treatment of recurrent self-injury. George has a master's degree from a prestigious university but has trouble holding down a job. He is bright, personable, interviews extremely well, and gets new jobs easily, despite his erratic job history and spotty resume. Invariably, he quickly begins to feel undervalued at the job, begins to question his supervisor's authority, and either gets fired or quits. He and his girlfriend live in an apartment that is owned by his parents, and he is required to pay his half of the mortgage payment each month. He currently has a part-time job that does not pay him enough to make the rent payment, and he has given them partial payment over the past few months. Recently, his parents informed him that they need the payment in full, on time, and that they need the money to meet their own expenses. This phone conversation led to urges to cut himself. He feels guilty that he is creating this burden for his parents. He feels that he is doing his best, that the part time job is less stressful for him and makes it more likely that he can maintain work. He is interpreting his parents' request as a sign that they feel that his inability to meet the rent payment is under his control, and that they do not recognize that it is all he can do right now to pay what he can. He also then begins to feel that they are right, that he is just slacking off and he could work full time and pay them if he just applied himself. He starts to worry that if he actually becomes able to pay them in full on time, then that will just confirm their idea that he could have done it all along.

In these case examples, the patients are very intellectually accomplished and capable. Their inability to follow through at school or at work may be partially due to depressive symptoms such as anhedonia, anergia, or inability to concentrate, but there are other important contributing factors. They are often quite motivated, and have energy to apply to a given task. There is little reason to doubt their success in these situations. However, the interpersonal aspects of the school and work environments can trigger emotional and interpersonal vulnerability that is not readily apparent. Furthermore, high internal expectations about performance can lead to self-condemnation in the face of what is felt to be acceptable performance. Negative self-comparisons with others, or distorted perceptions of the harmful intentions of others, lead to emotional dysregulation that becomes too difficult to tolerate. In Tara's and Lucy's case, school performance is disrupted by avoidance behaviors designed to provide escape from intolerable affect states. With George, the stress of a high-level job triggers a tendency to view his supervisors as undermining and not worthy of his respect. This leads to inappropriate expressions of anger, insubordination, and ultimate loss of the job.

The case of George illustrates some of the issues that need to be addressed in helping patients accept their limitations.

1. *Highlight the negative consequences of being skillful.* The inability of George's parents to recognize and accept his limitations creates a situation in which (apparently) skillful functioning has negative consequences for George. When George gets a full-time job, both George and his parents attribute his periods of lower functioning as deliberate and within George's control. For George, the idea of being able to hold down a full-time job and support himself financially becomes fraught with meaning – if he could do this now he could have done it before. If he can do it now, he will always be able to do it.
2. *Validate acceptance of limitations.* George's parents are validating and reinforcing his apparent competence, which leads George to take on full-time jobs that he cannot maintain and become self-hating when he cannot maintain them. The more realistic goal of maintaining a part-time job, a dialectic synthesis between not working/unrealistic full-time job, is not being validated. Accepting limitations, rather than maintaining unrealistic expectations, is an example of being skillful.
3. *Dialectic synthesis.* Of course, as in any dialectic formulation, although George has clear limitations (in the areas of interpersonal and emotional regulation), the opposite is also true and the perspective of George's parents is also valid. It is easy to understand how difficult it would be for George's parents to accept his limitations. They need him to pay the full rent, and they view him as someone who is talented and capable and they want to have high expectations for him. Since he is not classically depressed, the nature of his difficulties is less apparent. Expectations that are too low are just as invalidating as is not being able to recognize limitations. Acceptance of limitations in goals and expectations need to be balanced with expectations for change and progress; otherwise demoralization will result from feeling marginalized from the expected pursuits of peers.
4. *Consultation to patient.* George's therapist can help him reframe his attributions regarding his difficulties in holding down a full-time job. Once George understands that he is not simply slacking off or being lazy, he can approach his parents to explain the concept of mood dependency, and help them to understand the particular vulnerabilities and stressors that cause disruptions in his functioning.
5. *Consultation to family members.* Often, it can be helpful to have a family meeting in which the therapist conducts psychoeducation regarding BPD, mood dependency, interpersonal vulnerability, and the DBT approach of finding a dialectic synthesis between setting realistic goals and accepting limitations.

Summary

In order to reduce suicidal and self-harm behaviors in BPD, psychotherapy needs to promote a life worth living. In this chapter, we describe how DBT strategies and interventions are specifically applied to enhance treatment engagement and make improvements in the quality of life. DBT is unique in addressing the therapy-interfering behavior on the part of the clinician. In DBT, treatment-interfering behavior is not conceptualized as treatment resistance, but rather is attributed to skills deficits.

Medication noncompliance can sometimes be a form of treatment-interfering behavior. We have extrapolated from DBT how to set collaborative goals using commitment strategies and dialectic synthesis toward medication management and compliance.

Social and vocational goals are integral to building a life worth living. We illustrate the challenges to realistic goal setting for BPD individuals, largely due to mood-dependent functioning and interpersonal vulnerability. Although the evidence base for the efficacy of DBT does not address reduction in "quality of life"-interfering behaviors, we have developed DBT-based guidelines for effectively targeting social and vocational functioning in BPD patients. As in targeting suicidal behaviors, quality of life goal setting requires the clinician to maintain a dialectic stance, balancing validation with change, reciprocal and irreverent communications, and to constantly search for the dialectic synthesis.

References

1. Cabaniss, D.L., Cherry, S., Douglas, C.J., et al. (2011) *Psychodynamic Psychotherapy: A Clinical Manual*, Wiley-Blackwell, Oxford, pp. 205–206.
2. Schlesinger, H.J. (1982) Resistance as process, in *Resistance, Psychodynamic and Behavioral Approaches* (ed. P.L. Wachtel), Plenum Press, New York, p. 27.
3. Soloff, P. (2000) Psychopharmacological treatment of borderline personality disorder. *Psychiatric Clinics of North America*, 23, 169–192.
4. Paris, J. (2005) Borderline personality disorder. *Canadian Medical Association Journal*, 172 (12), 1579–1583.
5. Grossman, R. (2002) Psychopharmacologic treatment of patients with borderline personality disorder. *Psychiatric Annals*, 32 (6), 357–370.
6. Tadić, A., Wagner, S., Hoch, J., et al. (2009) Gender differences in Axis I and Axis II comorbidity in patients with borderline personality disorder. *Psychopathology*, 42 (4), 257–263.
7. Skodol, A.E., Gunderson, J.G., Pfohl, B., et al. (2002) The borderline diagnosis I: psychopathology, comorbidity, and personality structure. *Biological Psychiatry*, 51 (12), 936–950.
8. Linehan, M.M. (1993) *Cognitive Behavioral Treatment of Borderline Personality Disorder*, Guilford Press, New York, pp. 74–76.

Chapter 18

The end of treatment

It is often difficult to determine the appropriate point to terminate treatment with patients who have severe emotion dysregulation because it often seems that there are more issues that can be addressed. Also, patients often drop out of treatment against medical advice or at least before the clinician determines that they have achieved their treatment goals. Patients also stay in therapy but do not engage in a meaningful way to achieve progress. In DBT, there are guidelines for the clinician to determine when to recommend a "vacation from treatment" when the patient does not seem to be able to maintain the minimum commitment that will make the therapy viable. There is also a clear limit regarding when to consider a patient to be out of treatment when they do not explicitly quit. However, there are fewer guidelines for the clinician regarding when to determine when DBT may no longer be indicated, or when it is time to transition from Stage 1 DBT to later stages, 2 and 3.

In this final chapter, we consider the various circumstances regarding the end of treatment, as well as issues surrounding completed suicide and the experience of having a patient make a serious, high-lethality suicide attempt.

> **Key points**
> - Premature treatment dropout
> - Clinician-initiated therapy "vacation"
> - When treatment goals have been achieved
> - Completed suicide or very serious suicide attempt
> - Final thoughts about using DBT to treat suicide and BPD

Why BPD patients drop out prematurely

Individuals with BPD are notorious for premature treatment dropout [1]. As we have seen, DBT explicitly addresses treatment engagement and has shown some success in increasing treatment retention with these individuals [2]. We have made the argument that the

---

The Dialectical Behavior Therapy Primer: How DBT Can Inform Clinical Practice, First Edition.
Beth S. Brodsky and Barbara Stanley.
© 2013 John Wiley & Sons, Ltd. Published 2013 by John Wiley & Sons, Ltd.

experience of invalidation (either through overpathologizing on the part of the clinician, or over- or underemphasis on change) in TAU may contribute to early dropout. Thus, the emphasis on validation and the dialectic balance between validation and change may be a factor responsible for increased retention.

It is also very likely that mood-dependent functioning and extreme compartmentalization of negative and positive mood states make it difficult for these individuals to follow-through on their commitment to treatment. When they are in a negative mood state, they are aware of their suffering and not only more open to treatment, but are quite needy and help seeking (although often simultaneously help-rejecting). When in a positive mood state, however, they are not suffering and have difficulty remembering the times when they are in pain. Coming to a psychotherapy session to work on their problems challenges the coping mechanism that allows them to keep the suffering out of awareness (at least temporarily). As one patient who had a good week put it to her therapist, "Why would I want to come to a therapy session when I'm feeling okay this week? It would just remind me of my problems and make me feel bad. What are you trying to do? Make me feel so bad again that I try to kill myself?" Again, DBT targets mood dependency and encourages mood integration and the ability to maintain a simultaneous awareness of positive and negative mood states.

In many other forms of therapy, patients are usually held more responsible for their treatment failure, and the treatment frame does not encourage active pursuit of patients when they fail to attend their sessions. In contrast, as stated previously, a DBT assumption is that patients cannot fail in treatment. Either the clinician fails or the treatment fails. The clinician and the treatment are responsible for increasing motivation and commitment to treatment. In DBT, when patients miss a session, the DBT clinician takes a very active role in trying to reach the patient, seeks consultation from the DBT treatment team, and in general tries whatever it may take within their natural limits to enhance commitment to and engagement in the treatment.

Therefore, patients are not considered to be out of treatment unless/until they miss four individual or four DBT skills group sessions in a row. Although this may seem like an arbitrary limit (and it is), it is one that has adapted from research protocols that provides a useful clinical cutoff, in the absence of an explicit declaration or decision, for determining whether a patient is in or out of treatment. In that period of time, the DBT clinician will chase down, pine for, and basically beg their patients to come back, and will consult with the team to explore the possible therapy-interfering behaviors that may have prompted the patient to want to discontinue.

Clinician initiated "vacation" from treatment

Another scenario is when the patient continues to attend treatment and seek help, but continues to engage in life-threatening and/or therapy-interfering behaviors that impede the progress of the therapy. The clinician, after exhausting all possible interventions and contingencies, decides that a "vacation" from therapy is the next contingency necessary to ultimately enhance motivation and commitment to treatment [3].

Rather than unilaterally terminating the therapy, the clinician states that the therapy cannot continue either for a specified time or until a particular change is made on the part of the patient. The clinician must be extremely clear about what needs to change in order for the patient to return to therapy, and should help the patient as much as possible to make the change and avoid the vacation. The vacation should be presented as a result of the clinician's own personal limits, rather than the patient's failure to do well. The clinician will do whatever is possible to arrange an alternative treatment to provide support for the patient in achieving the required change, and the clinician will indicate that he or she is very open and waiting for the patient to return (Linehan terms this as "pining" for the patient to return).

When treatment goals have been achieved

There are no specific guidelines regarding how to determine when enough progress has been made in DBT treatment to warrant a mutually agreed upon ending of therapy. However, the explicit goal-setting progress, the behavioral definitions of treatment goals, the ongoing tracking and monitoring of goals using the diary card all provide objective data that can indicate when treatment goals have been achieved. If a patient is in Stage 1 DBT and exhibits a maintained cessation of life-threatening behaviors and therapy-interfering behaviors and has learned the requisite skills, the clinician may broach the subject of whether the patient feels ready to enter Stage 2 DBT, which would involve exposure therapy for past trauma. The evidence base suggests that this could take place following approximately one year of Stage 1 DBT psychotherapy [4]. Alternatively, the patient and clinician could agree to continue working on other quality-of-life goals, and develop a hierarchy of these goals to provide focused structure for the next phase of therapy.

If a patient indicates a desire to leave treatment and not continue to work toward other life goals, the patient and clinician can highlight the progress made by the patient, and identify goals that might be left for a future psychotherapy, if desired. There is no clear protocol regarding treatment termination under these circumstances. Often, the comorbidity and level of psychopathology of the typical DBT patient is such that they require long-term psychotherapeutic support of some kind. Despite progress in therapy and the achievement of certain goals, a complete cessation of treatment may not seem clinically indicated. It is difficult to determine whether a patient will be able to maintain therapy gains without ongoing support. Perhaps a transition to a more supportive psychotherapy might be an option for a patient who has gotten self-destructive behaviors under control and has demonstrated an ability to utilize skills.

Another obstacle to the idea of terminating treatment when treatment goals are achieved is that the patient may interpret a clinician's suggestion to transition to a different therapy as a rejection and abandonment. Thus, a contingency of the patient's progress is a perceived removal of support, which might result in a regression to old unskillful behaviors on the patient's part in order to keep the therapy going. Thus, any discussion of termination should be collaborative, and feelings of rejection or fear of the loss of support should be validated and addressed.

As in any termination process, it makes sense to devote a proscribed period of time to review the course of the therapy, to set a clear date for either termination or transition to a different phase of treatment, to anticipate how the change is going to feel, to plan ahead for the possibility of a regression, and to leave the possibility open for a resumption of work together in the future. Sometimes individuals with BPD have difficulty tolerating a prolonged termination period and they may feel the need to preempt the ending of the therapy by leaving earlier than the set date.

Serious suicide attempts and suicide

We would be remiss if we did not address the most devastating end to treatment, when it is due to the death of the patient by suicide. We are very aware of the likelihood of experiencing a loss to suicide given the population with whom we work. Many clinicians, particularly those working with "at-risk" populations, experience the suicide of at least one of their patients. This loss can cause therapists not only great distress but can lead to questioning their ability to work with suicidal patients. Naturally, this type of event always prompts a sense of deep sadness and a soul-searching assessment of what could have been done differently. Most of the time, in DBT, owing to the constant monitoring of suicidal ideation, availability for between-session coaching and contact, willingness to extend our limits for availability when a patient is in crisis, and an explicit focus on reducing suicidal behavior and safety planning, there is often a sense that, given the limits of knowledge, there was not much else that could have been done to prevent the act. Sometimes in hindsight a link in the chain of events where something could have been done differently can be identified. At these times, we need to radically accept that we cannot possibly know everything and prevent all self-destructive acts performed by our patients despite our best efforts. We also need to learn from our mistakes in order to prevent future suicide attempts. The DBT consultation team and our peer colleagues are also a source of support in this process.

We want to state clearly that a serious suicide attempt is NOT a reason in and of itself for ending an outpatient DBT treatment. On the contrary, these are the behaviors that indicate the need for treatment. A serious suicide attempt might cause an interruption in the outpatient DBT due to hospitalization and possibly a short-term partial hospitalization. However, the expectation is that the patient will ultimately return to outpatient DBT when there is no longer a need for a higher level of care.

In addition, we try to frame these losses in terms of those that occur in other medical disciplines. Patients die from illnesses despite the best medical care. The same is true in the mental health field. Unfortunately, the stigma surrounding mental health disorders prompts both patients and clinicians to attribute blame and fault for symptoms and behaviors.

We remind ourselves that someone has to treat these individuals, and that fear of losing them to suicide is not a good reason not to do so. How would it be if oncologists would not treat cancer patients because of their high mortality?

Final thoughts about doing DBT with suicidal individuals

This brings us back full circle. Individuals suffering with chronic suicidal ideation, and suicidal and self-harm behaviors, need clinicians who are well trained and willing to face the challenges of staying therapeutically engaged with them. If we have achieved anything through this book, we hope we have inspired you and have provided you with accessible DBT concepts and interventions to meet this challenge.

References

1. Linehan, M.M., Armstrong, H.E., Suarez, A., et al. (1991) Cognitive-behavioral treatment of chronically parasuicidal borderline patients. *Archives of General Psychiatry*, 48, 1060–1064.
2. De Panfilis, C., Marchesi, C., Cabrino, C., et al. (2012) Patient factors predicting early dropout from psychiatric outpatient care for borderline personality disorder. *Psychiatry Research*, 200 (2–3), 422–429.
3. Linehan, M.M. (1993) *Cognitive Behavior Therapy for Borderline Personality Disorder*, Guilford Press, New York, pp. 310–312.
4. Koerner, K. (2012) *Doing Dialectical Behavior Therapy. A Practical Guide*, Guilford Press, New York, pp. 29–31.

Index

Note: Page numbers in *italics* refer to Figures; those in **bold** to Tables.

acceptance
   consultation to patient and family
      members, 236
   dialectic synthesis, 236
   negative consequences, 236
   realistic quality of life goals, 235–6
   validation, 236
"apparent competence" *vs.* "active
      passivity", 228
arbitrary *vs.* natural limits
   activity, rescheduling therapy session, 174
   change in schedule, patient's request, 168
   hours of availability, 169
   immediacy, response to call, 169–70
   individual temperament and life
      circumstances, 167
   paging *vs.* phone contact, 170–171
   physical touch, 165–7
   self-disclosure, 165
   sense of burden, clinicians, 164
   "technical neutrality", 165

Beck Lethality Rating Scale, 179
behavioral analysis *see also* chain analysis
   diary card, 116–17
   therapy-interfering behavior, 163
   life-threatening behavior, 108, 112, 116–17
behavioral dysregulation, 209–10
between-session contact
   arbitrary *vs.* natural limits *see* arbitrary *vs.*
      natural limits, between-session
      contact

   clinician availability, 154–6, 173
   coaching call, 174
   dependency and autonomy balance, 171–3
   guidelines, 157
   in vivo skills coaching, 154
   reasons for, 79, 154–6
   relationship repair, 156
   reporting good news, 156
   skills coaching, 158
   therapy-interfering behavior, 162–4
   time-limited phone coaching interaction,
      158–61
   twenty-four-hour rule, 161–2
between-session phone coaching, 79
biosocial theory
   invalidating environment, 39
   overview, 93
   reviewing with patients, 94
   vulnerability, 39–40
borderline personality disorder (BPD)
   Axis I disorders, 36
   biosocial theory, etiology, 39–40
   characteristics, 37–8
   clinicians sympathy, 33–4
   and DBT *see* dialectical behavior therapy
      (DBT)
   definition, 35
   diagnosis, 34–5
   diagnostic criteria, **36**
   treatment retention, 239–40
   emotion dysregulation, 3–5
   evidence-based treatment, 30

The Dialectical Behavior Therapy Primer: How DBT Can Inform Clinical Practice, First Edition.
Beth S. Brodsky and Barbara Stanley.
© 2013 John Wiley & Sons, Ltd. Published 2013 by John Wiley & Sons, Ltd.

borderline personality disorder (BPD) (cont'd)
  mental illness, 37
  overdosing, 52
  safety planning *see* safety planning intervention (SPI)
  schizophrenia, 36–7
  self-definition and self-esteem, 4
  suicide risk assessment, 58–9
  suicide risk factors, 55
  treatment *see* dialectical behavior therapy (DBT)
  untreatability myth, 27–9
BPD *see* borderline personality disorder (BPD)

Centers for Disease Control (CDC), 48
chain analysis
  balancing validation with change, 107
  description, 106–7
  dialectic strategies and irreverent communications, 119–21
  inquiry method, 111
  life-threatening behaviors, 182
  links identification, 107
  positive consequences, self-destructive behavior, 108–9
  precipitants identification, 109–10
  skillful behavior, 112
  stylistic strategies, 118–19
  target behavior identification, 108
  trigger identification, 110–111
  vulnerability identification, 110
classical/respondent conditioning, 71–2
cognitive behavioral therapy (CBT), 6
cognitive dysregulation, 210
Columbia Suicide Severity Rating Scale, 179
commitment to treatment, DBT
  after suicide attempt, **89**
  "door-in-the-face" concept, 90–91
  "foot-in-the-door" concept, 90
  orientation to treatment, 97–9
  psychoeducation, etiology of BPD, 93–4
  review, BPD diagnosis, 91–3
  validation strategies, 94–6
conditioning
  classical/respondent, 71–2
  operant, 72–3

coordination of care, DBT model
  consultation to patient, 200–201
  patient and splitting, 201–3
  third-party clinicians, 203–4
coping strategies, 187–8

DBT *see* dialectical behavior therapy (DBT)
DBT case formulation
  dialectical dilemmas *see* dialectical dilemmas, DBT case formulation
  history, 206, 207–8
  presenting problem, 206–8
  primary treatment targets, 208–9
  secondary treatment targets, 209–10
  vs. psychodynamic formulation, 206
DBT consultation team
  balancing change with validation, 194–5
  functions, 194, 196–7
  support, 195
  team guidelines, 197–8
DEAR MAN interpersonal skills, 144–5
dependency and autonomy
  help-seeking behaviors, 171–2
  weaning between-session coaching, 172–3
Diagnostic and Statistical Manual of Mental Disorders (DSM)
  definition of BPD, 35
  DSM-IV-TR criteria, BPD diagnosis, **36**
dialectical behavior therapy (DBT)
  active clinician stance, 88–9
  agreements
    clinician, 98–9
    patient, 97–8
  case formulation *see* DBT case formulation
  and CBT, 80–81
  CbT *vs.* cBT approaches, 6
  clinical training, 7, 19–23
  clinician initiated patient 'vacation', 240–241
  commitment to treatment *see* commitment to treatment, DBT
  components, 6
  conditioning *see* conditioning
  definition, 5
  destructive behaviors, 16
  dialectic synthesis, 71
  "door-in-the-face" concept, 96–7
  eating disorders, 17
  empirically based indications for DBT, 17

evidence-based treatment, 16
goals, 241–2
interpersonal difficulties, 18–19
intervening with patients, 8
levels of validation, 68–70
posttraumatic stress disorder, 18
"pretreatment phase", 86
principles of, 6–7
"quality of life"-interfering behaviors *see* "quality of life"-interfering behaviors
reduction, self-harm behavior, 87–8
skills training, 128–9 *see also* skills training
stage 1, 76
stage 2, 76–80
staying alive, staying in treatment and stability, 86–7
suicidal adolescents (DBT-A), 16–17
suicidal individuals, 242–3
suicide attempts and suicides, 242
theory
  acceptance techniques, 63
  dialectics, 64–6
  mindfulness, 66–7
  validation, 67–9
therapists questions, 8
therapy-interfering behaviors *see* therapy-interfering behaviors
treatment drop out, 239–40
"treatment resistance", 9
validation and change, 70–71
dialectical dilemmas, DBT case formulation
  active passivity *vs.* apparent competence, 210–212
  adjunctive psychopharmacological interventions, 217
  communication strategies, 219
  contextual events/vulnerability factors, 214–15
  current stage, treatment, 213–14
  deficits, 215
  dialectical strategies, 217–18
  distress tolerance, 216
  emotional vulnerability *vs.* self-invalidation, 210, 212
  emotional regulation, 215
  entitled *vs.* undeserving, 211–12
  environmental precipitants, 214
  mindfulness, 215
  negative consequences, 216–17
  overly trusting *vs.* overly guarded, 211, 212
  problem solving, 218
  reinforcers, target to behaviors, 216
  secondary targets, excesses and deficits, 216
  stage 2 - treatment goals, 213
  treatment modes, 217
  unrelenting crisis *vs.* inhibited grieving, 211, 212
  validation, 218–19
dialectics
  accepting limitations, 236
  "apparent competence" *vs.* "active passivity", 228
  assumptions, 6–7
  capability and limitations, 232
  prescribing medication, 227–8
dialectic strategies and irreverent communications, chain analysis
  "enter the paradox", therapist, 119–20
  metaphors, 120
  negative emotions, 120
  wise and reasonable mind, 121
diary card
  balancing validation, 105–6
  behavioral analysis, 116–17
  chain analysis obstacles, 118
  description, 102, 103
  internal experience reporting, 103
  mindfulness and distress tolerance skills, 114, 116
  sample template, 103, **104**
  self-injury, 116
  setting the agenda, 106
  skills record, 114, **115**
  standard targets, 103
  versions, 103
disorder of dysregulation, 92–3
distress tolerance skills
  advantages and disadvantages, 141–2
  changing body temperature, 140
  crisis survival skills, 139
  improving the moment, 141
  radical acceptance, 142
  self-soothing, 140
  skillful distraction, 140
"door-in-the-face" concept, 90–91, 96–7

emotion mind, 121, 136–7, 139, 145
emotional dysregulation, components, 39

emotional pain, 53
emotional valence, 4
emotional vulnerability *vs.* self-invalidation, 210
emotion regulation skills
  function of emotions, 147
  mindfulness practice, 150
  model, observe and describe 147–8
  "myths", 146–7
  opposite action, 150–151
  positive emotions, 149–50
  vulnerability reduction, 148–9
environmental/interpersonal stress, 38

"foot-in-the-door" concept, 90

hierarchy of goals, DBT, 86–7

individual therapy
  chain analysis see chain analysis
  dialectic strategies and irreverent communications, 119–21
  diary card, 102–6, 114–18
  self-injury episode, 112, 113, 114
  stylistic strategies, 118–19
  suicidal ideation, 112, 114
In-session skills training, 156–7
International Classification of Diseases (ICD), 50
interpersonal dysregulation, 210
interpersonal effectiveness skills
  description, 142–3
  identifying and prioritizing goals, 143–4
  interaction objective skills, 144–6
  making/refusing, request, 144
  restructuring cognitions, 143
interpersonal goals
  DEAR MAN, 144–5
  maintaining relationships, 145
  maintaining self-respect, 145–6
in vivo skills coaching, 154

medication nonadherence
  dialectical approach, 227–8
  medication noncompliance, 226–7
mindfulness, 66–7
mindfulness skills
  cognitive control, 136
  "effectiveness", 138

increasing awareness, 138
vs. "mindlessness", 138
"non-judgmental" thinking, 138
"one-mindful", 138
readings, 139
reasonable mind and emotion mind, 139
requirements, 137
states of mind, 136–7
training, 136
wise mind, 136, 137

negative reactions, BPD patients, 19
nonsuicidal self-injury (NSSI)
  anger, 53, 56
  between session calls, 157
  BPD, 51–2
  cognitive factors, 55
  definition, 50–51
  dissociation and pain experience, 54
  distress tolerance, 216
  experience, 53–5
  external reinforcer, 216
  functions
    attention-seeking, 52–3
    experience, 53–5
    physiological factors, 54–5
    release, 54
  individual therapy, 78
  intent, 58
  multiple hospitalizations, 58
  neurobiology and neurocognitive factors, 54–5
  parasuicide, 50
  as risk factor for suicidal behavior, 179
  self-punishment, 53
  sense of control, 53
  vs. suicide attempts, 52
NSSI *see* nonsuicidal self-injury (NSSI)

operant conditioning
  maladaptive behaviors, 72
  reinforcement, 72–3
overdose, 52

paranoid ideation, 92
parasuicide, 50
positive emotions, 149–50
posttraumatic stress disorder (PTSD), 16
psychoeducation, 93–4

psychotherapy modification, 29–30
PTSD *see* posttraumatic stress disorder (PTSD)

"quality of life"-interfering behaviors
    acceptance of limitations, 229–31, 235–6
    capability and limitations, 231–3
    momentary lapses in behavior, 229
    mood-dependent functioning, 229
    progress toward goals, 233–4
    sensitivity to criticism, 229
    vulnerabilities and limitations, 229

radical acceptance, 142
randomized clinical trials (RCTs), 16
reasonable mind, 121
resistance, 3, 9, 29, 33, 66, 132, 222, 237

safety plan, form, **192**
safety planning intervention (SPI)
    BPD case example, 191, **192**
    description, 186
    implementation, 190–191
    internal coping strategies, 187–8
    means restriction, 189–90
    professional and agency contact, 189
    recognition, warning signs, 187
    risk assessment, 187
    social contacts, 188–9
    socialization strategies, 188
    steps, 187
    suicidal urges, 186
self-harm behaviors
    confusion between types, 46
    consequences, 58
    disclosure, 89
    history, 58
    interrupted attempts, 49–50
    nonsuicidal *see* nonsuicidal self-injury (NSSI)
    opioid deficiency, 54
    overreacting to, 47
    painful emotional state, 58
    reducing, 57–8, 87–8
    risk assessment and hospitalization, 58–9
    suicide *see* suicide
self-mutilation, 50
self-punishment, 53
skill modules
    distress tolerance skills, 139–42
    emotion regulation skills, 146–51
    interpersonal effectiveness skills, 142–6
    mindfulness skills, 136–8
skills coaching
    between-session contact *see* between-session contact
    clinician availability *see* arbitrary *vs.* natural limits, between-session contact
    24-hour rule, 161–2
    in session 156–7
    phone contacts, 158
    reporting good news, 156
    time-limited phone coaching interaction, 158–61
skills deficit model
    criticism, 126
    deficit compensation, 126
    etiology, 126
skills training
    behavioral analysis, 132
    between-session skills coaching, 157–61
    DBT, 128–9
    deficit model *see* skills deficit model
    description, 125
    format, 130–131
    homogeneous *vs.* heterogeneous groups, 130
    individual therapy, 131–3
    initial consultation and orientation, 130
    leaders, 129
    maladaptive behavior replacement, 131
    personal self-disclosure, 131
    principles, 127–8
    rationale, 127
    reluctant patients, 128–9
    Skills Training Manual, 129
    "stand-alone" treatment, 132
socialization, distraction and support, 188
SPI *see* safety planning intervention (SPI)
splitting
    consultation to patient, 201–3
    and DBT, 200
    definition, 199
    devalued clinician, 199
    "good" and "bad", 198
    idealization, 199
    psychopharmacologists, 199
stage 1 DBT, 18, 75–6, 86, 95, 206, 208, 209, 213, 221, 228, 239, 241
stage 2 DBT, 76, 206, 213, 239, 241

stylistic strategies
  irreverence, 119
  reciprocal communications, 119
suicidal behavior
  description, 88
  management
    assessment, 178
    commitment strategies, 181–3
    immediate crisis management, 183–4
    past suicide attempt *see* past suicide attempt
    safety planning, 181
  recurrent, 92
suicidal ideation
  depression, 111
  diary card, **113**
  levels, 103, 114
  SPI *see* safety planning intervention (SPI)
suicide
  note, 52
  intention, 51
  risk assessment and decision to hospitalization, 58–9
  underestimating risk, 47–8
suicide attempts
  aborted, 49
  clinical presentation, 55–7
  in BPD, 52
  cognitive factors, 55
  consequences, 180–181
  intention, 180
  interrupted, 49
  medical lethality, 179–80
  micro-overdoses, 50
  neurobiology and neurocognitive factors, 54–5
  NSSI, 50–51, 180
  precipitant, 180
  substance use, 181
  treatment implications, 57–9
  vulnerability, 180
suicide risk, management, 20–21

"talk" therapy, 16
"technical neutrality", 165

telephone contact, 157–8
  format, 158–9
  reluctance, patients, 159–60
  skills coaching, 160–161
therapist
  colleagues and peers collaboration, 22
  DBT, 19, 22, 24
  personal growth, 21–2
  positive therapy experience, 22
therapy-interfering behaviors
  behavioral chain analysis, 222
  chain analysis, 163, 223
  diary card, 222
  identification, 222, 223
  lateness, 223–5
  medication nonadherence, 226–8
  quality of life goals, 233–4
  rejecting suggestions, 162
  solution analysis, lateness, 225–6
  treatment "resistance", 222
  validation, 163–4
third-party clinicians, 203–4
three C's of consultation
  with colleagues *see* DBT consultation team
  non-DBT collaboration, 198–200
  to patient, 200–201
  to third-party clinicians, 203–4
"TIP" skills, 140
transference, 29–30
treatment by experts (TBE), 16
twenty-four-hour rule, 161–2

underestimating suicide risk, 47–8

validation strategies, DBT
  balancing with change, 95–6
  biosocial theory, 94
  empathy, 67
  levels, 68–9

wise mind
  description, 121, 137
  interpersonal interactions, 145
  quality of life goals, 234